FUNDAMENTAL SOCIAL RIGHTS AT WORK IN THE EUROPEAN COMMUNITY

Fundamental Social Rights at Work in the European Community

under the direction of
Alan C. Neal

for
The European Association of Labour Court Judges

Routledge
Taylor & Francis Group
LONDON AND NEW YORK

First published 1999 by Dartmouth and Ashgate Publishing

Reissued 2018 by Routledge
2 Park Square, Milton Park, Abingdon, Oxon, OX14 4RN
711 Third Avenue, New York, NY 10017, USA

Routledge is an imprint of the Taylor & Francis Group, an informa business

A Library of Congress record exists under LC control number: 99224608

ISBN 13: 978-1-138-31202-9 (hbk)
ISBN 13: 978-0-429-45846-0 (ebk)

Contents

Part II: Selected International Instruments

Preface

In the early 1990s a number of judges realised that throughout the European Union there were colleagues dealing with employment matters on a day-to-day basis who had no communication with each other. There also arose a feeling that too many decisions about the principles of employment law were being made by people who lacked practical experience of the real problems of workers and employers. In view of this, it was decided that the answer was to establish a European Association of Labour Court Judges, based mainly on judges of first instance who deal with the ordinary problems of ordinary people.

Having set up the organisation, we were asked by the European Commission to consider perhaps the most important question that an employment judge could be asked – namely, to identify, the fundamental rights of workers. This led us to set up an international conference, to discuss this subject. The book which we have now produced is the result of this conference. It contains input from employment judges from the Member States of the European Union and also from members of the European Economic Area.

The resulting book is a synthesis of the views of all these very different people. We quickly became aware that, although the traditions and experience of judges from different countries were very different, their views of what is "just" and what is "fundamental' are very similar. This demonstrates that there is a common European experience, possibly even a common universal experience, of what is and is not "just".

The word "fundamental" raises philosophical questions. We have studiously avoided these. If everyone agrees with a principle, we have regarded it as fundamental without consideration of whether some past, present or future society might not agree.

These results are by no means complete, but we hope that they amount to a framework from which some European Declaration could emerge which would not just be a pious aspiration but a genuine statement of principle with which all true Europeans would agree.

Colin Sara
(Secretary-General, EALCJ)

Editor's Foreword

The opportunity to present the results of the discussions undertaken during the 1997 Seville colloquium of the European Association of Labour Court Judges has been made available through the generous support of DG/V of the European Commission whose initial idea it was to organise a specialised judicial forum to consider the report of the *Comité des Sages*, and whose helpful input has been invaluable in focusing and structuring the various issues which were dealt with at that Seville meeting.

In the volume which has been prepared on the basis of the Seville proceedings, the "scene-setting" material is presented in the form of an introductory chapter, prepared by the Editor, setting out some of the background to the current debate over the development of fundamental social rights at work, followed by a chapter describing the composition and work of the *Comité des Sages*, being a revised version of the presentation given at Seville by Professor Eduardo Garcia de Enterria, himself a member of the *Comité*. This is then followed by five chapters dealing with the specific technical matters considered by the gathering of judges in Seville – much of the work for which has been co-ordinated by the Spanish team of Federico Jimenez Ballester, Victoriano Valpuesta Bermudez and Alfonso Martinez Escribano. The final statement of conclusions has been drafted by Colin Sara.

The technical chapters were drawn up on the basis of information provided by colleagues from the Member States in response to a questionnaire initially prepared by the Spanish team. Lengthy national reports were prepared in order to inform the discussions at Seville, and the detailed exchanges of views on their technical content were then infused into the chapters during the course of editing. The final versions were then scrutinised by the national delegates.

In the course of preparing this volume, the Editor has received tremendous support and assistance from numerous colleagues belonging to the Judiciaries of the Member States of the European Community and of the EEA States. To all of them a sincere vote of thanks is owed. Thanks also go to Douglas Crump and Colin Sara for their help in the initial stages of the editing process. Finally, a personal debt of gratitude is owed to Mandy Archer who, as Personal Assistant to the Editor, must have drawn one of the shortest possible straws when it comes to the "exploitation of workers"!

Alan C. Neal
Lucca, 1998

Part I

Fundamental Social Rights at Work in the European Community

Stimulating The Debate over Fundamental Social Rights at Work in the European Community

1. Introduction

This volume addresses some of the issues developing in the modern debate over the potential for formulating a "social constitution" for Europe, in the context of the legal order of the European Community. It contains the combined reflections of various members of the judiciaries of the Member States of the European Community and of the EEA States – particularly those with direct experience of judicial dispute resolution in relation to rights at work and the relations between employers and workers within the European Community.

Building upon the agenda offered by the 1996 Report of the *Comité des Sages*, "For a Europe of Civic and Social Rights", a selection of issues is addressed from the perspective of implementing and giving practical effect to "rights" of workers at work in the European Community. Consideration is given to the international framework of rights, as these have impacted upon work relationships and rights of workers, and questions are posed as to the enforceability of particular putative "rights", given the experience to date in other supra-national contexts.

Beneath all of the discussions reflected in the following pages flows a strong stream of "judicial scepticism", concerned to ensure that any progress in this area is placed upon sound practical evolution of effective rights, rather than upon the shifting sands of vague declarations of principle. In consequence, some of the conclusions reached do not obviously share the aspirational heights put forward by some commentators who have gone before. On the other hand, far from indicating a lack of enthusiasm for the development of a clearly settled rights regime for European Community workers at work, the reservations voiced serve to emphasise the care which needs to be taken in the difficult task of future development for the kinds of "social rights" which are under consideration here.

This study does not pretend dramatically to develop the theoretical dimensions of the "human rights" debate, nor does it put forward any kind of "agreed judicial line" in respect of the policy implications of developing "social rights at work" or as regards any of the specific rights proposed to be established. What it does, however, is to offer some reflections from a uniquely qualified group of actors on the stage of European labour law – members of the judiciaries of the Member States and the countries of the EEA – commenting in their personal capacities, and pooling the wealth of their direct experiences of legal dispute resolution in this vital area.

Within these limited boundaries, therefore, the European Association of Labour Court Judges offers its contribution to the debate on Civic and Social Rights for Europe.

2. The Seville Colloquium

The organisation of a colloquium to bring together Labour Court judges from the Member States of the European Community was an idea initially floated by DG/V of the European Commission. It was seen as part of the follow-up process to the debate sparked by the report of the *Comité des Sages* on civic and social rights,[1] and as providing an opportunity to explore links between the declaration of broad concepts of social and civic rights and the practical giving of effect and enforcement to any such rights.

In particular, a forum was sought which could address practical issues touching implementation and enforcement of the kinds of rights under discussion, hopefully without some of the natural reservation which accompanies public discussions between members of the judiciary. It was therefore not surprising that the proposal was eventually made for the European Association of Labour Court Judges to host the meeting, so that an existing infra-structure for bringing together judicial representatives from the various labour courts and tribunals throughout the Community could be utilised to this end.[2] The Spanish section of the European Association undertook the hosting of the colloquium,[3] and the technical direction was undertaken by the Association's Secretariat.[4]

1 European Commission, *For a Europe of civic and social rights (Report by the Comité des Sages chaired by Maria de Lourdes Pintasilgo)*, (Luxembourg 1996). The report of this body was presented in February 1996.

2 The European Association of Labour Court Judges includes amongst its objects "...(b) To provide a forum for the exchange of information and views in relation to the fields of social policy and labour law", and "... (c) To provide a technical forum in which to compare and contrast national practice as to the adjudication of employment and labour disputes". Its underlying purpose is "...To act as an association of judges and other judicial officers and those acting as judicial officers in matters concerning employment and labour law within the states which are members of the European Union and the European Economic Area".

3 Particularly in the persons of Federico Jimenez Ballester, Victoriano Valpuesta Bermudez and Alfonso Martinez Escribano (currently the President of the European Association).

4 The Secretary-General, Mr. Colin Sara, the Convenor, Professor Alan Neal, and the Treasurer, Mr. Douglas Crump, supported administratively by Miss Mandy Archer.

One point should be made, at the outset, as regards the scope of the discussions which took place in Seville. As is well known, the establishment of a *Comité des Sages* came about as one component in the European Commission's medium-term social action programme of 1995.[5] That programme was, itself, the third stage of a process which had been set in train with publication of the 1993 Green Paper,[6] and continued through the 1994 White Paper on European social policy.[7] The appointment of the *Comité des Sages* came hard on the heels of a joint hearing, organised in April 1995, between the European Commission and the European Parliament, looking at the future of the 1989 Social Charter.[8]

Given that the *Comité des Sages* focused particularly upon examining and developing questions raised during the joint hearing between the Commission and Parliament, it will be appreciated that their initial remit had the appearance of being rather narrowly concerned with labour market and employment-centred issues. However, as appears clearly from the eventual report of the *Comité des Sages*, such a perspective quickly became broadened to enable the deliberations of the *Comité* to address various "focal" employment rights in a context of "fundamental rights" and a more universal notion of social and civic rights.

Thus, in its report, the *Comité des Sages* identified eight rights which it proposed should be given full and immediate effect – namely, equality before the law; a ban on any form of discrimination; equality between men and women; freedom of movement within the Community; a right to choose one's occupation or profession and educational system throughout the territory of the Community; a right of association and a right to defend one's rights; and a right of collective bargaining and action. Alongside these "immediate" rights, the *Comité* proposed a range of further rights, in the form of objectives to be achieved. These cover a right to education; a right to work; a right to social security; a right to protection for the family; and a number of other matters which are set forth as forming "an integral part of the European social model".[9]

The focus of the Seville colloquium was, by comparison, significantly narrower. In particular, it was recognised that a number of the putative rights enumerated by the *Comité des Sages* go well beyond applicability only in the world of work, and call for consideration of much wider values and policies

5 See *Medium-term social action programme 1995-97*, 12 April 1995, COM(95) 134 final.

6 *Green Paper on European social policy: Options for the Union*, COM(93) 551 final.

7 *White Paper on European social policy: A way forward for the Union*, COM(94) 333 final.

8 Community Charter of the Fundamental Social Rights of Workers, 9 December 1989, COM(89) 471 final.

9 See the Report of the *Comité des Sages*, at p.17.

than those concerned "purely" with working relationships and the rights of workers at work. Furthermore, some of those putative rights enunciated by the *Comité des Sages* are, themselves, hybrid in nature, and require substantial further elaboration before any notion of justiciable and enforceable rights is capable of deriving from their declaration.

Consequently, the Seville colloquium concentrated, in terms of studying "live" rights in the Member States, upon four "key" areas of social rights at work in order to exemplify the matters under discussion. These were described, for the purposes of structuring the discussions, as covering *(i)* security of employment and freedom to dismiss; *(ii)* exploitation of workers – this being taken to encompass health and safety at work, along with the insistence upon "equitable" working conditions (including the regulation of working time); *(iii)* discrimination – in a multitude of guises; and *(iv)* rights of association (trade union freedom) and collective bargaining.

The Seville colloquium also sought to approach the application and enforceability of these various social rights against a detailed backcloth of the international institutional framework for rights recognised by the Member States of the European Community. For this purpose, therefore, the first part of the discussion in Seville dealt with the whole range of social rights recognised in international law, in national Constitutions and laws, and in Community law.[10] The frame of reference adopted, therefore, coincides with the more global "rights" framework to which the report of the *Comité des Sages* makes specific reference in the context of the revision of the Treaties.

The eventual Seville colloquium was attended by some fifty judges, drawn from all levels of the judiciary, from Supreme Court judges, through Presidents of Labour Courts, to first-instance judges in a variety of labour tribunals. As well as representatives from the legal systems of the fifteen Member States of the European Community, the colloquium was attended by judges from Iceland and Norway, representing Member States party to the Agreement on the European Economic Area.

Several of the individual participants also brought with them experience of activity within the frameworks of human rights systems apart from those directly touching the European Community. Thus, amongst the participants were members of Committees of Experts sitting in Strasbourg in relation to the European Convention, as well as a number of colleagues concerned with the supervisory work of the International Labour Organisation in Geneva, in relation to the relevant instruments of that body.

10 See *infra*, p.45 ff.

3. The Background Debate I:

Discovering a "Social Dimension" for the European Community

During the last decade, a debate has been intensifying within the European Community as to whether it can be possible to introduce a variety of "fundamental right" into the legal order of the Community as a legal instrument upon which workers within the community might be able to rely. The debate has been particularly stimulated in recent years by concern for a re-thinking of the nature of social and Community rights, in the lead-up to the Inter-Governmental Conference which was intended to give rise to a revision of the Treaties. That process reached its climax with the emergence of a draft treaty which was eventually signed by all of the Member States on 2 October 1997.[11]

Much more narrowly, however, there has been debated the hoary issue of whether it has been possible to identify an authentic "social dimension" for the European communities at all. That debate has concerned the scope of the various powers contained in the treaties, and has been concerned to plot the course of an increasing openness on the part of politicians to recognise that the economic and legal order being put into place since 1957 is not confined to an "economic dimension" purely concerned with a single European market, but which contains a "social dimension" running alongside that economic dimension and of particular concern in relation to issues such as the environment, public health, and working conditions. By now, as one writes in the late 1990s, the orthodox view clearly recognises not only the existence of a "social dimension" to the European Community but also recognises that this is not merely an "add-on" to that economic dimension. Indeed, it as precisely in order to address the challenge posed to the integrated economic entity which has progressively been brought into being at the European level, that changes to the Community's treaty powers have been brought about and that there has been witnessed an increased recognition of this reality in the case-law of the European Court of Justice.

The emergence of a generally recognised sets of norms which may be said to reflect the "social dimension" of the community has, in great measure, helped to legitimise and to stimulate the search for coherence in relation to the body of rules which may be said to constitute the legal provisions dealing with "social Europe".

In the present context, the discussion has moved on from the debate of the 1970s and early 1980s over whether it was possible to identify and classify

11 *Treaty of Amsterdam amending the Treaty on European Union, the Treaties establishing the European Communities and certain related acts*. For a comment on the new instrument in the context of social policy arrangements, see *Lammy Betten*, "The Amsterdam Treaty: Some General Comments on the new Social Dimension", (1997) 13 *International Journal of Comparative Labour Law and Industrial Relations* 188.

"fundamental principles of Community law". That discussion, developing in parallel with the case-law of the European Court of Justice in cases such as *Stauder*,[12] *Nold*,[13] or *Hauer*,[14] concentrated to a great extent upon the question of from where the European Court of Justice might draw upon as sources of "general principles". It was developed, as general recognition spread that the Court was willing to have recourse to "general principles", in the direction of classifying the kinds of matters which would make up the range of "general principles" of Community law, and, inevitably, led on to discussion of the relationship between Community legal provisions and other international orders embodying such matters under the general rubric of "fundamental rights".

Certainly, therefore, one is able to find express statements underlining this development, as in *Nold*,[15] where it was put in terms that:

> "respect for fundamental human rights is one of the general principles of Community law the observance of which [the court] has a duty to secure".

Similarly, in the *International Handelsgesellschaft* case,[16] the European Court of Justice declared that:

> "...respect for fundamental rights forms an integral part of the general principles of law protected by the Court of Justice. The protection of such rights, whilst inspired by the constitutional traditions common to the Member States, must be ensured within the framework of the structure and the objectives of the Community".

Nevertheless, the limits upon the Court of Justice are well known, particularly in relation to "fundamental rights" deriving from instruments such as the Council of Europe's 1950 Convention for the Protection of Human Rights and Fundamental Freedoms – as indicated, for example, in the *Cinetheque* case:[17]

12 Case 29/69, *Stauder* v. *City of Ulm, Sozialamt*, [1969] ECR 419.

13 Case 4/73, *Nold* v. *Commission*, [1974] ECR 491.

14 Case 44/79, *Hauer* v. *Land Rheinland-Phalz*, [1980] ECR 3727.

15 Case 4/73, *Nold* v. *Commission*, [1974] ECR 491, at p.507.

16 Case 11/70, *International Handelsgesellschaft*, [1970] ECR 1125.

17 Cases 60/84 and 61/84, *Cinetheque* v. *Federation Nationale des Cinemas Français*, [1985] ECR 2605. It may be noted, however, that in Case C-260/89, *ERT*, [1991] ECR I-2925, the Court of Justice observed that: "On the other hand, where such rules do fall within the scope of Community law, and reference is made to the Court for a preliminary ruling, it must provide all the criteria of interpretation needed by the national court to determine whether those rules are compatible with the fundamental rights the observance of which the Court ensures and which derive in particular from the European Convention on Human Rights".

"Although it is true that it is the duty of this court to ensure observance of fundamental rights in the field of Community law, it has no power to examine the compatibility with the European Convention of national legislation which concerns, as in this case, an area which falls within the jurisdiction of the national legislator."

However, it was not until some time afterwards that consideration began to be given in any detail to the identification specifically of "social rights", and, even more narrowly, "fundamental rights at work". In this context, much depended upon the development and increasing recognition of a "social dimension" to the European Community order, alongside the hitherto predominantly "economic" imperative of that body.

Indeed, it was effectively with the overt recognition at the political level of the parallel status of the "social" dimension of the Community that the groundwork could be laid for such a labour market oriented consideration of the debate over "fundamental rights". However, what constitutes that "social dimension" has been a matter of some controversy for well over twenty years.[18]

Whether one finds a ready answer to this question in the words of a President of the ETUC, looking towards "a Europe which links democracy, social justice and economic success",[19] or one shares the puzzlement of the commentator who questions:

"... Does it all mean that the "social dimension" comprises those measures which are a natural part of the economic market — the welfare without which the competition will not work? Or does it go further and include measures of social justice and priorities based on human need which may take precedence even over the bottom line of the accountants' judgments on efficiency?".[20]

This much vaunted "social dimension" of the European Community is, for all its high profile, surprisingly difficult to pin down with any exactitude. Nonetheless, something lies behind the rhetoric – particularly following upon

18 For discussion of this issue, see *Alan C. Neal*, "In Search of the 'Social Dimension", in K.Källström (ed), *Festschrift för Tore Sigeman* (Iustus Förlag, Uppsala 1993) 219. Some of the standard literature on the subject can be found referred to *inter alia* in M.Gold (ed), *The Social Dimension: Employment Policy in the European Community* (Basingstoke 1993) and R.Nielsen & E.Szyszczak, *The Social Dimension of the European Community* (2nd edition, Copenhagen 1993). See also the contributions in Alan C. Neal & S. Foyn (eds), *Developing the Social Dimension in an Enlarged European Union* (Scandinavian University Press, Universitetsforlaget AS, Oslo 1995).

19 Ernst Breit, President of the ETUC, in *1988 Trades Union Congress Annual Reports, General Council Reports and Congress Debates*, p.570.

20 Lord Wedderburn, *The Social Charter, European company and employment rights: An outline agenda* (The Institute of Employment Rights, London 1990), p.6.

various political declarations made on the occasions of the meetings of Heads of States and Governments of the European Community.

For present purposes, therefore, it is as well to remind oneself of precisely what was said on those oft-cited occasions when the political leaders of the European Community were at pains to stress the "human face" of the economic structure which they were in the process of completing – most notably, at the Madrid summit in June 1989, where it was proclaimed that: [21]

> "... in the course of the construction of the single European market, social aspects should be given the same importance as the economic aspects and should accordingly be developed in a balanced fashion".

4. The Background Debate II:

"Fundamental Social Rights" and "Fundamental Rights of Workers"

Once having set the "social dimension" scene for the modern developing debate, one of the first controversial strands which needs to be taken into account concerns the basic question as to whether it is possible to recognise "fundamental rights" amongst the principles of European Community law. This is a question which has regularly been addressed in the context of seeking to identify "general principles" of Community law as that legal order has developed during the past 40 years. Indeed, it may be recalled that it was in the face of this issue of "definition" that the *Comité des Sages*, at the very outset of taking up its remit, sought to broaden the formal scope of its activities in order to provide a more complete context within which to conduct its consideration and put forward its proposals.

A follow-up issue concerns the identification of "social rights of workers", and the inevitable question as to which, if any, of these might be regarded as "fundamental" rights within a supra-national system. Assistance for those addressing this matter in the context of the emerging legal order of the European Communities tends to be sought with particular reference to the 1989 Community Charter of the Fundamental Social Rights of Workers, and the continuing debate over how to give more pragmatic effect to the provisions contained therein.[22] Here, again, it should be noted that the original focus for the remit of the *Comité des Sages* was directed towards this 1989 instrument and

21 Madrid Summit "Conclusions", 26/27 June 1989, Point 2.

22 In relation to this instrument, and some of the problems raised in the context thereof, see, for example, the contrasting views expressed by *B.Bercusson*, "The European Community's Charter of Fundamental Social Rights of Workers", (1990) 53 *Modern Law Review* 624, and *Bob Hepple*, "The Implementation of the Community Charter of Fundamental Social Rights", (1990) 53 *Modern Law Review* 643.

to its future development and "incorporation" into the Community legal order. Such an approach is not, it should be noted, without controversy. However, if one is looking for some measure of justification in the adoption of this path, it might be observed that, while, in the eyes of various critics, its adoption serves artificially to narrow the technical scope of the debate, for those concerned with policy development and problems of implementation of the ambitions in this field, it does at least provide some steady point of reference for discussion of specific "rights" relating to workers at work in the European Community.

These issues have been addressed in a variety of settings, including recently during the European Social Policy Forum's meeting in Brussels during the Summer of 1998.[23] From the contributions to that meeting, indeed, mention may be made of one general reporter's approach, within the framework of looking at "participation and citizenship" of the Community, which sets out with a fair degree of clarity many of what might be described as the "orthodox" underlying propositions, to the effect that:[24]

> "Citizenship refers to a triad of rights.
>
> A first generation is that of civil rights, which were born in the XVIIIth century and the philosophy of the self determination of the self sufficient and individual; they consist of "liberties from" and impose upon others, including the government authorities, negative obligations (*e.g.* not to curb property rights or freedom of speech).
>
> The second generation is that of social rights, which consist of powers ("liberties to") and can only be attained through the imposition upon others, including the government authorities, of a certain number of positive obligations.
>
> Social rights are a comparatively recent phenomenon compared to civil rights. Not until the twentieth century, and really not until after the Second World War, did constitutions and legislation begin to reflect the idea that workers' or citizens' health, for instance, is a social good and that citizens accordingly have the right to health (attached to workers (or derived from rights of workers) or attached to citizens). The different models of welfare state have had different ways of providing for these rights; however, they generally recognised the principle that the health care, the education, and the welfare of each individual is a good for the entire community and that its members should enjoy a certain basic standard of living: this is the founding principle of social rights.
>
> In recent years, a fair number of new rights (third generation rights) have emerged, mostly through the drafting of relatively specific charters.

23 This took place in Brussels between 24 and 26 June 1998.

24 See the background paper prepared for Workshop 3 of that meeting, by Mme. Giannicheda, entitled "Promoting participation and citizenship".

> Some, such as the UN Convention on the Rights of Children and Adolescents, are endowed with quite strong statutes. Others are declarations stemming from the work and discussions of social movements and voluntary or community associations (ranging from charters of rights of patients or homeless persons to charters of environmental rights)."

Once again, critics might regard such a frame of reference as being inadequate to embrace all of the possible strands of debate which might be undertaken under the umbrella of considering fundamental rights at work within the European Community. Nevertheless, the quotation serves to remind the observer of how the debate at the European level has tended to be structured, and of where some of the "assumptive limits" of that debate are sometimes perceived to run.

It almost goes without saying that the literature on this area is enormous, and here is not the place to rehearse in outline the major lines of argument adopted by various distinguished commentators.

Amongst the earliest areas to receive treatment at the Community level was the crucial field of equal treatment between men and women. That area has proved to be a rich vein both for developing "rights" and for case-law at the level of the European Court of Justice. Essentially, the Community approach has been to adopt as its point of departure a "non-discrimination" approach – whether in relation to the exercise of "economic" rights such as the right to free movement and the provision of services within the Common Market, or in respect of the treatment of goods moving between Member States of the Community. To this has been added an approach seeking to ensure "equal opportunities" between men and women. However, what has been absent here has been any trend (until very recently) towards a goal of substantive "sex equality" or anything in the nature of provisions intended to afford "positive discrimination" in the pursuit of quantitative equality between the sexes.

The focus of debate in recent years has alighted upon "how" there should be incorporated various forms of "fundamental right" into the Community legal order, rather than "whether" this should be an objective for concern. This discussion has included views propounded by those who regard it as a natural part of the Community legal order that "fundamental rights" should enjoy a place, without need for express spelling out of the definition or extent of such "rights", as well as contributions by those who would see the construction of an express "Bill of Rights" at the Community level, with a view to declaring and spelling out the "rights" regarded as core in this context. In support of the various views, experience with other international instruments (*e.g.* the European Social Charter, or the UN Declaration of Fundamental Rights and Freedoms) has been drawn upon to support differing viewpoints. Common to all of the views, however, is the acceptance that there is a role to be played at the level of the European Community for "fundamental rights" at work, and that the achievement of establishing such a chapter of "rights" requires something more than the present extent of Treaty powers and the interpretative powers of the European Court of Justice currently made available under the Treaties establishing the European Community. Attention has, consequently, centred upon not just what the content of the list of "rights" should be, but also upon the powers available to introduce and sanction such phenomena. This has developed, in recent years, into an active agenda which, as part of the "lobbying" process accompanying the Inter-Governmental Conference on the revision of the Treaties in 1997, has seen some degree of formalisation in the preparatory process over possible inclusion of "fundamental rights" provisions in any new version of the Treaties.

A number of contributions have been made to the debate, some of which have taken a "theoretical" starting point, and others of which represent much more of a "vested interest" pleading in the context of the balance of power in industrial relations within the Community order. Amongst the matters to have found common accord in these contributions have been the acceptance of the limited scope of "Treaty powers" available to the institutions of the Community, together with a growing preparedness to regard mechanisms such as the "social dialogue" as a vehicle for promoting the achievement of some of those objectives. It is also relevant to point to the fact that a lively academic debate has been stimulated as to the proper scope of the "social dimension" of the Community, and in relation to the role and function of "fundamental rights" in a social setting such as the labour market of the unified single market established since 1992.

Suffice it, for present purposes, to say that, during the course of the Seville colloquium, the participants found it necessary to bear in mind a variety of specific practical problems in this area. Thus, concern was had to the general notion of developing "fundamental" and "human" rights, and, in particular, their effective enforcement.[25] In the European setting, this – not unnaturally – involved close consideration of experience with the

25 In respect of the practical issues of developing enforceable rights at the national legal system level, see, for example, the material contained in B.Conforti & F.Francioni (eds), *Enforcing International Human Rights in Domestic Courts* (The Hague 1997). The approach of placing such developments in a framework of "social justice" also formed part of this debate – see, for example, the (arguably somewhat dated) contributions of A.Glenn Mower Jr., *International Cooperation for Social Justice* (Westport 1985). As regards one of the widely recognised "motors" behind calls for development of such rights regimes in the world of work, see the narrower discussion offered in *T.E.McCarthy*, "Transnational Corporations and Human Rights", in A.Cassese (ed), *UN Law/Fundamental Rights – Two Topics in International Law* (Alphen aan den Rijn 1979), p.175.

Council of Europe's Convention rights.[26] So, too, was there concern for the identification and development of "new" contemporary rights areas – as, for example, in relation to "sexual harassment" or "disability discrimination".[27] More ambitiously, and reflecting much of the debate in the run-up to the Inter-Governmental Conference, there was specific concern for the problems involved in developing a "social constitution" for Europe – something which carries with it an unavoidable political agenda, depending upon where the contribution originates.[28]

Indeed, with this latter question, one is led back to the central task initially given to the *Comité des Sages* – for it should, of course, be recalled that the original intention with the setting up of the *Comité des Sages* as part of the Commission's 1995 Medium-Term Social Action Programme was to address the issue of how to transform the basis offered by the 1989 Community Charter into a more institutionalised and effective "floor of rights" for workers within the European Community. Bearing this in mind, therefore, a word should be said about that instrument, its genesis, and the results which have accrued in the area to which it addresses itself in the period since the Strasbourg summit of December 1989.

5. The Significance of the Community Charter of the Fundamental Social Rights of Workers 1989, and the European Commission's Follow-up Social Action Programme of 1989

With a basis for a more pro-active approach to social policy having been

26 For overall coverage of this instrument, see, for example, F.Jacobs & R.White, *The European Convention on Human Rights* (2nd edition, Oxford 1996). In the context of specific matters discussed in Seville, particular note may be taken of Chapter 13, "Freedom of Assembly and Association", p.237. For some of the experience derived in the course of operating the provisions of this instrument at the national level, see, for example, A.Drzemczewski, *European Human Rights Convention in Domestic Law – A Comparative Study* (Oxford 1983).

27 See, for example, in relation to problems in developing such notions, the contribution by E.Heinze, *Sexual Orientation: A Human Right* (Dordrecht 1995). Some of the general issues are also taken up by contributors to T.Degener & Y.Koster-Dreese (eds), *Human Rights and Disabled Persons* (Dordrecht 1995) – see, for instance, the section by *A.Hendriks*, "The Significance of Equality and Non-discrimination for the Protection of the Rights and Dignity of Disabled Persons", p.40, and that by *P.Alston*, "Disability and the International Covenant on Economic Social and Cultural Rights", p.94.

28 See, for example, the offerings in *M.Rodriguez-Piñero* & *E.Casas*, "In Support of a European Social Constitution", in P.Davies *et al* (eds), *European Community Labour Law: Principles and Perspectives* (Oxford 1996), p.23. That piece can also be seen against offerings such as R.Blanpain, B.Hepple, S.Sciarra & M.Weiss, *Fundamental Social Rights: Proposals for the European Union* (1996), or that produced under the auspices of the ETUC by B.Bercusson, S.Deakin, P.Koistinen, Y.Kravaritou, U.Mückenberger, A.Supiot & B.Veneziani, *A Manifesto for Social Europe* (Brussels 1996). For a more sceptical view on "declarations" of this kind, see *Alan C. Neal*, "Labour Law in the 1990s: An Unweeded Garden that Grows to Seed?", (1997) 13 *The International Journal of Comparative Labour Law and Industrial Relations* 11.

laid by revisions to the Treaties implemented through the 1986 Single European Act, and with increasingly express political recognition of the need for direct recognition of a "social dimension" for the European Community, as manifest in the conclusions of the European Councils of Hanover and Rhodes, it was clear, as the 1980s drew to a close, that the time might be ripe for an initiative on this front.[29] The eventual manifestation of that initiative was to be seen in the 1989 Community Charter of the fundamental social rights of workers, which was agreed between eleven of the (at that time)[30] 12 Member States at their meeting in Strasbourg on 9 December 1989.[31]

The Preamble to that Community Charter made express reference to the internationally recognised sources of rights to be found in Conventions of the International Labour Organisation and in the European Social Charter of the Council of Europe. It also made clear that the aim of the instrument was to "declare solemnly that the implementation of the Single European Act must take full account of the social dimension of the community", and went on to declare that it was necessary, in this context,

29 The genesis of this "social dimension" is traceable from the emphasis placed by the European Council at the Hanover summit in June 1988 upon "social aspects of the single market", through the declaration at the Rhodes summit of December 1998 that "realisation of the single market should not be regarded as a goal in itself", and, subsequently, to the declaration at the Madrid summit of 1989 *(supra)* that, in the context of establishing the single market, a like emphasis should be placed upon "the social aspects" as upon the economic aspects.

30 The undertakings contained in the Community Charter were subsequently extended to Austria, Finland and Sweden, following their entry into membership of the Community in 1995. An acceptance of the principles underlying the Charter had already been expressed by the States of the EEA which did not seek full membership of the Community after 1994.

31 Community Charter of the Fundamental Social Rights of Workers, 9 December 1989, COM(89) 471 final. This eventual instrument had emerged from a process which commenced in November 1988, with the Commission inviting the Economic and Social Committee to look into the possible content for a "Community Charter of the fundamental social rights of workers" – a process which gave rise to the Opinion of the ESC on that subject, adopted on 22 February 1989. Shortly thereafter, on 15 March 1989, the European Parliament adopted a resolution on "the social dimension of the single market", including a call for adoption of "fundamental social rights". Following informal discussion of a draft "Charter" at the European Council meeting in Madrid (12 June 1989), the European Parliament then demonstrated a high level of activism in the field of promoting "social rights", with a group of resolutions being adopted in September 1989, and an eventual resolution of 22 November 1989 proving to be the precursor to the instrument which was eventually adopted by 11 of the 12 Member States at the Strasbourg summit on 9 December 1989. Various topics arising out of the Community Charter have been discussed by European commentators. Amongst the contributions in the English language, mention may be made of Lord Wedderburn, *The Social Charter, European company and employment rights: An outline agenda* (The Institute of Employment Rights, London 1990), and *Bob Hepple*, "The Implementation of the Community Charter of Fundamental Social Rights", (1990) 53 *Modern Law Review* 643.

"to ensure at the appropriate levels the development of the social rights of workers of the European Community, especially employed workers and self-employed persons".

The Community Charter, as agreed in December 1989, covered twelve categories of "fundamental social rights". These touched upon, respectively: *(i)* Freedom of movement;[32] *(ii)* Employment and remuneration;[33] *(iii)* Improvement of living and working conditions;[34] *(iv)* Social protection;[35] *(v)* Freedom of association and collective bargaining;[36] *(vi)* Vocational training;[37] *(vii)* Equal treatment for men and women;[38] *(viii)* Information, consultation and participation for workers;[39] *(ix)* Health protection and safety at the workplace;[40] *(x)* Protection

32 The right to freedom of movement would be restricted only on grounds of public order, public safety or public health. It would give workers from one Member State, working in another Member State, the freedom to work in any occupation or profession on equal terms and with the same working conditions as nationals of the host country.

33 In each Member State, workers would receive fair remuneration, sufficient for a "decent" standard of living. Protection would be given to part-time workers. There would be limits on the withholding of wages, and workers would have free access to job placement services.

34 There should be an improvement in working conditions, particularly in terms of limits on working time such as minimum annual paid leave and a weekly break from work. Particular mention is made of the need for improved conditions for those not on open-ended contracts (for example part-time or seasonal workers).

35 Workers, including the unemployed, should receive adequate social protection and social security benefits.

36 This involves the right to organise trade unions and to choose whether or not to join them, to conclude collective agreements, and to take collective action. Such action includes the right to strike, except where existing legislation stipulates exceptions (including the armed forces, the police and government service).

37 It is noteworthy that this was set out to embrace most university courses and some secondary education. Workers should be able to train, and re-train, throughout their working lives.

38 Action should be intensified to remove discrimination and provide support to prevent a clash between responsibilities in the home and at work.

39 This should apply especially in multinational companies and in particular at times of re-structuring, redundancies or the introduction of new technology. Worker participation would be developed "in such a way as to take account" of existing rules and traditions.

40 Perhaps the most successful of all of the areas set out in the Community Charter – though note also the controversy aroused over the scope of the legislative powers granted by Article 118a of the revised Treaties in relation to matters concerning "health and safety", as eventually addressed by the European Court of Justice in Case C-84/94, *United Kingdom of Great Britain and Northern Ireland* v. *Council of the European Union*, Judgment of the Court, 12 November 1996 (the Working Time Directive case). See, for more detail and a consideration of the historical development, Alan C. Neal & Frank B. Wright, *The European Communities' Health and Safety Legislation* (Chapman & Hall, London 1992), and, on the most recent position, *Alan C. Neal*, "Regulating Health and Safety at Work: Developing European Union Policy for the Millennium", (1998) 14 *The International Journal of Comparative Labour Law and Industrial Relations* 147.

of children and adolescents;[41] *(xi)* Elderly persons;[42] and *(xii)* Disabled people.[43]

The final provisions of the instrument covered issues relating to implementation of the Charter. In line with the provisions set out there, Member States were given responsibility "in accordance with national practices" for guaranteeing the rights in the Charter and for implementing the necessary measures. Meanwhile, the Commission was asked to submit proposals on areas within its competence.[44]

Developments since 1989 have witnessed a wide range of measures introduced in fields dealt with by the Community Charter – many stemming directly from the Commission's 1989 Action Programme – although during this period there has indisputably also been a heightening of controversy over the appropriate "way forward" in this sphere, given clear political divisions between the Member States. Indeed, it is quite a remarkable tribute to the energy and persistence of the European Commission that a significant proportion of the measures outlined in its Action Programme of 1989 have come to fruition in legislative or (as the jargon would have it) in "soft law" form.[45]

If one were to offer a generalised comment upon the achievements of the 1989 Community Charter, it might be to the effect that a wide range of relatively uncontroversial matters touching protection rights to be enjoyed by individual workers has been developed into Community legislation, while an accompanying body of more contentious – but still, essentially, "individual" – rights has been introduced notwithstanding various reservations and some substantial resistance on the parts of particular Member States.[46]

41 The minimum employment age should be no lower than the minimum school-leaving age, and in any case not lower than 15 years. The hours which those aged under 18 can work should be limited, and they should not generally work at night. Once compulsory education is over, young people must be entitled to receive adequate vocational training. If they are already working, this should take place during working hours.

42 Workers should be assured of resources providing a decent standard of living in retirement. Others should have sufficient resources and appropriate medical and social assistance.

43 All disabled people should have additional help towards social and professional integration.

44 This opportunity for the Commission to set the active agenda was taken with the Communication from the Commission concerning its Action Programme relating to the implementation of the Community Charter of Basic Social Rights for Workers (COM(89) 568 final).

45 The "official" progress in relation to this aspect of social policy can be traced through the Annual Reports and surveys produced by the European Commission. See, for example, *Commission Report on the Community Charter of the Fundamental Social Rights of Workers and on the Protocol on Social Policy Annexed to the Treaty Establishing the European Community* (COM(95) 184 final).

46 The most commonly identified Member State in this context being the United Kingdom. See, for example, the events surrounding the challenge to the validity of the Working Time Directive before the European Court of Justice, Case C-84/94, *United Kingdom of Great Britain and Northern Ireland* v. *Council of the European Union*.

However, what is particularly noteworthy to the observer familiar with labour law regulation in the Member States of the European Community is the almost total absence of any "collective" dimension to these developments. Thus, for example, the 1989 Community Charter itself set out with a highly restricted scope of ambition in relation to matters touching collective bargaining and collective agreements between the industrial relations actors at national level.[47] Even where mechanisms which might appropriately be described as "collective" in nature – *e.g.* consultation arrangements with the representatives of workers – the limits of these had already been established during the process of legislating on measures contained in the 1974 Social Action Programme,[48] and could hardly be said to take the form of any radical new departure in terms of impact upon collective labour relations within the Member States of the European Community. Indeed, it may be argued that, even were one to take the more creative view that the provisions on information and

47 The reasons for this clear policy of abstentionism in relation to such matters are clearly identified in policy studies and research undertaken for the European Commission prior to the revision of the Treaties through the 1986 Single European Act. Such a reluctance had been developed over time on the basis of comparative studies of the industrial relations systems of various of the Member States, leading to the conclusion that cultural and contextual differences between the national systems were such as to render it improbable that co-ordinated harmonisation or integration initiatives could successfully be introduced from the Community level. In particular, a study of "collective wage agreements" by Professor Lyon-Caen, published for the Commission in 1972, formulated this view in strong terms, and, having put forward the view that "according to the present legal situation in the European Community the validity of collective wage agreements is limited to the territory of the individual Member States", went on to conclude on the more general front that, "As things stand at present, the conclusion of genuine European collective bargaining agreements is *unlikely*. None of the functions which the collective agreement fulfils currently exist at this level and the observable trends are not in that direction". See, Commission of the European Communities (DG/V/D/3), "In search of the European Collective Bargaining Agreement. Study of Mr. Lyon-Caen", (Doc. V/855/72-E). A study comparing "the rules of the game" for industrial relationships within the Member States prior to the 1986 Treaty revisions also made clear what seemingly intractable problems were faced in the context of industrial relations systems demonstrating so much of the particular national values and contexts in which they had been conceived and developed: F.Furstenberg, M.Grandi, A.C.Neal & J.D.Reynaud, *Les regles du jeu: Industrial Relations in Four Community Countries – Similarities and Uncertainties as Regards the Rules Governing Them* (Commission of the European Communities, Brussels, V/1433/86).

48 Council Resolution of 21st January 1974 concerning a social action programme of the European Communities (74/c 13/1). As part of the labour law component of this programme were included the two Directives which set the pattern for "collective" consultation procedures of this kind – namely, Council Directive 75/129 of 17 February 1975, on the Approximation of the Laws of the Member States relating to Collective Redundancies (OJ 1975 L48/29) and Council Directive 77/187 of 14 February 1977, on the approximation of the laws of the Member States relating to the safeguarding of employees' rights in the event of transfers of undertakings, businesses or parts of businesses (OJ 1977 L61/26). The nature of the consultative obligations created by these instruments was considered by the European Court of Justice in Joined Cases C-382/92 and C-383/92, *Commission of the European Communities* v. *United Kingdom*.

consultation contained in the 1989 "framework Directive" on health and safety should be taken to reflect the policy thrust associated with the 1989 Social Charter,[49] it has to be recognised that those particular mechanisms had already been well developed in the context of social policy measures dealing with health and safety at work, and, in the eyes of many, touched upon relatively "uncontroversial" matters in respect of which it is difficult to conceive of a "conflictual bargaining" forum for their agreement and resolution between the industrial relations actors.[50]

Meanwhile, a variety of matters covered by the list of "fundamental rights of workers" in the 1989 Community Charter were not approached directly, in the sense of being presented by the European Commission in the form of a list of proposed legislative acts, but, instead, were taken up for development in the framework of a number of "policy action areas", such as the "Helios II" programme (directed towards disabled people)[51] – a device which has been regularly resorted to and which can be seen, most recently, with the current 4th Equal Opportunities Action Programme,[52] or the Commission's Action Plan for free movement of workers.[53] In consequence, any "political" controversy which might be stirred in connection with such initiatives was, arguably, sufficiently "dampened" as to avoid open disputes when action eventually came to be required.[54]

It was, however, with the stage designed to follow the completion of the Single Market in 1992 that the most significant "hiccup" in this process of developing a "social Europe" occurred. Thus, at the negotiations over revision of the Treaties undertaken by what eventually became the 1992 Treaty of Maastricht, a head-on conflict between the government of the United Kingdom and the remaining eleven Member States could not be avoided, and, as a consequence, the technical compromise which was eventually adopted – in the form of a Protocol and Agreement on Social Policy annexed to the Maastricht Treaty – left the Community with the unsatisfactory position of

49 See Council Directive 89/391/EEC, of 12th June 1989, with a view to the introduction of measures to encourage Improvements in the Safety and Health of Workers at Work.

50 It may be suggested that, even for the most resolute proponent of the proposition that "the market mechanism" should determine policy choices in the field of social affairs, there is some political difficulty with the presentation of a proposition to the effect that there is virtue in unsafe working conditions, or that fatalities at work constitute "a price worth paying" for economic efficiency.

51 The programme was adopted by the Council on 25 February 1993 for a period of four years.

52 COM (95) 381.

53 COM (97) 586.

54 Or, *a fortiori*, when budget lines were being sought for their continuation and implementation!

having given birth to two parallel systems of labour law.[55] The political rhetoric of this period has been well documented, although it should be noted that the only productive use made of the 1992 legislative powers created by the Agreement on Social Policy was in relation to two matters, dealing respectively with European works councils and with parental leave.[56]

Since the election to office in the United Kingdom of a Labour government in the Spring of 1997, the publicly voiced position of that Member State has shifted, towards an acceptance of the values underlying the 1989 Social Charter and the 1992 Protocol and Agreement on Social Policy. Indeed, the two instruments legislated for under the powers contained in the 1992 Agreement have also subsequently been re-addressed, and both have now been enacted so as to extend their effect to the United Kingdom under powers in the Treaty to which the United Kingdom has expressly given its consent.[57]

Most significantly, following the most recent Inter-Governmental Conference, the Treaty of Amsterdam,[58] once ratified by all of the signatory States and brought into force,[59] will regularise this position, drawing the 1989 Community Charter more closely into the legal order of the European Community, and bring about the Treaty revisions aspired to at Maastricht but temporarily frustrated by the interregnum of the Protocol and Agreement on Social Policy.[60]

55 *Protocol (No. 14) on social policy*, together with the *Agreement on social policy concluded between the Member States of the European Community with the exception of the United Kingdom of Great Britain and Northern Ireland* – the two systems consisted of that which was applicable for the (then) twelve Member States, by virtue of the existing Treaty provisions (Articles 117 – 122), and that which was created in the Protocol and Agreement for "the Eleven" (excluding the United Kingdom). For comments on this situation and a variety of theoretical observations about the "constitutionality" of the arrangement, see *inter alia E. Whiteford*, "Social Policy after Maastricht", (1993) 18 *European Law Review* 202, and *D.Curtin*, "The Constitutional Structure of the Union: A Europe of Bits and Pieces", (1993) 30 *Common Market Law Review* 17.

56 Respectively, Council Directive 94/45/EC of 22 September 1994, on the establishment of a European Works Council or a procedure in Community-scale undertakings and Community- scale groups of undertakings for the purposes of informing and consulting employees, and Council Directive 96/34/EC of 3 June 1996, on the framework agreement on parental leave concluded by UNICE, CEEP and the ETUC. Work in relation to part-time work regulation has been in progress since 1997 - see COM(97)392 final.

57 See Council Directive 97/74/EC of 15 December 1997 extending, to the United Kingdom of Great Britain and Northern Ireland, Directive 94/45/EC on the establishment of a European Works Council or a procedure in Community-scale undertakings and Community-scale groups of undertakings for the purposes of informing and consulting employees, and Council Directive 97/75 /EC of 15 December 1997 amending and extending, to the United Kingdom of Great Britain and Northern Ireland, Directive 96/34/EC on the framework agreement on parental leave concluded by UNICE, CEEP and the ETUC, both adopted under the "unanimity" powers contained in Article 100 of the Treaty of Rome.

58 See *supra*.

59 *Editor's Note:* Which is still not the case at the time of writing.

60 The result is to be achieved through what should become a revised (and renumbered) Chapter of the Treaty entitled "Social Provisions", made up of Title XI, Articles 136 – 145.

6. The Variety of Actors in the Establishment of Generally Applicable Rights Frameworks

Of natural concern to those involved with the debate over developing a "social constitution" of rights for workers at work in the European Community – particularly given the European geographical context and the changing political face of Central and Eastern Europe – have been the developing principles contained in the 1961 European Social Charter. That achievement of the Council of Europe, entered into by *(inter alia)* each of the Member States of the Community, stands alongside the 1950 European Convention for the Protection of Human Rights and Fundamental Freedoms (the "Rome Convention") – widely regarded as the "jewel in the crown" of the Council of Europe.

So, too, has direct concern been held to provisions developed on a global basis at the level of the United Nations, in the form, particularly, of the stipulations concerning civil and political rights. That consideration has, generally speaking, been in terms of having regard to "human rights" and "fundamental freedoms" applicable across the totality of society.

The mere mention of such instruments serves to illustrate that the sources for establishing rights in this area have been fragmented, with global activity at the level of the United Nations, as well as regional activity, such as that of the Council of Europe. As the European Community has developed and undergone progressive enlargement since the signing of the Treaty of Rome in 1957, a number of issues have arisen in relation to the connections between (as well as the boundaries dividing) these various supra-national institutional arrangements.

Indeed, even though the focus of discussion may be overwhelmingly Euro-centric, it is increasingly important also to keep a close eye upon progress in other regional contexts – such as the NAFTA States[61] or the MERCOSUR[62] and ASEAN[63] frameworks – as well as upon other major recent developments at

61 Canada, Mexico and the United States of America. The NAFTA Agreement contains, *inter alia*, provisions relating directly to rights and standards at work. See, for example, the labour side agreement of NAFTA, the North American Agreement on Labor Cooperation (NAALC).

62 Bringing together Argentina, Brazil, Paraguay and Uruguay – and soon to be extended so as to include Chile.

63 The Association of Southeast Asian Nations (ASEAN) was established on 8 August 1967 with the signing of its founding agreement in Bangkok. Its current membership comprises Brunei Darussalam, Cambodia, Indonesia, Laos, Malaysia, Myanmar, Philippines, Singapore, Thailand and Vietnam.

the global level (most notably, the activity of the WTO).[64]

One reason for taking note of relationships within and outside the geographical sphere of Europe has been highlighted recently with a technical dispute over the extent to which the developing European Community legal order enables that entity to adhere to, or subsume itself to, a rights regime external to its established decision-making and legislative powers. This issue came to the fore, most notably, with the reference to the European Court of Justice of the question whether powers existed under the current form of the Treaties for the European Community to accede to the European Convention – in response to which the Luxembourg Court delivered an unequivocal negative, stating that:

> "as Community law now stands, the Community has no competence to accede to the European Convention for the Protection of Human Rights and Fundamental Freedoms".[65]

Nor has this been the only issue upon which relations between the European Community and international standard-setting organisations have been under the spotlight. In particular, the position of the Community in respect of the International Labour Organisation has also been closely considered, notably in respect of the competence of DG/V of the European Commission and the standing of individual Member States of the Community in their individual national dealings with the ILO.[66]

Eventually, therefore, in Opinion 2/91, the European Court of Justice was asked for its view on the nature of the respective Community and Member State competencies in relation to conclusion of ILO Convention No.170 concerning safety in the use of chemicals at work. The subject-matter of this case offered the opportunity to consider the issue of internal and external competence, as well as to take stock of the legislative scope of Article 118a of the Treaty.[67] Following formal reference to the Court of Justice, an eventual decision was reached that:

64 The World Trade Organisation Agreement has been ratified by all of the Member States, as well as by the European Community in its own capacity, following the delivery of Opinion 1/94 of the European Court of Justice on 15 November 1994. See [1994] ECR I 5267. The arrangements for the WTO came into effect on 1st January 1995. For comment on this, see *J.Bourgeois*, "The EC in the WTO and Advisory Opinion 1/94 – an Echternach Procession", (1995) 32 *Common Market Law Review* 763. The significance of an organisation such as the WTO in the context of the present debate over fundamental rights at work has recently been emphasised by the Director-General of the ILO, who commented that "...the latest important recognition of the particular significance of fundamental rights in the context of trade liberalisation was at the Ministerial Conference of the World Trade Organisation in Singapore; in their declaration, the ministers of trade, while agreeing that the comparative advantage of countries, particularly low-wage developing countries, should in no way be called into question, renewed their "commitment to the observance of internationally recognised core labour standards." See *The ILO, standard setting and globalization*, Report of the Director-General to the 85th Session of the International Labour Conference (Geneva 1997).

65 Opinion 2/94, delivered on 28 March 1996, on Community competence to accede to the Convention for the Protection of Human Rights and Fundamental Freedoms.

"the conclusion of ILO Convention No.170 is a matter which falls within the joint competence of the Member States and the Community".[68]

Whatever the view taken of the particular disputes which have arisen in relation to the European Convention and as regards relationships with the International Labour Organisation, the very existence of these controversies serves to remind the observer that any process towards creating a regime of fundamental social rights, and embodying such a framework within the structures of the European Community, is not necessarily a matter which beckons with open arms. In addition to any controversy over the identification and definition of relevant rights, the "constitutional" position of the European Community has constantly to be borne in mind, and the Opinions of the European Court of Justice in 1991 and 1994 provide a timely reminder of the obstacles which have to be overcome in this particular context.

Nevertheless, as is indicated below,[69] the daunting task of constructing a basis upon which a "social constitution for Europe" might be founded has formed an explicit element in recent policies and programmes, and the political process tending in such a direction would appear to have been gathering pace for some considerable time.

66 To the dismay of many, it has been evident for many years that there has been an uneasy relationship between the International Labour Organisation and the social affairs directorate of the European Commission. As an organisation founded in 1919, the ILO has tended to regard itself as the key global player in social protection standard-setting, and suggestions that, from time to time, the European Community was seeking to "re-invent the wheel" have often been in evidence. This uncomfortable duality has been particularly noticeable in the field of occupational health and safety, where a variety of ILO instruments have been developed over more than half a century. In addition, there has been a lingering dispute between the European Community and a number of its Member States over how their respective interests should be represented within the ILO — particularly since each Member State is a member of the ILO, but the Community enjoys observer status only.

67 The preceding history of disputes over the respective competencies is set out in Opinion 2/91 (especially in Part IV), which notes previous problems which had arisen in relation to ILO Convention No.153 and ILO Convention No.162 (the latter of which had given rise to Commission action — later withdrawn — for annulment of a Council Decision concerning the appropriate procedural approach to be adopted by the Community and the Member States).

68 During the course of its consideration, however, the Court of Justice had given express indications that, in cases of joint competence such as that under consideration, it was necessary, in order to ensure unity in the international representation of the Community, to ensure close co-operation between the Community institutions and the Member States, both in the process of negotiation and conclusion and in the fulfilment of the obligations entered into. In relation to the context of this dispute, and for further details of *inter alia* the own-initiative Opinion on relations between the EU and the International Labour Organisation, issued by the Economic and Social Committee in the wake of the Court's Opinion in relation to ILO Convention No.170, see *Alan C. Neal*, "Regulating Health and Safety at Work: Developing European Union Policy for the Millennium", (1998) 14 *The International Journal of Comparative Labour Law and Industrial Relations* 147.

69 See *infra*.

7. A Note on the International Instruments in the Field

Much of the background to the discussions in the Seville colloquium drew its frame of reference from experience and values to be found in specific international instruments touching social and civic rights at work. In particular, the well-established instruments of the United Nations, its specialised International Labour Office, and the Council of Europe, formed a significant part of the backdrop for consideration of particular issues.

A selection of the most significant of these international instruments has been included in this volume as an Appendix, amongst which is also to be found the most recently adopted declaration of the International Labour Organisation, dated June 1998, concerning follow-up measures in relation to instruments promulgated through that organisation.[70]

In relation to the modern framework of international instruments,[71] the post-Second World War starting point is the United Nations' Universal Declaration of Human Rights of 1948,[72] which, in turn, was the direct predecessor to the Council of Europe's 1950 European Convention for the Protection of Human Rights and Fundamental Freedoms.[73] That European Convention sets out "the first steps for the collective enforcement of certain of the rights stated in the Universal Declaration", with the contracting States undertaking to ensure for everyone within their jurisdiction the range of civil and political rights and freedoms set out in the Convention. Subsequent protocols have extended the list of rights originally set out in the Convention when signed in 1950.[74]

In terms of adjudication and enforcement of disputes over the rights contained in it, the Convention provides for a European Commission and a European Court of Human Rights to deal with individual petitions.[75] It is generally recognised that

70 See *infra*, p.175 ff.

71 It may be mentioned that, amongst those instruments whose influence is most keenly perceived from a longer historical perspective, and which, in consequence, necessarily shape the context of any debate in this field, are the English Magna Carta of 1215, which asserted the right to a fair trial and a just legal system; the Declaration of Independence of the United States of America of 1776; and the French Declaration of the Rights of Man and the Citizen of 1789.

72 See *infra*, p.118 ff.

73 See *infra*, p.180 ff.

74 In particular, to provide for the power to give advisory opinions (Protocol No.2 of 1963). See *infra*, p.200 ff.

75 Provision is also made for the bringing of inter-state cases. Although there have been few of these to date, where they have occurred, they have concerned allegations of serious violations of human rights. It should be noted that the Commissioners who sit in the European Commission of Human Rights and the Judges of the European Court of Human Rights are entirely independent, and are elected by the Committee of Ministers and the Parliamentary Assembly respectively.

the case-law of the European Court and European Commission of Human Rights have reinforced and developed the Convention rights, thereby providing a measure of dynamism for the system so established and enabling a degree of evolution to take place without the need for recasting of the terms of the Convention itself.[76]

Also emanating from the Council of Europe is the 1961 European Social Charter,[77] which, following a number of amendments in the three-and-a-half decades since its inception, has recently been updated to provide for a Revised Charter taking into account various additional protocols, and enunciating 31 basic rights enshrined in the instrument itself.[78]

The other major source of international standards in this field – particularly when one is considering this area in the context of the states of Europe – is the International Labour Organisation, based in Geneva. This part of the United Nations initially developed its Conventions and Recommendations in the area of labour and workers' rights in the post-1919 era following the ending of the First World War. Since the Declaration of Philadelphia, in 1944,[79] its activism in the field of fundamental social rights at work has become concentrated, in particular, upon the development of a group of "core standards", now generally manifested in seven instruments.[80] Some notion as to the extent of the success gained in this area can be gauged from the 1997 Report of the Director-General, presented to the 85th Session of the International Labour Conference.[81]

76 All of the contracting States, with the exception of Ireland, Norway and the United Kingdom (all three of which were represented at the Seville colloquium), have incorporated the Convention into their own law, thereby enabling the domestic judiciary to take full account of its provisions when considering a grievance. It should also be noted that, once domestic judicial remedies have been exhausted, an individual may thereafter still seek redress before the institutions in Strasbourg for an alleged breach of the Convention by a contracting State. Such a facility has given rise to the observation that "the Strasbourg machinery is not a substitute for national courts, but is, in a sense, an extension of them".

77 See *infra*, p.203 ff. for the 1996 revised version of this instrument.

78 Amongst the various additional Protocols consolidated into the revised version of the Charter are those adding new rights (1988), revising the supervision procedure (1991), and adding a system for collective complaints (1995).

79 See *infra*, p.115 ff.

80 Respectively, ILO Convention No. 29 concerning Forced or Compulsory Labour (1930), *infra*, p.125 ff.; ILO Convention No. 87 concerning Freedom of Association and Protection of the Right to Organise (1948), *infra*, p.138 ff.; ILO Convention No. 98 concerning the Application of the Principles of the Right to Organise and to Bargain Collectively (1949), *infra*, p.145 ff.; ILO Convention No. 100 concerning Equal Remuneration for Men and Women Workers for Work of Equal Value (1951), *infra*, p.151 ff.; ILO Convention No. 105 concerning the Abolition of Forced Labour (1957), *infra*, p.157 ff.; ILO Convention No. 111 concerning Discrimination in Respect of Employment and Occupation (1958), *infra*, p.161 ff.; and ILO Convention No. 138 concerning Minimum Age (1973), *infra*, p.166 ff.

81 *The ILO, standard setting and globalization*, Report of the Director-General to the 85th Session of the International Labour Conference (Geneva 1997).

8. A Comment on the "Academic" Debate over Fundamental Social Rights of Workers

A number of components have been present during the course of the development of that debate over fundamental social rights. Not surprisingly for a debate which includes amongst its chief participants a number of academic authorities in the relevant field, there has been a "legitimate voice" dispute over who should be entitled to participate in any debate concerning "fundamental rights". At one end of the spectrum, there appear acknowledged writers and researchers in the field of "human rights" and associated topics (amongst which may be the notion of "fundamental human rights" or fundamental rights in general) while towards the other end of the range can be found recognised authorities in the areas of social and employment law. While the former accuse the latter of "reinventing the wheel" in relation to the debate over "rights", or of over-simplifying the issues involved in that debate, the latter retaliate with complaints of rigid formalisation by the "human rights" scholars which fails to take into account the particular needs of workers in the community labour market.

Into this maelstrom enter some of Europe's most senior labour court judges, concerned to identify some of the subject-matter to which this debate relates, and charged with producing an account of the current "state of play", together with some preliminary assessment of the prospects for judicial embracing in the future of any "fundamental social rights" phenomenon into the employment law and legal orders of their respective national systems.

9. The "Amsterdam Process", the Comité des Sages and the Future of Fundamental Social Rights at Work – "Effective" Rights or "Aspirational" Declarations

Self-evidently, the Seville discussions which have given rise to this volume took place during the currency of the Inter-Governmental Conference considering revision of the Treaties – the task which was eventually achieved with the Amsterdam Treaty of 1997.[82] In consequence, it is important to bear in mind the varying agendas of those involved in that process – particularly, the European Commission, which was instrumental in providing the background for addressing the enormously significant issue of establishing explicit fundamental rights provision within the Treaties making up the European Communities. This was a time of much lobbying and "headline" political declarations in the field. Indeed,

82 *Editor's note:* Although, as has already been indicated, it remains unclear, at the time of writing, how and when the Amsterdam Treaty will eventually be brought into effect through the necessary process of ratification by the Member States of the Community. See *Lammy Betten*, *supra*, note 11.

one has only to consider the stream of publications being issued by various interested parties to appreciate the pressures under which this attempt at considered debate was being undertaken.[83]

Undoubtedly, one of the most significant steps in this process was the establishment of a specialised group of experts, under the format of a "Comité des Sages", and, indeed, the very fact of the setting-up of this *Comité des Sages* can be seen as indicating a number of important matters. First, the natural inclusion of this issue on the agenda for the Inter-Governmental Conference was underscored. Second, this issue was not viewed as merely a matter of technical application of standards to be discovered elsewhere and incorporated into Community legal form. Instead, it was conceived of as a matter calling for philosophical consideration of the underpinning rationale for embarking upon any process of identification of, and development for, a regime of fundamental social and civic rights for the citizens of the Community.

Since the publication of the report prepared by the *Comité des Sages*, the follow-up activity of, in particular, the European Commission, has gone even further to impress how important this issue is perceived as being. Indeed, there has been established a group of (essentially academic) specialists in the field of human and fundamental rights who have been continuing the work towards consideration of appropriate and timely steps towards the development of such a regime for the enlarged European Community of the next millennium.

However, it is a matter of pure speculation as to whether there will eventually be created some "Charter" of fundamental rights, of the kind envisaged and proposed by the *Comité des Sages*, or whether this matter is destined to tantalise for many years to come. Certainly, the overt result to date – if measured in terms of the input into the Amsterdam Treaty – cannot be said to be substantial, or, even, to carry the promise of any dramatic future development within the foreseeable future.

While it is right to have regard to the wording of the new Article 136,[84] to the effect that:

83 Amongst the documents relevant to the present matters, mention has already been made *supra* of contributions such as *M.Rodriguez-Piñero* & *E.Casas*, "In Support of a European Social Constitution", in P.Davies *et al* (eds), *European Community Labour Law: Principles and Perspectives* (Oxford 1996), p.23; R.Blanpain, B.Hepple, S.Sciarra & M.Weiss, *Fundamental Social Rights: Proposals for the European Union* (1996); and the ETUC's voice in B.Bercusson, S.Deakin, P.Koistinen, Y.Kravaritou, U.Mückenberger, A.Supiot & B.Veneziani, *A Manifesto for Social Europe* (Brussels 1996). There was also a host of polemical contributions, containing a variety of proposals, with a wide range of argumentation – from the carefully reasoned to the blatantly propagandist!

84 Inserted as a replacement for the existing Article 117, and subsequently renumbered as Article 136. As indicated above, it should be noted that this provision, at the time of writing, is still awaiting the full ratification of the Amsterdam Treaty by all of the Member States before it will be able to come into force.

> "The Community and the Member States, having in mind fundamental social rights such as those set out in the European Social Charter signed at Turin on 18 October 1961 and in the 1989 Community Charter of the Fundamental Social Rights of Workers, shall have as their objectives the promotion of employment, improved living and working conditions, so as to make possible their harmonisation while the improvement is being maintained, proper social protection, dialogue between management and labour, the development of human resources with a view to lasting high employment and the combating of exclusion."

It might prove wise, in the cold light of day, not to anticipate too much as flowing from this provision.[85] One might prefer to look, instead, towards a continuation of the steady progress made through European Commission initiatives designed to develop and stimulate an extension of the "social dimension" alongside the economic dimension of the Single Market.

Perhaps, indeed, such a sceptical approach would reflect, in many ways, some of the reservations expressed during the course of the discussions at the Seville colloquium. As members of the judiciary, the group gathering in Seville might be considered to approach issues concerning "rights" from a particular (and, arguably, narrow) perspective – namely, that of identifying and giving effect to justiciable rights read out of classical legal sources. Indeed, when one considers the various legal backgrounds making up the experiences of this group, it might be wondered whether some, at least, of the group might not be severely hidebound by limitations upon the creativity of judges imposed within their own national contexts.

Certainly, there is clear evidence that the approaches adopted by these judges includes a strong element of that suggested scepticism, and, on occasions, an unwillingness to venture with great commitment into some of the more fanciful realms of potentiality for "fundamental rights" propounded in certain theoretical or "critical" writings.

This is manifest in the search for "effective" rights, rather than major concern for "aspirational" declarations or the like. Yet, this is not necessarily to suggest that various aspirations are not shared by the members of the judiciary faced with such issues. Instead, it serves to remind us of the need for any framework of rights, whether fundamental, social, or whatever, to be capable of delivery in order to carry with it the ability to convince citizens of its relevance and value in a modern social setting.

85 See the observations in *Alan C. Neal*, "Labour Law in the 1990s: An Unweeded Garden that Grows to Seed?", (1997) 13 *The International Journal of Comparative Labour Law and Industrial Relations* 11.

Some voices have spoken out in recent years to indicate perceived shortcomings – or even "dangers" – in approaches which concentrate too strongly upon "high sounding pronouncements" or "glorious declarations" on rights. In this sphere, perhaps more than any other, appeals to the notion of Marshall McLuhan that "the medium is the message", without more, falls far short of realistic defensibility.[86] So, too, are the dangers apparent in raising too high the hopes of citizens, only to have promises dashed by the realities of short-term politics, economic constraints, or the superficial machinations of those whose only concern is a cynical establishment of immediate electoral advantage.

Whatever the eventual outcome of the debate over fundamental rights at work in the European Community, one thing emerges clearly from the discussions at the Seville colloquium – just as the same message emerges from the Report of the *Comité des Sages*. Any "rights", whatever their form and scope, must be clear, effective, and sanctionable. Towards that goal the energies of the European Commission and all of those concerned to promote and develop a vision of "Social Europe" will have to be channelled.

86 See, *inter alia*, H.Marshall McLuhan, *The Gutenberg Galaxy: The Making of Typographic Man* (1962).

The Report of the *Comité des Sages*: "For a Europe of civic and social rights"*

My purpose here is to present the Report of the *Comité des Sages*,[1] "For a Europe of civic and social rights" – a document which has constituted a part of the process of the Inter-governmental Conference on the revision of the Treaties, which has been the prelude to the signing of the Treaty of Amsterdam, on 2 October 1997.[2] That document will continue to have an influence well beyond the conclusion of the Inter-Governmental Conference, since, as we shall see, one of its proposals is specifically concerned with the establishment of a new Inter-Governmental Conference on the revision of the Treaties, dealing specifically with social rights.

Background to the Debate

As is well known, the history of the Community – now the European Union – has been a progressive and long drawn out process: It began forty-six years ago, in 1951, with the signing of the Treaty of Paris, which set up the European Coal and Steel Community.[3] A number of Treaties – numbering some seventeen in all – then followed, slowly giving rise to this unprecedented organisation into which every European has invested his hopes. Thus was brought into being this phenomenon called the European Community – or, rather, the "European Union", which, of course, in addition to the "European Community", consists of two further so-called "pillars".[4]

The progressive nature of the Community's formation, as compared with that of normal constitutional processes, meant that the issue of the protection of fundamental rights was not accorded formal consideration, either by the

* Eduardo Garcia de Enterria, Emeritus Professor of Administrative Law in the Universidad Complutense de Madrid, Spain, and a member of the *Comité des Sages* October 1995 – February 1996.

1 European Commission, *For a Europe of civic and social rights* (Report by the Comité des Sages chaired by Maria de Lourdes Pintasilgo), (Office for Official Publications of the European Communities, Luxembourg 1996).

2 Treaty of Amsterdam amending the Treaty on European Union, the Treaties establishing the European Communities and certain related acts, 2 October 1997.

3 Treaty establishing the European Coal and Steel Community, 18 April 1951.

4 To use the term which has become the norm since the agreement to the Maastricht Treaty.

constitutional bodies or by the States, since these were working in the domain of Community law. Indeed, although there is reference, if rather minimalistically, to one typical social right in the 1957 Treaty of Rome – where Article 119 of the Treaty prohibits discrimination on the ground of sex,[5] albeit only so far as concerns the remuneration for a particular job – in virtually every Treaty up until the 1986 Single European Act,[6] such a "constitutional" or "higher" level is nowhere to be found, save for that minimal recognition of an anti-discriminatory principle.

The 1986 Single European Act was a first attempt to revise the whole system of the Community. Furthermore, it includes in its Preamble an important declaration concerning "fundamental rights".[7] This has to be seen in conjunction with the formula by which the Treaty of Rome defines the function of the Court of Justice in Article 164, such that, "The Court of Justice shall ensure that in the interpretation and application of this Treaty the law is observed". This is all that is said concerning the function of the Court of Justice. It is thus evident that the Preamble to the Single European Act, which "fundamental rights" the Court of Justice is obliged to guarantee, implicitly safeguards human rights and fundamental freedoms.

Even before this "solemn declaration" was incorporated into the Treaties, the Court of Justice itself had already stated, in the *Stauder* judgment of 1969,[8] that fundamental human rights are enshrined in the general principles of Community Law. As is well known, the Court of Justice states that the basis of its decisions is not merely the written laws, but also the general

5 Article 119 of the Treaty of Rome (unchanged by the Single European Act 1986 or by the Treaty on European Union 1992) provides that:

"Each Member State shall during the first stage ensure and subsequently maintain the application of the principle that men and women should receive equal pay for equal work.

For the purpose of this Article, 'pay' means the ordinary basic or minimum wage or salary and any other consideration, whether in cash or in kind, which the worker receives, directly or indirectly, in respect of his employment from his employer.

Equal pay without discrimination based on sex means:

(a) that pay for the same work at piece rates shall be calculated on the basis of the same unit of measurement;

(b) that pay for work on time rates shall be the same for the same job."

6 Single European Act, signed at Luxembourg on 17 February 1986 and at The Hague on 28 February 1986.

7 The third indent to the Preamble declares the determination of the Member States "to work together to promote democracy on the basis of the fundamental rights recognised in the constitutions and laws of the Member States, in the Convention for the Protection of Human Rights and Fundamental Freedoms and the European Social Charter, notably freedom, equality and social justice".

8 Case 29/69, *Stauder* v. *City of Ulm, Sozialamt*, [1969] E.C.R. 419.

principles of Community law, which its jurisprudence has progressively moulded from various sources (including, in particular, principles common to the Member States); generally recognised and accepted principles of law, such as legal certainty; and the constitutional principles common to the Member States. Amongst these general principles, to which the Court of Justice regularly makes reference before reaching a decision, the *Stauder* judgment had already stated that fundamental human rights had to be included. This was justified not on the basis of some kind of abstract principle, but on a concern for the source and instrumental means of establishing these basic human rights. The Court suggested two sources – first, the common constitutional traditions of the Member States, and, second, international Treaties on fundamental rights (particularly the 1950 Rome Convention, established by the Council of Europe).[9]

The function of these fundamental rights in the Community order was to force the institutions of the Community to respect them; to fill the gaps;[10] and, in like manner, to impose obligations upon the Member States whenever they acted in the sphere of Community Law proper. By means of this dual approach, and as general legal principles, the jurisprudence of the Court of Justice has declared as part of Community Law the right of ownership; the right to the "free exercise of financial activity"; the right to privacy and to the inviolability of the home and of correspondence; the right to freedom of expression; the right to the non-retrospectivity of penal laws; and a whole series of protective rights in relation to administrative procedures.

This legal activity eventually culminated – notably by way of the revisions to the Treaties introduced at Maastricht – in Article F of the Treaty on European Union. In stark contrast to the rather vague formulation to be found in the Preamble,[11] paragraph 2 of Article F states the following:

> "The Union shall respect fundamental rights, as guaranteed by the European Convention for the Protection of Human Rights and Fundamental Freedoms signed in Rome on 4 November 1950 and as they result from the constitutional traditions common to the Member States, as general principles of Community law."

9 Council of Europe, Convention for the Protection of Human Rights and Fundamental Freedoms 1950, adopted in Rome on 4 November 1950.

10 For example, in all matters concerning defence rights in administration procedures brought before the Community administration.

11 In terms, for example, whereby the signatory States recite "Confirming their attachment to the principles of liberty, democracy and respect for human rights and fundamental freedoms and of the rule of law"– by which the Court of Justice always reserved the power to determine which rights might be considered principles of Community law

The wording "The Union shall respect..." is mandatory, and the problem seems to have been resolved, thereby acquiring a weight which was hitherto lacking. Astonishingly, however, we then go on to find that the Maastricht Treaty itself includes a further provision, in the shape of Article L, which defines in restrictive terms the extent of the jurisdiction of the Court of Justice of the European Communities in relation to the provisions of the Treaty on European Union. That Article L expressly provides that the powers of the Court of Justice extend only to the following provisions of the Treaty on European Union, namely:

- the provisions amending the original Treaties of the three Communities;[12]
- the third sub-paragraph of Article K.3(2)(c);[13] and
- Articles L to S, inclusive.

When looking at this list it can easily be appreciated that Article F, paragraph 2 (stating that fundamental rights, in their mandatory forms, linked the European Communities) has, unexpectedly, been excluded. In other words, what we are faced with is a series of rights which have been spelled out but which lack any legal guarantees or sanctions. This is a strange situation, indeed, by the standards of any jurist! Rights being subject to arbitration – a truly paradoxical state of affairs!

The Treaties, as we are constantly told by the Court of Justice, have the consistency of a Constitution, but it is a Constitution which lacks fundamental rights – an apparent contradiction in terms, particularly when one thinks of the Constitutional paradigm formulated in Article 16 of the Declaration of the Rights of Man and of the Citizen,[14] which maintains that:

> "Any society in which no provision is made for guaranteeing rights or for the separation of powers, has no Constitution."

It could therefore be said that the Maastricht Treaty on European Union, by virtue of this unexpected "sterilising" clause comprising Article L, gives rise to a constitution without fundamental rights, thereby lacking an essential element of a true Constitution.

12 *i.e.* the Coal and Steel Community (ECSC), the Economic Community (EEC) and the Atomic Energy Community (EURATOM).

13 Concerning issues in the fields of justice and home affairs, falling within Article K.1.

14 Declaration of the Rights of Man and of the Citizen 1789.

Pressure for Accession to the Rome Convention

In order to fill this enormous gap, an increasingly firm proposal has evolved at the heart of the European institutions to the effect that the Community (now in the guise of the European Union) should undertake the step of accession as a co-signatory to the 1950 Rome Convention for the Protection of Human Rights and Fundamental Freedoms.

That Rome Convention, which currently also consists of a further ten Protocols, possesses, above all else, an historically unique institutional system, offering an international guarantee of protection for the rights proclaimed in these international instruments against potential violations by States signatory to the Convention. The system thus enables any citizen to request the protection of the Court in Strasbourg against any violation perpetrated against him by his own State. Indeed, it is not even necessary to be a national of the country to make this request,[15] since any person alleging violation in the territory of any of the signatories to the Rome Convention has the right to seek protection from two specialised institutions – namely, the European Commission of Human Rights,[16] and, of course, that great institution, the European Court of Human Rights.

The proposal for the European Communities to accede to the Rome Convention, thus becoming part of the institutional system in Strasbourg, found echoes in every European institution and official body.[17] Eventually, therefore, in 1994, the European Council initiated a process with a view to possible accession for the Communities to the Rome Convention. This was undertaken by making use of Article 228 of the EEC Treaty, which provides, in paragraph 6, that:

> "The Council, the Commission or a Member State may obtain the opinion of the Court of Justice as to whether an agreement envisaged is compatible with the provisions of this Treaty. Where the opinion of the Court of Justice is adverse, the agreement may enter into force only in accordance with Article N of the Treaty on European Union".[18]

It should be remembered that it was the Council of Ministers which initiated the proceedings by consulting the European Court of Justice on the issue of the compatibility of the Rome Convention with the Community Treaties. The

15 *i.e.* as a legitimising condition.

16 What might be described as a first "filtering" body.

17 The Commission, the Council, and the European Parliament voiced this proposition repeatedly.

18 *i.e.* only in the event of prior amendment of the Treaties, following ratification by all of the Member States.

proceedings before the Court of Justice were of extraordinary complexity,[19] but, finally, (and most surprisingly, given that there seemed to be a common opinion at the heart of the Community) in March 1996, the Court of Justice issued its "Opinion",[20] to the effect that the Common, as the Treaties stood in their current form, could not accede to the Rome Convention.

This outcome – and, on this point, the Report of the *Comité des Sages* concurs[21] – could have been reached by means of Article 228, paragraph 6; *i.e.* by revising the Treaty. Moreover, the timing had been opportune, just as the Inter-Governmental Conference had begun, specifically with the competence and ambition to achieve a revision of the Treaties. It would therefore appear that the simplest solution would have been to have gone along this route – *i.e.* simply charging the Inter-Governmental Conference with the task of eliminating the formal obstacles noted in the Opinion issued by the Court of Justice, and pursuing the path in respect of which there seemed to be a general consensus. This would have enabled a position to have been reached whereby the European Union could have acceded as an additional member of the Strasbourg system. In that way, the Union could have taken to itself all of the consequences which flow from accession, including, above all, the essential feature of so-called "external control", which would ensure, in the area of Human Rights, the supremacy of the European Court of Human Rights over judgments of the European Court of Justice in Luxembourg.

Coincidentally, however, just a week prior to the issuing of the Opinion of the Court of Justice, in March 1996, the Report by the *Comité des Sages* was published. That Report, and the *Comité des Sages* which gave rise to it, had been envisaged in Spring 1995, in the context of the European Commission's Social Action Programme,[22] and the arrangements for the work of the *Comité des Sages* had been put into place in October 1995. Thereafter, work progressed at an intensive rate over the course of the following six months.

The Report which eventually emerged in March 1996 consisted of a re-examination of the entire issue of Social Rights, at precisely the time when a revision of the Treaties was being undertaken within the framework of the Inter-governmental Conference.

19 All fifteen Member States and each of the Commissions were heard.

20 Opinion 2/94, delivered on 28 March 1996, on Community competence to accede to the Convention for the Protection of Human Rights and Fundamental Freedoms. A so-called "Opinion" but, in fact, binding.

21 And which is not, furthermore, simply established incontrovertibly.

22 See Medium-term social action programme 1995-97, COM (95) 134 final, issued on 12 April 1995.

The Composition of the Comité des Sages

Before turning to the content of the Report which was produced by the *Comité*, I should say a word about the individuals who made up that body. First, it should be emphasised that the formula *"Comité des Sages"*, which was adopted for this group, has to be seen as no more than an administrative formula. It just happens to be the case that, within the structure of the European Communities, there are committees of "Experts" and committees of "Sages". This is not, in any sense, to suggest that the latter category are some variety of "super-experts", for it is not a question of being "knowledgeable" in any special, qualified manner.[23] Rather, the use of the term renders it somewhat closer to the French term *"sagesse"* – *i.e.* a notion of persons who are expected to exercise and demonstrate "good sense", or "wisdom".[24]

Certainly, in the selection of these "Sages" – amongst whom I was honoured to be one – "learning" was clearly not the main criterion. Indeed, when one considers the profiles of these seven "Sages" – a number which might possibly serve to evoke the seven wise men of Ancient Greece – one discovers quickly that they came from a selection of completely different backgrounds, and lacked any formal technical qualification particular to the context in which they were being called upon to act.

The chairwoman of the *Comité des Sages* was Mrs Maria Lourdes Pintasilgo, who has been the only female President of the Council of Ministers in the Iberian Peninsula.[25] An extraordinary woman, of enormous vitality and with an wonderful capacity for leadership, she came from a career background in Economics. Joining here were another two women, in the persons of the Greek Louka Katseli – a Professor of Economics who was a graduate of Harvard, where she had also lectured – together with Shirley Williams, who had at one time been a Minister of Education in the United Kingdom under a Labour government.[26] To these was added a prominent (and, in many ways, an unusual) French businessman, Frederic Pascal – a man endowed with an extraordinary concern for social issues, who made a major contribution to the work of the *Comité* – along with the eminent Swede, Bengt Westerberg, who had been a former Minister of Labour in the Swedish government. These were joined by

23 As the term is used in Spanish, for example.

24 Or, perhaps, as one might say in French to a child, "sois sage" – "be sensible, be reasonable in what you do".

25 For a number of months, some years ago, under the Presidency of the Republic of General Leales.

26 Baroness Williams had been granted a life peerage by that Labour government, by virtue of which she entered and held her seat in the House of Lords. Subsequently, she abandoned the Labour Party and went on to become a prominent figure as a founding member of the British Social Democratic Party.

Hartmut Kaelble – a German Professor of Contemporary History – and, finally, a Spanish Professor of Law, in the person of myself.

Such was the "line-up" of the *Comité*. However, it has to be said that, if ever there was one truly "wise man" involved with the work of the group, it was not one of the "seven", but the person unanimously nominated by us as our Rapporteur and the author of the Report. This was the Frenchman, Jean-Baptiste de Foucauld, who for many years had been a commissioner on the French Development Programme, and who is a prominent intellectual, well known for his work as a social philosopher.[27] While, of course, duly following the dictates of the Committee, Jean-Baptiste de Foucauld contributed true wisdom indeed.

The *Comité* concluded its work in March 1996, and its conclusions were eventually presented at the European Social Forum of that Spring. Since then, a great deal of effort has been dedicated to promoting awareness of the Report of the *Comité des Sages* and the debate surrounding it, as we shall now see.

Outline of the Report

The Report begins by noting that social issues are, and from now on will remain, at the centre of the challenges which must be faced in the building of Europe. To put it bluntly, a Europe based upon social exclusion, or upon large-scale unemployment, is simply not an option.

Admittedly, the economic and social conditions which formed the basis upon which the "welfare state" was conceived – based on full employment – have undergone radical change in the face of the globalisation of economies, the challenges posed by technological advances, and the like. However, this must not give rise to an abandonment of the European social model. It is highly significant that Europe has distinguished itself in relation to other economies – such as those of the United States of America, Japan, the former socialist countries of Eastern Europe, and the economies of South-East Asia – as a particular social system, and this must not be lost. Consequently, social exclusion must not be the price to pay for economic success – particularly since, far from being an obstacle to competitiveness, it constitutes, on the contrary, a factor which serves to increase competitiveness (as European history itself has demonstrated).

The situation currently facing us, therefore, is that there is a need for us to renew our labour and employment policies. In doing so, we have to create a social model which strengthens (or, at least, is capable of strengthening), rather than weakens, the economic system.

27 And, indeed, also well known as the Chairman of a political association of some reknown!

The present state of affairs in relation to social rights is particularly complex. Thus, the various individual States recognise social rights through their own constitutional regimes. At the same time, however, every Member State has also undertaken to adhere to the various international treaties and agreements in this field – from the important fundamental United Nations instruments to the Council of Europe's 1950 Rome Convention,[28] as well as in respect of the numerous Conventions of the International Labour Organisation.[29] This fact has, consequently, promoted an understanding between the Member States of the Union, who thus share a basically common view of the matter. Nevertheless, in spite of this, it remains the case, as has already been mentioned, that this vast problem has still not been addressed either through the Treaties or through the law derived from them. There exists, in other words, a "social deficit" in Community Law – and one which, as a matter of urgency, has to be resolved.

While the Maastricht Treaty refers to a strengthening of the aims of the Union – notably, of reinforcing economic and social issues – it also introduces a basic concept of European citizenship.[30] Furthermore, it realises a whole series of social policies[31] – notwithstanding the fact that efforts on this front may be regarded as being handicapped by the requirement for unanimity, which effectively establishes a power of veto which enables any one Member State to halt the progress of a Community policy. Yet, this whole situation clearly fails to provide for the needs to which I have referred. In particular, it fails to provide for those which are especially critical in the face of the phenomenal transformation being experienced in the world of work and by virtue of the radical economic developments which are being witnessed on a continuing basis.

It is essential, in the view of the *Comité des Sages*, to clarify matters and to take this situation forward. With that in mind, therefore, three progressive steps are suggested in order to achieve this:

1. A first step would be to create, on a firm foundation,[32] a pedestal of minimum fundamental rights, which would be applicable immediately.[33]

28 Council of Europe, Convention for the Protection of Human Rights and Fundamental Freedoms 1950 *(supra)*.

29 Of which, to date, there have been over 175. The so-called "core" Conventions on fundamental rights (Nos. 29, 87, 98, 100, 105, 111 and 138) are set out in Part II of this volume. See also the comments contained in the report of the Director-General to the 85th session of the International Labour Conference, *The ILO, standard setting and globalization* (Geneva 1997).

30 I shall return to the issue of citizenship *infra*.

31 From Articles 117 *ff*.

32 *i.e.* solidly (not with the weakness of the current conception of the general principles of law, each freely interpreted by the Court of Justice).

33 This, as will become clear, is precisely the problem concerning whether there should be accession or not to the Rome Convention, to which I shall refer *infra*.

2. The second step would be to integrate into the Treaties an initial list civil and social rights, drawing a distinction between those rights which would derive immediate benefit from legislative protection and those which would require policies and a significant investment of resources in order to become effective.

3. Finally, the third phase would consist of initiating a large-scale collective process involving all of the European countries in the development of a modern register of civic and social rights. As the Report makes clear, given that "economic Europe" has taken almost fifty years to build (and, indeed, is still evolving), the building of "social Europe" cannot be expected to be achieved by means of a single constitutive act of will. Consequently, a collective process must be set in train, which will actively involve the societies of each and every Member State.[34]

The First Stage

The first of these phases involves the question of accession to the European Convention for the Protection of Human Rights and Fundamental Freedoms (the 1950 "Rome Convention"). On this point, the *Comité des Sages*, breaking with the tradition of every specialised European institution and commission before it, comes out against European Union accession to the Rome Convention.

To achieve such accession would require the revision of a multi-national Convention, currently embracing some fifty member States. Following the fall of the "Iron Curtain", the countries belonging to the Strasbourg system – and, thus, also to the framework supervised through the European Court of Human Rights – include all of the former Soviet states, encompassing not only those that might have been considered as occupied by the Russian Army but, indeed, most of the States which made up the former USSR. This fact alone would make any revision of the Rome Convention an extremely complex process, given the involvement of fifty states and with the likelihood that it would take several years to complete. Moreover, the outcome of such a process would remain uncertain.

At the same time, within the established institutions of the Council of Europe and the European Court of Human Rights,[35] the European Union Member States are already a minority.[36] Consequently, while the Report does not make this observation outright, there is a clear implication that, in practice, the majority of States making up the Council of Europe lack a liberal democratic tradition. In consequence, therefore, it would seem inappropriate to impose

34 Something, indeed, which would be totally new in the entire history of the evolution of Europe.

35 Which, in their present form, consist of 40 members.

36 A minority of fifteen States.

upon a body of this nature the level of respect to be observed for the fundamental rights of the European Union.[37]

Furthermore, up until recently, there has been a broad uniformity of juridical and political perceptions. That consensus, however, has now virtually broken down. Recent events indicate the extent of this. Thus, there has been talk of "turbulence" in the Strasbourg system,[38] while, in the United Kingdom, a judgement delivered in 1995 by the European Court of Human Rights gave rise to loud protests denouncing the Rome Convention and calling for that country to seek to withdraw from its provisions.[39]

Consequently, rather than talking of accession or incorporation,[40] it has been suggested that there is, more importantly, a perceived lack of cohesion in the existing system, which gives rise to problems for the European Court of Justice when reviewing Community acts. Instead, therefore, of arguing in favour of accession to or incorporation for the 1950 Rome Convention, the Report of the *Comité des Sages* proposes working with Article F, paragraph 2, and Article L of the Treaty on European Union. Article F, paragraph 2, already refers to the Rome Convention, but could be extended in scope to allow for indirect incorporation of the Community Charter of the Fundamental Social Rights of Workers,[41] as well as the provisions contained in the Masastricht "Social Protocol",[42] while the elimination of the "sterilising" preventative clause of the

37 Note that, while expressing itself in "politically correct" terms, the Report does make clear insinuations.

38 As suggested by a French professor in a recently published article.

39 See the decision of the Court in *McCann and others* v. *United Kingdom* (27 September 1995). This judgement ruled against the United Kingdom in respect of a violation of the right to life, in the context of the death of three Irish terrorists in Gibraltar, after criminal proceedings in Gibraltar had completely exonerated the British government. Such a situation is possible only where there is a lack of cohesion as between political and juridical doctrine, for it would be inconceivable in a European state to review an acquittal of murder in a criminal court (by, for example in Spain, invoking the right of habeas corpus – the right to life is a fundamental right in the Spanish Constitution), or to invoke the right of ownership as a basis for an acquittal of burglary, misappropriation, *etc.*

40 And, it must be stressed, the author is explaining this in his own terms.

41 Community Charter of the Fundamental Social Rights of Workers (COM(89) 471 final).

42 Protocol No. 14 on social policy, annexed to the Treaty on European Union, together with the Agreement on social policy concluded between the Member States of the European Community with the exception of the United Kingdom of Great Britain and Northern Ireland. At the time of writing, the Protocol and Agreement on social policy had been signed by only 14 of the Member States, since the United Kingdom had not done so by virtue of the British "opt out" negotiated at Maastricht.

(Editor's note). However, since the time of the meeting of the European Association of Labour Court Judges in Seville in May 1996, the newly-elected British Labour government has not only expressed its intention of joining the regime established under the Protocol and Agreement on social policy but has also taken steps to implement into United Kingdom law the legislative instruments which have, so far, emerged out of the procedures provided for in those instruments.

judicial guarantee contained in Article L has already been identified as being a matter of pressing concern.

There would, therefore, be a direct incorporation of the entire Rome Convention and its Protocols, together with the entirety of the other international agreements on social issues which have been subscribed to by every Member State. This, it is felt, would be preferable to entering upon the task of undertaking what has already been shown to constitute a complex revision of the Rome Convention and then attempting its incorporation into an institutional system which, for the time being, finds itself in something of a state of crisis.

It is also suggested that there are, indeed, advantages in subjecting the Court of Justice of the European Communities to some form of external control,[43] such as that to be found before the European Court of Human Rights – something which currently applies to every European Constitutional Court (or, as the case may be, High Court). However, rather than providing for recourse to the European Court of Human Rights, the Report of the *Comité des Sages* proposes the creation of a kind of *ad hoc* Court, consisting of representatives from each of the Member States, drawn from their respective Constitutional Courts (or, as the case may be, High Courts), which would contribute to reflecting those common constitutional traditions which are the source of the concept of Europe's fundamental rights.

It has to be observed, however, that to adopt this formula would require the resolution of an extremely serious problem which was raised most acutely by the German Constitutional Court in the course of its notorious "Maastricht judgement" of 12 October 1993.[44] That judgement – in relation to which veritable rivers of ink have flowed, and which still generates debate through all sorts of publications – preserves the power of the German Constitutional Court to declare Community decisions as anti-constitutional, thereby challenging the principle of the supremacy of Community law over national law. The Italian Constitutional Court has expressed opinions of a like nature in this respect, while similar propositions have been put forward even in the French Parliament.

The *Comité de Sages* takes the view that the best way to put a stop to these cracks in the Community system, given the unexpected pretensions of the national constitutional courts, would be to involve those very constitutional courts themselves, through the proposed *ad hoc* Court, in order for this to function as a sort of habeas corpus mechanism in relation to the work of the Court of Justice in Luxembourg.

43 Although this is a proposal which, in the view of this commentator, will undoubtedly be rejected by the ongoing Inter-Governmental Conference.

44 This judgement resolves the issue of the constitutionality of the Maastricht Treaty – *i.e.* its compatibility with the German constitution, Bonn's fundamental laws, in the light of the Treaty's ratification.

The Second Stage

The second step would be to include in the text of the Treaties itself an initial declaration of fundamental rights. First, there would be a statement of those rights which are already protected legally in the basic form of the Treaties – equality under Community law; the outlawing of all forms of discrimination (on the basis of sex, language, religion, *etc*); the possible provision of "positive discrimination" measures; freedom of movement and residence throughout the European Union; the right of access to employment throughout the European Union; the right to a choice of education throughout the European Union; the right of association (in particular, of workers); the right to participate in collective bargaining and to embark upon collective action (in particular, the right to resort to industrial action). There would then be set out the principles establishing those rights which would require specific policies and the investment of resources in order to implement – the right to employment; the right to education; the right to lifelong education and training; the right to equitable conditions of employment, to health and to social security, and so on.

The Third Stage

Finally, the third phase of these proposals is to set in motion a vast collective participatory process, involving all of the European countries in developing a modern register of civic and social rights and duties, in order to take account of the changed nature of our modern developing economies and societies.

For this purpose, the Report works on the basis of the concept of "citizenship". That concept was proposed by, and is contained in, the Maastricht Treaty.[45] However, it is only to be found there as a purely formal phenomenon, defined in terms of three simple consequences – namely, the right to vote in local elections;[46] the right to diplomatic protection by diplomatic bodies of countries other the citizen's own;[47] and the right to complain to the Ombudsman.[48]

That is the sum extent of the references to citizenship contained in the Maastricht Treaty. However, the Report of the *Comité des Sages* suggests that those references should be fleshed out with a substantial social content, wherein

45 As introduced into Part II of the Treaty Establishing the European Community by Article G, point C, of the Treaty on European Union. In particular, Article 8 proclaims that "Citizenship of the Union is hereby established", and goes on to provide that "Every person holding the nationality of a Member State shall be a citizen of the Union".

46 By virtue of Article 8b. All European citizens may vote in the local elections of their place of residence, even if that is not their own country.

47 By virtue of Article 8c.

48 Article 8d.

would be found the idea of a collective society, which is the true concept of citizenship. Such a concept is one of truly collective solidarity and of rights to participate in things which are common to all, and which are of interest to all.

It is precisely on this basis of citizenship that the Report proposes that a collective process should be set up throughout Europe, sponsored (it is suggested) by the European Parliament, and in which NGOs,[49] traditional social partners, and new social players representing social trends and all points of view,[50] should participate in a process of collective reflection over a period of at least five years.

This period of collective reflection would gradually culminate in a sort of "European general social states", sponsored by the European Parliament, and which would come forward with a "charter" of civic and social rights and duties adapted to the new circumstances. It is not a question of experts or civil servants: This must be something which is born out of the very heart of society.

It has to be said that this part of the Report of the *Comité des Sages* is the one which has received – perhaps most surprisingly – the best reception. For the first time in the history of the European Communities, the European Parliament has set in motion this process of collective reflection. It has called upon the society of the European States; and it has asked those societies about their ideas, their fears, their ambitions, and also for their suggestions about this new project on the conception of a society adapted to current circumstances. The European Parliament has also sponsored meetings at which those involved in producing the Report are being asked to announce these glad tidings.

Indeed, I myself have been present at a number of these,[51] and, in my view, this is moving some substantial way towards creating a true state of Union. At one meeting which I attended in Paris, for example, a document signed by important intellectual, moral and religious figures was drawn up and promulgated. Similarly, in Madrid, such a concrete outcome was achieved with social leaders and non-governmental organisations. The whole aim is to create a state of Union which goes beyond the purely rhetorical.

Strangely enough, therefore, it has proved to be this third proposal – which had seemed the most rhetorical and the least tangible of the proposals contained in the Report of the *Comité des Sages* – which has turned out to be the most workable. Thus, while the Report itself is a work of pure reflection – a reflection designed to be offered to the current ongoing Inter-Governmental Conference – now, by virtue of this third phase, that reflection is also being offered to the citizens of Europe. Indeed, if anything, it now appears that we should be more hopeful of success through this avenue than may be expected,

49 Non-Governmental Organisations.

50 It should be noted that this is not intended necessarily (or even predominantly) to focus upon official bodies.

51 Some ten or more, at the time of writing.

so far as we are presently aware, from the current proceedings at the Inter-Governmental Conference.[52]

A Final Comment

By way of conclusion, this author would merely like to make reference to an extract from the final section of the Report of the *Comité des Sages*, which he believes to be extremely evocative and highly pertinent:

> "The European Union once again stands at the crossroads. It will only be able to take up the present challenge if it is prepared to give appropriate status to the social dimension. This is not something that can happen at a stroke, but neither are there any grounds for taking the easy option and continuing past practice. Europe has to innovate in terms of social policy, just as it has done in other policy sectors. The only way we shall build an attractive social model is by being prepared to make ongoing changes, reflecting the enhanced need for a competitive edge to cope with the increasing globalisation of social developments – both demographic and sociological – and the basic human needs which acquire their main expression in the form of rights and duties."

52 *(Editor's note)*. An observation which, following the outcome of the IGC, appears even more starkly to be the case than when it was made in May 1997 during the Seville colloquium.

Social Rights Recognised in International Law, in National Constitutions and Laws, and in Community Law

1. Introduction

The basic aim of the first part of this report is to examine how the fundamental rights of workers appear in the national legislation of the Member States and in international instruments.[1] The Report is concerned with social rights in general, as well, in particular, as rights enjoyed by workers or others associated with them, such as rights relating to social security or to protection in old age, generally associated with those who are or have been workers.

It is necessary to start with the proposition – which will come as no surprise – that there is in Europe a very high degree of correspondence between the rights guaranteed by national legislation and those recognised internationally. This is true of individual rights and public freedoms in general. As regards social rights, economic rights and cultural rights, or so called "third generation" rights (relating to the environment or information technology), the correlation with international provisions is greater in recent national texts than in older ones, depending on the time when those rights of a social nature appeared in contemporary constitutions.

As well as similarities, however, there are also differences in various aspects between national and international regulations. It is therefore necessary also to stress the complementary nature of some with others. To this end, it is appropriate to examine the catalogue of rights to be found in the international texts, particularly in the European area, and then to take a look at the national catalogue.

1. In the context of this Report, the expression "Member States" is used to include all of the national systems considered in the national reports produced for the Conference of the European Association of Labour Court Judges in Seville, Spain, 18 - 21 May 1997. This should therefore be taken to encompass the fifteen Member States of the European Union, together with Iceland and Norway, in the context of their membership of the European Economic Area.

2. The International Catalogue of Rights

(a) The United Nations

In this section the starting point is the United Nations Declaration of Human Rights (1948), where mention is made of rights of a social nature.[2] The same content later appears reiterated and applied in the New York Agreements.[3] Amongst these, reference must be made to the agreement concerned with Civil and Political Rights, since this deals with rights of non-discrimination, equality before the law, and the equal and non-discriminatory protection of the law;[4] the prohibition of slavery and forced labour;[5] the right to due process of law;[6] the right to freedom of association, including the right to establish trade unions;[7] and the protection of the family and infancy.[8] Other rights are provided for alongside these which have, in many cases, to be observed by the state and the employer. These would include the right to privacy,[9] or the rights of freedom of thought and freedom of opinion.[10]

However, it is the International Convention on Economic, Social and Cultural Rights which is the international text of universal scope which refers specifically to many of the fundamental rights of workers. This instrument includes mention of the right to work,[11] the right to equitable working conditions,[12] and the freedom to join a union.[13] It also encompasses the right to social security protection,[14] as well as the rights to protection of the family,[15]

2 See, in particular, Articles 7, 8, 10, 18, 19, 20, 22-25 and 28.

3 This, of course, leaves aside any discussion as to their value, given that they are seen as being merely declarations of principles, without the direct force of legal regulation behind them.

4 Articles 2.1 and 26.

5 Article 8.

6 Article 14.1.

7 Article 22.1.

8 Article 23 and Article 24 respectively.

9 Article 17.

10 See, respectively, Article 18.1 and Article 19.

11 Article 6.

12 Article 7.

13 Article 8.

14 Article 9.

15 Article 10.

maternity (with special reference to working mothers),[16] and minors (with a prohibition on their working in harmful working environments).[17] Other rights include the right to physical and mental health (which includes health at the workplace and the prevention of occupational diseases).[18] In addition, there is mention of nutrition,[19] education,[20] and cultural, scientific or artistic rights.[21] Particular mention should also be made of the international Conventions on the Elimination of all Forms of Racial Discrimination (1965) and the Elimination of Discrimination against Women (1979).

The most notable characteristic of all of these provisions is their acceptance by all European countries, (albeit with certain reservations, which do not, however, affect social rights).

(b) The International Labour Organisation

Turning to International Labour Organisation instruments relating to the fundamental rights of workers, there are five which are ratified by all of the European Member States. These are Conventions No. 29 and No. 105 on forced labour, Conventions No. 87 and No. 98 on freedom of association and collective bargaining, and Convention No. 100 on equal pay. There are, however, some exceptions in relation to Convention No. 87 (Iceland), or reservations from some States concerning Convention No. 98. There are also differences provided for in many, depending upon whether the conventions are or are not directly applicable ("self-executing" or "non-self-executing"). Together with these, there are numerous ratifications of Convention No. 135, which guarantees the rights of workers' representatives in companies. By contrast, however, ratifications of Convention No. 158 on the termination of the employment contract at the initiative of the employer are few and far between (ratified by Spain, Finland, France, Portugal and Sweden, with ratification recently being considered in Luxembourg).

16 Article 10.2.

17 Article 10.3.

18 See, in particular, Article 12.2.b and Article 12.2.c.

19 Article 11.

20 Article 13.

21 Article 14.

3. The European Catalogue of Rights

The regional system of protection of fundamental rights provided for by the Council of Europe extends, on the one hand, to civil and political rights, and, on the other, to economic, social and cultural rights. The primary instrument for this purpose is the European Convention on Human Rights (1950). A particular feature of the system is the existence of an institution – in the shape of the European Court of Human Rights (ECHR) – whose pronouncements have given rise to a body of case-law which is also a regulatory source of the rights and freedoms dealt with in the Convention. This has come about notwithstanding that the essential purpose of the system is to protect individuals against interference by the authorities in their private and social lives.

In the context of the 1950 Convention, interest centres upon the right to due process exercised within a reasonable time-scale – "the right to a fair and public hearing"; the right to freedom of thought, conscience or religion; the right to freedom of expression; and the right to freedom of assembly and association, including the right of individuals to form and to join unions for the protection of their interests. The ECHR has interpreted the expression "for the protection of their interests" in Article 11 as meaning that the freedom is guaranteed in order to protect the professional interests of union members through the action of their unions, in the exercise of which the unions must be consulted on public matters affecting those interests and be entitled to take action to protect their members.

From the case-law of the ECHR, it is interesting to note, in spite of the fact that the rights protected in the system are essentially civil and political, that many of them have social and economic implications. On the other hand, the ECHR has pointed out that the purpose of the Convention is the protection of rights which are not theoretical or illusory, but which can be real and effective. Moreover, many of those rights require States to agree upon positive actions which involve affecting the relationships between individuals, the scope of which interventions have to be determined by weighing up the respective general and individual interests affected, in the light of the particular circumstances of the case and having regard to the social reality of the time.

It may be noted that, in the social field, it has been concerned with the freedom of association which has given rise to most pronouncements.

The special regulatory force of the 1950 Convention is reflected in the reception given to it by certain legal systems. This is the case, for example, in Austria, where it has enjoyed constitutional status since 1964, and in Iceland, where it has had the force of law since 1994.

It should be pointed out, however, that the Council of Europe guarantees specifically social rights by way of another treaty – the European Social Charter of 1961, along with associated instruments dealing with social matters (such as the Additional Protocol of 5th May 1988). As indicated, the European Social

Charter is a separate treaty, specifically devoted to social rights – although without the guarantees of protection or the force of those recognised in the 1950 Convention. Thus, by signing up to the European Social Charter the signatory States bind themselves, in Part I, to certain social policy principles or objectives, and to a minimum list of rights (at least five of those indicated in Part II). This is also the situation in respect of the Additional Protocol to the Charter of 5th May 1988.

By virtue of Part I of the Charter, the States are bound to recognise, as an objective of social policy to be pursued by all additional means, the establishment of the conditions to allow the following rights and principles to be made effective:

1. All persons are to have the opportunity to earn a living by means of a freely chosen job.
2. All workers are entitled to equitable working conditions.
3. All workers are entitled to health and safety at work.
4. All workers are entitled to sufficient remuneration to provide themselves and their families with a decent standard of living.
5. All workers and employers have a right to associate freely in national or international organisations for the protection of their economic and social interests.
6. All workers and employers are entitled to collective bargaining.
7. Children and adolescents are entitled to special protection against the physical and moral dangers to which they are exposed.
8. Female workers, in the event of maternity, and other female workers, where appropriate, are entitled to special protection in their work.
9. All people are entitled to appropriate professional orientation, to help them to choose a profession according to their personal aptitudes and interests.
10. All people are entitled to appropriate professional training.
11. All people have a right to benefit from measures to allow them to enjoy the best state of health they can achieve.
12. All workers and people in their charge are entitled to Social Security.
13. All people that lack sufficient resources are entitled to social and medical assistance.
14. All people have a right to benefit from social services.
15. All disabled people are entitled to professional training and to professional and social re-adaptation, whatever the origin and nature of their disability may be.
16. The family, as the fundamental unit of society, is entitled to appropriate social, legal and economic protection, to achieve its full development.
17. Mothers and children, irrespective of their marital situation and family relations, are entitled to appropriate social and economic protection.

18. The nationals of each of the contracting parties have a right to exercise, in the territory of another party, any lucrative activity on equal terms with the nationals of the latter, subject to restrictions based on overriding reasons of an economic or social nature.
19. The migrant national workers of each of the contracting parties and their families are entitled to protection and assistance in the territory of any other contracting party.

On top of these provisions, Part I of the Additional Protocol of 5th May 1988 added the following items to the list of principles:

1. All workers have the right to equal opportunities and equal treatment in matters of employment and occupation without discrimination on the grounds of sex.
2. Workers have the right to be informed and to be consulted within the undertaking.
3. Workers have the right to take part in the determination and improvement of the working conditions and working environment in the undertaking.
4. Every elderly person has the right to social protection.

Part II of the Charter sets out a list of minimum rights (as provided for by Article 20.1.b) of which at least five must be recognised by a signatory State. That list consists of:

- Article 1 – Right to work.
- Article 5 – Freedom to join a union.
- Article 6 – Right to collective bargaining.
- Article 12 – Right to Social security.
- Article 13 – Right to social and medical assistance.
- Article 16 – Right of the family to social, legal and economic protection.
- Article 19 – Right of migrant workers and their families to protection and assistance.

Finally, the Charter establishes the obligation to subscribe to additional Articles or paragraphs – to the extent of a minimum total of 10 Articles or 45 paragraphs. So far as the Additional Protocol of 5th May 1988 is concerned, this only makes it obligatory for one of the four recognised rights to be ratified.

In accordance with these provisional measures, declarations and reservations have been formulated by all of the States of the European Union, as well as Iceland and Norway at the time of their signature or ratification. From these, one can see, in brief: (a) almost total ratification in the cases of France, Italy or Spain; (b) extensive ratification in a majority of cases (Austria, Denmark,

Germany, Iceland, Ireland, the Netherlands, Norway, Sweden, and the United Kingdom); and (c) limited ratification in exceptional cases, such as Cyprus.

From all this it may be concluded that the European system is extensive as regards its catalogue of social rights, but that it suffers from certain imperfections. This is not, however, so much the case in relation to the matters dealt with by the 1950 Convention – which provides a good demonstration of the importance of having a mechanism, such as the ECHR, to ensure that the rights referred to do not remain "mere declarations" but, instead, are turned into "reality". However, it should also be noted that recent steps have been taken to improve the effectiveness of rights provided for, particularly through the Additional Protocol to the Social Charter of 9th November 1995, establishing a system of collective claims. So, too, is there the system which would result from the proposed fusion of the Commission and the Court, with a view to bringing about other improvements.

4. The Reception of International Norms into Internal Law

At first glance, internal or Community law regulations might be thought of as unnecessary, in view of declarations in international texts that many of the fundamental rights contained therein are expected to be applied to all. It might thus appear that universal international or European treaties are already a sufficient instrument for achieving uniform regulation in relation to the fundamental rights of workers.

Such issues can only, however, be addressed after studying the systems of incorporation or reception of international regulations into internal law. Reception creates two issues: one with regard to the procedures for incorporation into the internal legal systems, the other relating to the level at which the international regulation is incorporated.

In respect of the procedures, it is interesting to note that, while each country has its own methods for incorporation of international regulations into internal law, there are strong or important similarities between all of them. In all places one finds the same techniques of approval and ratification. Distinctions begin to appear, however, once one begins to analyse the constitutional provisions, where these exist, on the procedures for, or recourse to, popular referendum. In general, such procedures include deliberation over and approval of the relevant international regulation in the appropriate legislative bodies, which will then authorise ratification by the Head of State. On less significant matters, the consent of the State may be granted by the government.

As for the level of incorporation of international norms into internal law, the various theories concerning the complex problem of the relations between the two are well known. Thus, the first (a monistic system) proclaims the supremacy of internal law,[22] while the second (also monistic) proclaims the priority, pre-eminence and supremacy of international law.[23] The third, sustained by contemporary doctrine, is dualistic, recognising that they are separate and different disciplines.

Turning to various specific cases, one thus sees that, in Germany, the general rules of international law are considered part of internal law, and treaties need parliamentary approval in order to be transformed into national law. In Austria, ratification is required by the National Council, who may decide that the treaty must be implemented with the adoption of laws. Meanwhile, in Iceland and Sweden the effects of treaties depend upon legislation for their national incorporation. However, in The Netherlands, as well, broadly, as in Spain, the treaty is incorporated into national regulations upon ratification, without the need for legislation – although the nature of many provisions (especially on employment matters) means that there is a requirement for additional national regulations in order for them to be given full effect.

One interesting problem is the "status" of the norms of international law which become incorporated into internal law. In this context, there are four options: legislative, supra-legislative, infra-constitutional, or constitutional. These four options are all to be found among the various solutions which States have adopted. Thus, while most of the States recognise the primacy of international norms over national provisions, few recognise their constitutional "status", and, indeed, in some systems the international norm may be subjected to checks in order to ensure its constitutionality. At the same time, however, there are some countries which accord international norms no higher status than those of national law.

5. The National Catalogue of Rights

In order to appreciate the similarities or differences between international and European norms and national regulations, this section presents a catalogue of rights in the various national legislations, indicating all of those which are applicable, subject to the respective regulatory system, in accordance with the Constitution.

5.1. Germany

In Germany many of the general principles of rights at work are set out in the Constitution.[24] These include respect for the dignity of the person and

22. As presented at the turn of the century by theorists such as Jellinek – See, for example, G.Jellinek, *The Declaration of the Rights of Man and of Citizens* (New York 1901).

23 See, *inter alia*, the works of Hans Kelsen or George Scelle.

24 The German "Basic Law" of 1949, as revised in 1994.

the free development of the personality;[25] freedom of association, including the right to form unions and to collective bargaining;[26] the right freely to choose a profession;[27] freedom of expression, applicable in the working context or environment;[28] as well as the guaranteeing of the social and welfare system as a whole.[29] One should also highlight, following recent reform, the right to equality between men and women at work,[30] and the prohibition of discrimination affecting workers.[31]

5.2. Austria

The constitutional provisions in Austria recognise as fundamental rights particularly the freedom to choose and exercise a profession, the freedom of choice of professional training, and rights of association and assembly, as well as a prohibition on forced labour. They also provide for the right to equality before the law, and, in particular, prohibit privileges by virtue of sex, position and class.[32]

5.3. Belgium

Articles 10 and 11 of the consolidated Belgian text of 17 February 1994,[33] refer to equality and non-discrimination. Meanwhile, Article 23 recognises the right to live with human dignity, and declares, to that end, that the infra-constitutional regulations guarantee inter alia social rights, including the right to work, freedom of choice of profession, the promotion of the maximum possible level of employment, as well as rights to equitable working conditions and remuneration, information, consultation and collective bargaining, social security, protection of health, social, medical and legal assistance, and to the individual's own social development. The right of association is specifically recognised.[34]

25 Articles 1 and 2.

26 Article 9.3.

27 Article 12.

28 Article 5.

29 Which derives from the principle of "the social state" in Article 20.

30 Article 3.2.

31 Article 3.3.

32 See Article 7 of the *Bundes-Verfassungesgesetz in der Fassung* 1929.

33 *Texte co-ordonné.*

34 Article 27.

5.4. Denmark

The 1953 Danish Constitution recognises the freedom to work, and includes a prohibition against restrictions in that freedom, as well as declaring equality of opportunity of access to work.[35] The Constitution also proclaims, as an object of common endeavour, that all citizens not prevented from working through disability may do so under conditions which guarantee their maintenance, and provides for them to receive the assistance of the authorities should they lack the necessary resources to guarantee subsistence.[36] The right of association and the right to equality are also recognised specifically.[37]

5.5. Spain

The 1978 Spanish Constitution lists almost all of the rights mentioned in the international texts, and declares that regulations relating to fundamental rights will be interpreted in accordance with the Universal Declaration of Human Rights and the international treaties on the subject. Included among these social rights are those relating to freedom of association, unionisation, the right to strike, work, collective bargaining, social security, health, protection of the family, and protection for mothers.

5.6. Finland

Article 5 of the Finnish Instrument of Government proclaims the rights of equality and non-discrimination, with particular reference to equality between the sexes in working life, especially with regard to wages and other conditions of employment.[38] In Article 15 it recognises the right to work and to earn an income by this means, as well as the right to training for employment and professional freedom. It also obliges the State to protect workers and develop employment, and concludes by indicating that nobody is to be dismissed from their work without legal cause. The Instrument of Government also recognises the right to a minimum obligatory level of resources and assistance for those who cannot achieve a decent living, and the right to receive essential resources in the event of unemployment, illness, unfitness for work, age, maternity, and loss of the support of the family, as well as social and health services.[39] It also recognises the right to professional freedom of association and the right to organise in order to safeguard one's interests.[40]

35 Article 74.

36 Article 75.

37 Respectively, by Article 78 and a combination of Article 70 and Article 8.

38 Instrument of Government, 17th July 1919, with subsequent modifications.

39 See Articles 15 and 15.a.

40 Article 10.a.

5.7. France

Included among the social rights provided for in France are equality (particularly as between the sexes); the right to have employment and the right not to be discriminated against in work or employment due to one's origins, opinions or beliefs. Also recognised is the right to form unions, the right to join the union of one's choice, and the right to engage in trade union activities, as well as the right to strike. Other rights include those to social security, maternity protection, and protection of infancy, as well as protection of health, safety, and the right to breaks, especially for elderly workers, with the declaration that all persons who, for reasons of age, physical or mental state, or situation, are unfit for work, will have the right to obtain the appropriate means for their subsistence from the community.[41]

5.8. The United Kingdom

The United Kingdom has no written Constitution, with the consequence that social rights do not exist as a coherent body of fundamental rights which are set down. However, some social rights are to be found in early historical constitutional texts. Rights of this kind are to be found established in "statute" or written law, and in the "Common Law".

5.9. Greece

The Greek Constitution of 1975, after proclaiming the principle of equality before the law,[42] recognises the right of association,[43] as well as the right to work. There is also reference to the right to equal remuneration for work of equal value, without distinction on the ground of sex or other circumstances, as well as to the right to collective bargaining.[44] Article 23 of the 1975 Constitution regulates both the freedom to join a union and the right to strike.

5.10. Ireland

Although the Irish Constitution of 1st July 1937 devotes few provisions to social rights, there is recognition of certain key items. These include the right to equal treatment before the law, without differential discrimination

41 These rights are contained in the Introduction to the Constitution of 27th October 1946.

42 Article 4.

43 Set out in Article 12, and regulated extensively in Article 22.

44 The relevant regulation provides for a system of labour conditions in which the general working conditions are determined by Law and are then complemented by collective agreements, or, failing this, which are determined through a process of arbitration.

due to physical capacity,[45] as well as the right to form associations and unions.[46] Particular attention should be drawn to Article 41.2 of the Irish Constitution, as this constitutes a unique feature amongst the constitutional laws that have been compared for the purposes of this Report. That provision, after recognising that "with her life in the home, a woman offers support without which the common good could not be achieved", declares that "the State will endeavour to guarantee that mothers are not obliged by economic needs to devote themselves to work, thereby neglecting their duties in the home".[47] Other social principles dealt with by the Irish Constitution are the protection of the disabled, widows, orphans and the elderly, the non-existence of abuse, and the protection of the health of workers.[48] Many rights are considered to be guaranteed by the Constitution, in as much as they are rights which are latent or are tacitly recognised in Article 40.3, which refers to defence by the State of the personal rights of citizens ("personal rights"), as would be the case with the right to work and the right to earn a living.

5.11. Iceland

The 1944 Icelandic Constitution deals with a number of social rights.[49] These include equality and non-discrimination, with reference to equal rights for men and women;[50] the right to freedom of association and to form unions;[51] the freedom to choose an occupation, with provision for the right to negotiate "terms of employment and other employment-related matters";[52] and rights to receive assistance in the event of illness, disability, or need due to old age, unemployment and similar circumstances.

5.12. Italy

One of the fundamental principles of the Constitution of the Italian Republic of 22nd December 1947 is the right of all citizens to work and the obligation

45 Article 40.1.

46 Article 40.6.1.iii.

47 It is thought, however, that this regulation – leaving aside its doubtful effectiveness and current validity – must be interpreted in accordance with Article 45.2.i. of the Constitution, where it is provided that men and women, being equal, will be entitled to the appropriate means to earn a living.

48 See, in particular, Article 45.4.

49 Constitution of 17th June 1944, with subsequent modifications, especially those introduced by Law no. 97/1995.

50 Article 65.

51 Article 74.

52 Article 75.

of the State to put in place the necessary conditions to make this effective.[53] This is to be achieved by regulating a range of specified rights between parties to economic relationships *(rapporti economici)*. These include the protection of work in all its forms;[54] sufficient and proportionate retribution, and a maximum duration for the working day, as well as provision for breaks and holidays;[55] equality of rights for woman workers and minors, with special reference to equal pay for equal work, as well as maternity protection;[56] the right of the disabled to work in order to provide the means for their maintenance and social security, alongside protection for workers in the event of injury, illness, disability, age and unemployment;[57] as well as the right to freedom of association and the right to engage in trade union activity, including the ability both to enter into collective agreements of general validity and to strike.[58]

5.13. Luxembourg

The Constitution of the Grand Duchy of Luxembourg brings together, in its Article 11, the right to equality (section 2), the right to work (section 3), to social security, protection of the health and breaks of workers, as well as trade-union freedoms (section 5, including the right to strike, according to judicial interpretation).

5.14. Norway

The Norwegian Constitution of 17th May 1814 did not contain any social or labour rights. However, subsequent reforms have included some rights, having the character of proclamations or principles, whose extension depends upon the enactment of ordinary legislation. Examples of these include the right to work (1954), the right of workers to participation or co-determination in their employing enterprise (1980), and a general provision placing responsibility upon the State to respect and guarantee human rights (1994).

5.15. The Netherlands

The revised text of the Fundamental Law of the Kingdom of the Netherlands includes a number of rights with social significance.[59] These include the

53 Article 4.

54 Article35.

55 Article 36.

56 Article 37.

57 Article 38.

58 Articles 39 and 40, respectively.

59 Fundamental Law *(Grond Wet)* of the Kingdom of the Netherlands, revised 19th January 1983.

right to freedom of association and to freedom of expression,[60] a prohibition against discrimination, and the freedom to choose work freely.[61] It also deals with the right to the social assistance of the State, the promotion of opportunities for sufficient employment, and the right to the benefits of social security,[62] as well as the duty of the legislator to establish the legal system of workers, regulations for their protection, and to facilitate their participation in the administration of their employing enterprises.[63] There is no constitutional provision in The Netherlands for collective bargaining, or dealing with collective action.

5.16. Portugal

Alongside other fundamental rights, such as those relating to equality and to freedom of choice of profession,[64] the 1976 Constitution of the Portuguese Republic[65] undoubtedly contains the most extensive list of "rights, freedoms and guarantees of workers", dedicating an explicit heading to these matters in its Title II.[66] Amongst the matters set out as rights in Title II are employment security, with the prohibition of dismissals without legal cause or for political or ideological reasons;[67] the right to form associations of workers for the defence of their interests and participation in companies;[68] the freedom to join a union, with extensive provisions dealing with individual rights and those of trade-union associations,[69] and, in concrete terms, with rights to trade union action;[70] and the right to strike, along with a prohibition on the use of lock-outs.[71] Of the economic and social rights figuring in Title III, mention may be made of the

60 Article 8 and Article 7, respectively.

61 Article 19.3.

62 All of which are to be regulated by law, as provided for by Articles 19 and 20.

63 What is described as the "regulation of the legal status of workers".

64 Which are set out, respectively in Article 13 and Article 47.

65 As amended most recently by Constitutional Law 1/1992, of 25th November 1992.

66 This includes Articles 53-57, in addition to which there are, in Title III, further economic and social rights and duties set out in Articles 58-72. Without doing more than making brief reference to what is an extremely extensive list, it may be noted that the rights provided for in Title II appear to have greater legal force accorded – by virtue of the system referred to in Article 17 and the selection of subjects in Article 288.

67 Article 53.

68 Article 54.

69 Article 55.

70 Article 56.

71 Article 57.

right to work, with special reference at the beginning to equality of opportunities without limitation due to sex;[72] the treatment of rights of workers during employment, with specific provisions on pay (with safeguards for the principle of equal pay for equal work), health and safety, arrangements for breaks and holidays, unemployment, a national minimum wage, the duration of the working day, maternity protection, and protection for minors;[73] the right to social security, with specific mention that the protection will encompass illness, old-age, disability, widowhood, orphanhood, unemployment, and any other absence of, or decrease in, livelihood or the capacity to work;[74] and the right to health protection.[75]

5.17. Sweden

The Swedish Law of 24th November 1994, by means of which the country's basic constitutional law, the Instrument of Government, was most recently reformed, brings together equality for men and women, personal and economic well-being, and the rights to work, social assistance and security.[76] It also recognises the rights to freedom of assembly and freedom of association,[77] develops the prohibition on discrimination,[78] provides for the right of association for workers and for employers – including coverage of procedures for industrial disputes[79] – and deals with the freedom to exercise a profession, with a general reference to the 1950 European Convention, whose content is declared inviolable by the laws.[80] There is also, it may be noted in passing, a curious provision to defer to the law the regulation of the right of Lapps to breed reindeer.[81]

6. Common Considerations in Relation to Constitutional Texts

Certain groups of social rights can be identified on the basis of congruity between the sets of constitutional rules,[82] and from the extent to which the sets

72 Article 58.

73 Article 59.

74 Article 63.

75 Article 64.

76 With reference among the Fundamental Constitutional Principles, in the First Chapter, Article 1.

77 Chapter 20, Article 1.

78 Save for positive efforts to obtain harmonisation between men and women. See Articles 15 and 16.

79 Article 17.

80 Article 23.

81 Article 20.

82 Naturally, with the exclusion of the United Kingdom.

of rules are regarded as consistent. These criteria are not necessarily of huge significance, however, since, in certain constitutions, the laws replace or fill lacunae. The following groups may be classified:

(a) Generally Agreed Rights

(i) Equality, non-discrimination, and particular rights relating to equality between the sexes. The first of these rights is unanimously to be found, the second is to be found very extensively, while the third receives express mention in over half of the national systems.
(ii) Freedom of trade union association, which is given express recognition in half of the countries considered, and which, in the rest of the systems, is taken to be included in the general right of freedom of association.
(iii) The right to work, which is recognised in almost all of the systems, with the exceptions of Austria and Ireland.
(iv) The rights to protection of health, social security and social assistance, which are recognised in nearly all systems, with, once again, the exceptions of Austria and Ireland.

(b) High Level of General Agreement on Rights

This category represents rights which are to be found in five or more constitutional texts, and comprises:

(i) Express freedom to join a union.[83]
(ii) Right to collective bargaining.[84]
(iii) Freedom of choice of profession.[85]
(iv) Seeking full employment.[86]
(v) Right to strike.[87]
(vi) Right to a minimum living or minimum subsistence income.[88]
(vii) Right to participate in the administration of the employer enterprise.[89]

83 Found in 7 constitutional texts.

84 Found in 5 constitutional texts.

85 Found in 6 constitutional texts.

86 Found in 5 constitutional texts.

87 Found in 6 constitutional texts.

88 To which there is explicit reference in 4 constitutional texts, with implicit reference in a number of others.

89 Found in 5 constitutional texts.

(c) Low Level of General Agreement on Rights

This category embraces rights which are to be found in between two and four constitutional texts, and extends to the following:

(a) Right to professional training.[90]
(b) Right to employee protection.[91]
(c) Provision of a Workers' Statute.[92]
(d) Right to equitable working conditions.[93]
(e) Right to equitable remuneration.[94]
(f) Equal remuneration for equal work.[95]
(g) Reference to the length of the working day, breaks, and holidays.[96]
(h) Prohibition on dismissal without legal cause.[97]
(i) Maternity protection.[98]

(d) Rights Recognised in Isolated Cases

This final potpourri category includes various isolated references to matters such as:

(i) Reference to a national minimum wage.
(ii) Prohibition on lock-outs.
(iii) Right to negotiate working conditions individually.

7. Procedures for Protection

There is wide agreement that all of the rights dealt with here are exercisable through judicial processes before courts which constitute part of the general legal system. In addition, there are some cases where non-judicial bodies have been established with jurisdiction to deal with complaints over violations of certain fundamental rights — most notably, in the case of discrimination, as in The Netherlands or Iceland.

90 Found in 3 texts.

91 Found in 4 texts.

92 Found in 3 texts.

93 Found in 4 texts.

94 Found in 4 texts.

95 Found in 3 texts.

96 Found in 2 texts.

97 Found in 2 texts.

98 Found in 4 texts.

Eleven of the fifteen Member States of the European Union have Constitutional Courts or like bodies, although there is a great diversity between those systems and the extent of their intervention in relation to the protection of social rights. In some systems, this function is entrusted to all judges,[99] although it is rarely exercised. In others, a specific body exists, but this only carries out prior verification of the constitutionality of laws.[100] In the remaining States, constitutional jurisdiction has achieved greater development, including by way of specialised organs displaying widely differing characteristics. Thus, for example, in the cases of Germany and Spain, there is mention of recourse to the Constitutional Court when no appropriate legal remedy or protection has been obtained before the ordinary courts. In Belgium, Italy and Portugal, however, such direct recourse to protection is not available to ordinary citizens.

8. Promotional Legislation

The National Reports which have formed the basis for this General Report detail numerous laws and regulations of other kinds which regulate various civil rights. These are especially important in the United Kingdom, where there is no written Constitution.

Without going into the detail of these regulations, it is possible to highlight certain common elements in the different sets of rules. In this context, it should be noted that the principles or the foundations of the Constitutions are generally considered to provide generic clauses for the recognition of a great many rights, including even those which are not expressly recognised in the remainder of the provisions contained in those Constitutions.[101] This is the case, for example, with so-called "social status clauses", providing for rights to dignity and the development of the individual's personality, or providing for the right to life and physical integrity.

There is a two-way process here, since Constitutions have a decisive influence upon the development of legislation, which, in turn, allows the scope of the effects of the fundamental rights to be extended not only to encompass the relationships of citizens who exercise public powers ("vertical" efficacy) but also to relationships between individuals ("horizontal" efficacy), which is not provided for in some Constitutions.

A further point is that legislation for the development of social rights — and, indeed, labour legislation in general — tends commonly to be integrated

99 As is the case in Denmark, Greece and Sweden - as well as in Austria, provided that this does not raise any issue of validity of a statute.

100 See, for example, in Austria, France and Ireland.

101 Other, perhaps, than in relation to the rules for the interpretation of the meaning and content of those specific rights which are recognised.

with regulations which are specific, and which are commonly modern or are the result of recent reforms. This feature is a reflection of the increasingly common practice of dealing specifically with the regulation of one particular issue, on the basis of its special characteristics, and for providing at the same time a built in up-dating process, thereby following the rapid changes which are brought about by society and by the national economy in relation to the labour market and in respect of social policy. In some instances, these specific regulations are to be found in general legal volumes, such as, for example, in the relevant national Civil Code (albeit with the granting of some degree of autonomy and independence). In other cases, there will be particular statutes dealing with this subject matter, although these tend to be integrated into the remainder of the general legal system, and frequently provide supplementary provisions to regulations already provided for by the Civil Code or through the law of obligations.

Finally, in many countries, promotional legislation makes up for a silence on the part of the national Constitution in relation to these kinds of rights. The absence of any such provision in the various Constitutions tends to be due to the fact that these instruments were drawn up some considerable time ago. The consequence of having such compensatory legislation is that it permits the list of rights in force to develop, as a whole, along lines similar to other systems. Such promotional legislation, with provision for continuing development, has permitted the national catalogues of those systems concerned to come much closer to the catalogues found in the international and European systems.

9. The Nature and Effectiveness of Social Rights

Amongst the various social rights there are some whose effectiveness depends upon the way in which they are recognised in relation to workers or citizens, thereby enabling such workers or citizens to carry on their activities with the assistance of the authorities and in accordance with the opportunities provided by the law. This is particularly the case in relation to rights such as the right to equal treatment and the right to non-discrimination, as well as with the right to freedom of association, the freedom to join a trade union, or the right to strike. Such rights, of which these are perhaps the most significant, are those which most closely resemble what might be described as the "classical" fundamental rights with a political content, such as the right to freedom of thought, opinion, and expression, as well as rights to move freely, to enjoy the inviolability of the home, to communicate freely, and the like.

In relation to all of these, their effectiveness is dependent entirely upon the fact that the judicial and constitutional systems guarantee respect for such rights on the part of the public authorities. Other rights, by contrast, are merely institutional guarantees, whose effectiveness will depend upon protective actions taken by the State which appropriately enable their exercise and enjoyment. Amongst this latter kind of right, one might mention the right not to be dismissed without lawful or "just" cause.

Most social rights, however, are rights to benefits. These only come about when the law creates them, and their content is that which is attributed to them by that same Law. This will be the case particularly where a reference in a Constitution to a specific law is not explicit with regard to the particular right in question. Indeed, what is more, in some cases the Constitutional provision — irrespective of how this might be formulated — can only be described as "programmatic" or "aspirational", such that it is not possible to guarantee delivery of the right in real economic and social terms. For this reason, it may be suggested, a number of "more realistic" Constitutions limit themselves to entrusting the State with the task of promoting, or working towards, the highest possible level of effectiveness.

Consequently, therefore, some rights are born effective and directly out of the Constitution, even though the law may configure them or limit them, so that they have a jurisdictional guarantee of protection. However, for most of them, the constitutional proclamation, although of positive value, is not a suitable means for achieving their effectiveness. This is because their real creation remains in the hands of the legislator, whose actions or omissions cannot be checked efficiently by the judge, given that they depend upon decisions with a political content (especially, in relation to what economic and other resources are to be allocated for the purpose), and are thus decisions whose appropriateness, in practice, cannot effectively be controlled by the judge.

It is in the nature of things that there will always be fundamental rights whose effectiveness depends upon the economic possibilities and political criteria of the relevant public authorities concerned with them (be these national, international or in the context of the European Community). Consequently, it follows that a mere proclamation of social rights in Community regulations, even if supplemented by complementary agreements between all of the interested countries, cannot be sufficient to enable such social rights to be effective.

Security of Employment and Freedom to Dismiss

1. The Concept of Dismissal

There are various obstacles in the way of defining a uniform concept of dismissal. Thus, whilst, in principle, the phenomenon could be defined as "the unilateral act or decision of an employer, which, without the agreement of the other party, discharges *per se* the contractual relationship", this technical concept would not, however, include other principles which some national legal systems introduce into their particular rules regarding dismissal.

In some of those systems, indeed, one cannot speak of "contractual resolution", but of "discharge at the initiative of, or attributable to, the employer". Meanwhile, other legal systems treat such forms of termination as retirement, *force majeure, etc*. as autonomous means of discharge different from dismissal. The analysis of the phenomenon of "dismissal" must, therefore, involve identifying the ultimate or immediate, direct or indirect, author of the discharge. Consequently, the notion of dismissal includes not only unilateral decisions of the employer which have the effect of discharging the contract, but also the presumption of discharge at the initiative of, or under the responsibility of, the employer.

Legal systems which recognise the use of fixed-term contracts – whether exclusively or as an alternative to contracts of indefinite duration – will, of course, include in the concept of "dismissal" a termination of the contract before its anticipated expiry date or the non-renewal of a contract, paying special attention to termination with notice and to premature discharge on "reasonable" grounds. Meanwhile, the creation of concepts such as "suspension" of the contract while keeping the job open (in cases such as maternity), has broadened the concept of "dismissal" in some legal systems to include the refusal by an employer to re-employ workers who are supposed to have enjoyed such a right.

The concept of "constructive" dismissal or "indirect" dismissal must also be considered within the overall picture. This phenomenon is understood to mean a situation whereby the employer achieves the result of terminating the employment relationship without good cause by forcing the worker to take the decision to cease work, a decision which the worker would not have taken in the absence of the decisive conduct by the employer.[102]

Also of interest are those legal systems in which "indirect" or "constructive" dismissal is a form of resignation founded upon serious breach by the employer of his contractual obligations. The most frequently cited causes giving rise to such breach tend inter alia to be repeated or continuing non-payment of wages; non-compliance with regulations applicable to the work to be performed; contraventions in relation to the hours which the employee is required to work; default in relation to matters concerning health and safety at work; humiliating, degrading or offensive treatment; and the abusive exercise of the employer's powers.[103]

2. The Right to Stability in Employment and the Prohibition of Arbitrary Dismissal

The differences between the national legal systems with regard to the concept and legal basis of dismissal reflect their different approaches to the principle of stability in employment. From the national reports studied we may infer, in general, that there is no fixed right to permanent stability in employment. Some legal systems start from unconditional or absolute contractual freedom, on the basis that employment is no more than a temporary contract and, above all, that none of the parties can be forced to maintain the contract against their will.[104] The only regulatory limitation in these cases is the need for notice or for just cause for premature discharge. Most of the legal systems move somewhat away from this respect for absolute freedom, and contain real and theoretical limits on the right to discharge. However, they reserve the rule of mandatory reinstatement of the worker dismissed to cases of dismissals which are contrary to fundamental rights, in which exceptionally a principle of real stability is applied to employment when faced with dismissal by the employer.

102 This concept is not known in all the legal systems, nor is it always treated in the same way. There are countries which do not consider it at all, although they apply the civil law technique of "termination by breach" for such conduct. In other legal systems, there is specific protection for the worker against such conduct, based on the model of protection designed for dismissal. Under this model, the discharge is regarded as being attributable to the employer, and imposes upon him any consequential duties of compensation.

103 As a general rule, there is a need for a judicial process which declares the existence of "indirect" or "constructive" dismissal – with the result that in some systems there can be dismissal by judicial dissolution – and the appropriate compensation is awarded in favour of the worker, even though in most countries it is regarded as resignation without notice and in others a judicial resolution is necessary to declare the employment contract discharged. Finally, the legal consequence of indirect dismissal is compensation, and this is calculated on the basis of the economic remedies established in each country for dismissal.

104 This is the situation, in particular, in the cases of Austria (but with the benefit of any "severance pay" and the possibility to challenge certain dismissals if they are "socially unjustified" - *i.e.* relating to substantial interests of the employee) and Iceland.

In most cases, the injustice of the employer's action is only translated into economic compensation.

There is, however, agreement on the prohibition of arbitrary dismissals that are manifestly unreasonable, illicit or without just cause, with in a wide range of categories which are considered as unjustified dismissal.

3. Regulatory Sources

A comparative analysis of dismissal must take into account the different sources of regulation in the national legal systems and, therefore, its constitutional treatment. Generally, Constitutions are limited to recognising freedom of work. The explicit recognition of the right to work only exists in some Constitutions, although it takes concrete shape not in an effective right to a job with immediate effectiveness, but in efforts that the public powers must make to promote employment and occupation. Significant differences exist in the constitutional values and principles in this respect and in the level of intervention by the respective organs of constitutional control. A recognition of the right to work does not exist as a universal rule giving a constitutional right to stability in employment. Nor does the European Social Charter make any contribution to the legal basis of dismissal. It should also be noted that ILO Convention No. 158 has not been generally ratified.[105]

The Constitutions of Finland and Portugal, however, constitute important exceptions to this general proposition. Provisions in those instruments prohibit dismissal without legal cause or for political or ideological reasons.[106]

In the realm of sources below constitutional level, the evolution of national legal systems as regards dismissal began with a belief in the right of contractual freedom, including freedom of discharge and of regulation of such discharge by the parties. Both these freedoms have tended to become limited, restricting the role of unilateral will on the discharge of contracts and introducing disciplines that would not be available where there is pure private contractual autonomy. In the majority of cases, the Law is the main source of regulation of the basis of dismissal, in both its substantive and its procedural aspects. In addition to this, the rules contained in collective agreements have lesser importance. Generally, these rules are important where they are more favourable than the law in that there is no absolute right to discharge on payment of appropriate compensation. It is usually understood that the limitations on freedom of dismissal amount to the re-legitimation of the employer's powers of dismissal through an appropriate, more reasonable and less arbitrary exercise thereof.

105 ILO Convention No. 158 concerning Termination of Employment at the Initiative of the Employer, and see *supra*.

106 As already noted, *supra*.

In some countries, the legal principles are contained in the Civil Code, but together with this they have specific legislation in the general labour laws, or sometimes in laws specifically relating to dismissal, notably in terms of discriminatory dismissals. It has been a common phenomenon for there to have been a revision of the rules in the 1990s. It is also common to find that an important role is performed by the interpretation of these Regulations by the Courts as complementary to the written regulations, when it is presumed that a major modification in the actual application of these was not intended.

4. Notice of Dismissal

In beginning to examine the rules concerning dismissal, especially in the Community countries, it is necessary first to analyse notice of dismissal. The establishment of notice is linked historically to the *"ad nutum"* or "at will" character of dismissal, the idea of notice being to make dismissal less painful and to facilitate the search for new employment for the worker. Originally, there was a single period of notice, relatively brief, required both for resignation by the worker and dismissal by the employer, which could be extended by contract and which the first collective agreements would also attempt to extend. Subsequent development consisted of the progressive unification of the term of notice for all types of employment contract and in the progressive separation of the required periods of notice for resignation and dismissal. As regards minimum established periods, it is not easy to find a common quantitative denominator as a criterion for harmonisation, as the periods vary from one country to another, and within each country, depending on length of service in the company, age or sector of activity.[107]

The differences in the national legal systems regarding the non-enforceability of notice and the consequences of not giving the required notice must also be taken into account. As regards the former, most legal systems tend to acknowledge the idea of dispensing with notice in cases of dismissal due to causes attributable to the worker. However, this varies depending on the category of reason for dismissal, based on the degree of deliberate conduct or culpability. So they treat in different ways causes of termination relating to the person or the worker (illness) and causes based on flaws in conduct (serious misconduct, serious non-compliance with contractual obligations). Neither do the national legal systems agree about the effect of force majeure on the immediate termination of contract without notice, creating the distinction between circumstances relating to the

107 Taking into account these factors and bearing in mind their importance in the absolutely free systems mentioned above, these range from 1 to 3 months in Iceland and from six weeks to 5 months in Austria for white-collar employees. In other systems, such as Italy, one must refer to the provisions in collective agreements, custom and practice or equity. In Spain and Holland, as a minimum, it is one month. In Sweden, there is no general uniform provision, it depends on the circumstances.

company, due to the needs or in the interests of the employer, and frustration which prevents not only the continuation of contracts but also the observance of notice. The most widespread rule is that non-observance of notice gives rise to the right to receive the legal remuneration that would have been received during the notice period.[108]

5. The Justification for Dismissal

One of the matters of the greatest significance in the comparative examination of dismissal is that of the justification for dismissal. The perspective of the legal systems for labour law in different countries is centred in the idea of justification for dismissal as a validation of the employer's decision. Thus the decision of the employer is not treated as a purely contractual resolution for non-compliance, with effects only in contractual terms, but rather that it affects important interests of both parties and of the company itself. Although there is great scope for allowing the employer to free himself from the working relationship when any grounds have occurred to justify this, some systems seek to safeguard what they call the "weaker" side of the contract; *i.e.* the interests of the employee. Dismissal ceases to be a contractual faculty of freeing from the contract, but is framed in a more functional context, as serving the interests of the employer and being used as an instrument for the administration of the company. The implicit pre-supposition of this transformation seems to be based upon the presumption of the indefinite utility for the employer of the labour relationship or on the responsibility of the employer for guaranteeing permanence or stability in employment. From *"ad nutum"* dismissability there is a move to the requirement for non-unlawful grounds or grounds justifying the dismissal, in an evolution with various stages in each place and time, to the point of the current co-existence of the various possible concepts.

6. The Prohibition of Dismissal on Certain Grounds

In many legal systems, the primary protection from dismissal is centred on prohibiting dismissal under certain circumstances or on certain grounds. Thus the protection of national defence leads to the prohibition of dismissal in the

108 However, differences or exceptions exist, such as in the United Kingdom, where we are informed that dismissal without notice is presumed to be wrongful, or, as in Finland or Ireland, where, when termination is required by law, under judicial criteria or by agreement, the absence of notice will be taken into account in considering whether the dismissal is lacking in sufficient cause; in Belgium, Denmark and Norway, although notice is not considered necessary for the validity of the termination, it is useful as part of the testing of the validity of the grounds for dismissal in unilateral dismissals of this type.

event of military service, where this exists, there being a general provision which suspends the employment contract, though some legal systems require a minimum length of employment service for this right to be enjoyed. A second type of prohibition on dismissals (technically, it is a suspension) is for maternity, for which leave of variable duration is provided in all the Member States. To render it effective there is at the same time a prohibition on dismissal for the corresponding period. Banning the dismissal of women in the event of pregnancy also exists in most countries. As regards illness, the national legal systems, while excluding the explicit prohibition of dismissal, follow the more widespread formula of suspending the contract, with heterogeneous temporal limits, it being lawful to consider dismissal in the event of illness that lasts for a long period or is intermittent for a prolonged period. There are other grounds that are forbidden in some legal systems, such as those involving disabled people or marriage. Some countries, also, provide special means or forms of protection, such as the need for approval of the dismissal by judicial or administrative bodies when the employer wishes to dismiss people who come within this category.

Special mention is merited for those dismissals that place constitutionally significant benefits at risk. The first case is that of discriminatory dismissals, in relation to which the prohibition of discrimination already exists in most of the national legal systems and is inferred from ILO Convention No. 111 of 1958.[109] In general, all distinctions founded on race, colour, sex, religion, political opinion, national origin or social origin are prohibited as regards employment. The prohibition of discrimination on the grounds of sex in the various national legal systems also has a specific basis in European Community Law, in the guise of Directive 76/207/EEC, interpreted rigorously by the Court of Justice, so that it has given rise to specific legal rules on the subject.[110] It may be noted that the Dutch legislation arguably presents the most extensive list of forbidden factors, including matters such as civil status and sexual orientation.

The national legal systems also accept the principle of the unlawful nature of dismissals as a reprisal, the clearest case of which is anti-trade union dismissal due to activity in or membership of unions. In this connection, the final unlawful grounds for dismissal are those relating to strikes, because the existence of the right to strike requires the non-termination of the employment contract due to its exercise. Substantial differences exist with regard to the right to strike, however, because the majority recognise the right to strike, while others speak rather of

109 ILO Convention No. 111, concerning Discrimination in Respect of Employment and Occupation.

110 Directive 76/207/EEC on the implementation of the principle of equal treatment for men and women as regards access to employment, vocational training and promotion, and working conditions.

freedom to strike. In some legal systems there is provision for the possibility of dismissal due to active participation in illegal strikes.

Making a final reference to the unlawfulness of the grounds for dismissal, mention must be made of the significant step that has been taken in many legal systems which prohibit the anti-social and improper use of dismissal, applying the principle of abuse of the law and anti-social exercise thereof, enabling the social validity, legality and morality of the dismissal to be verified. This concept requires that the employer demonstrates conformity with the guidelines of the legal system. The basis of this is that it is in the employer's interest to discharge the contract of employment, and so the employer has to prove the causes or grounds that make the employer's decision legitimate *iuris et de iure*. These reasons may then be verified externally by the courts.

7. The Reasons or Grounds for Justified Dismissal

One last step is "justified dismissal", which requires the employer to state the reason for dismissal. The reasons for the dismissal are then objectivised and controlled judicially. The dominant model in European countries, to put it in general terms, is that of a requirement that legitimate grounds for the dismissal are to be shown. It is possible to distinguish, depending on the importance of the reason, situations where the dismissal might be operative immediately and others where a period of notice must be respected. This general rule is accompanied by the provision of some exceptions which exist in various national legal systems, due either to the characteristics of the employment relationship, to the size of the company, to the requirement of a minimum length of service, or finally to the special circumstances of a trial period, during which in most countries there exists a freedom to dismiss.

Summing up the references to grounds justifying dismissal, the employer's interests which are worthy of safeguarding and the corresponding reasons justifying dismissal are protected in the legal systems in various ways, with different degrees of precision and determination, some using the method of general grounds, others that of a specific list of justifiable causes and others a list of examples. Despite the extraordinary diversity of assumptions and of their legal interpretation, two common elements are highlighted – one that these causes may be related to the capacity or qualification of the worker, with their conduct, or with the economic, technical or organisational reasons of the company, in line with Article 4 of ILO Convention No. 158, and the other that the grounds, in all these assumptions, must be of a real, serious, reasonable and proportional nature to justify the dismissal.

It is appropriate here to consider the various reasons for dismissal in the national systems, starting from the distinction between reasons relating to the conduct of workers, to their capacity and to the needs of the company, which are the general categories or types employed in general terms or with a subsequent listing by the legal systems.

First, in all the national systems the dismissal may be justified of workers who do not comply with their obligations or who are guilty of a breach which is sufficiently significant to destroy the relationship. The conduct of the worker in breach of contract will justify dismissal where it amounts to a serious violation of the contractual obligations. In this category of grounds, the dismissal has a disciplinary character, being an instrument at the service of the company's disciplinary system, although its consideration as a disciplinary sanction is not expressly recognised in most of the systems – though it is so recognised in collective agreements or company rules. It is common practice for there to be disciplinary rules, from various sources, which set out what conduct justifies sanctions and how to assess their seriousness in order to guarantee that the sanction is proportional to the breach, as well as procedures for regulating employers' decisions.[111]

These groups of types of breach are categorised using different formulae, such as those of "seriously inappropriate conduct by the worker" (The Netherlands); a reason which "relates to the conduct of the employee" (United Kingdom); "reasons concerning the behaviour of the worker" (Germany); "serious reasons" (Belgium); "especially powerful reasons" (Finland, which defines the reasons negatively by indicating those that may not be justifiable grounds); "just cause" (Norway and Portugal, the first also with negative delimitation, the second with a defined list, to which this residual general cause is added – as is also done by the legal system in Ireland, which mentions "other substantial grounds"). These categories are developed by the case-law pronouncements of the courts.

A second group of reasons which may justify dismissal are those relating to the personal circumstances of the worker, not consisting of culpable non-compliance with the contract. This applies to professional ineptitude (whether innate or supervening), which may derive from changes in the production organisation to which the worker does not adapt. All legal systems are agreed as to the scope of this reason for justifying dismissal, although with variables as regards notice and economic compensation. The same occurs with long-term or persistent illness, which in all legal systems provides possible grounds for dismissal, once certain time limits are exceeded. Some legal systems include decrease in output or productivity here, which others regard as a disciplinary matter, requiring the decrease to be wilful and continuous, although this is not compatible with the dismissal being for objective reasons as set out in the next paragraph.

111 Summarising examples from the different legal systems, the following are included in this group of breaches: unpunctuality, absence from work, negligence at work, revealing secrets or breach of the duty of confidentiality or discretion, causing offence to the employer or to other employees, certain criminal acts, misconduct.

The last type of ground for dismissal is that of "dismissal for objective reasons in the interests of the company". Its peculiarity lies in the inclusion of reasons relating to the company's own collective organisation. In these cases there is no longer a need for the job to be done due to circumstances that have developed in relation to the need for that function within the production process as a whole. That amounts to reasons which are either economic or of financial equilibrium, or relating to the profitability or efficiency of the company, due to a change in the organisation or in the technology. The definition and limits of these economic, organisational or technological reasons show significant differences in the various systems, because the balancing of the interests of the worker in conserving jobs against that of the employer in achieving management objectives is not identical in all systems. Some countries are more rigorous in the requirements to show the need for dismissal, considering dismissal as a last resort, while in others there is a greater willingness to accept the needs of the company.

Lastly, we can must take into account the existence of a specific legal basis for collective dismissals in the community sphere – Directive 75/129/EEC – the transposition of which into national legislation has had a decisive influence on the homogeneity of national rules on the numerical and temporal dimensions of the personnel affected, the need for consultation and negotiation with the representatives of the workers and the intervention of the competent public authority, whose decisions are open to appeal before the administrative courts in some countries.

An international formula exists – that set out in Article 7 of ILO Convention No. 158 – which has caused difficulties in most European countries. On the other hand, common elements do not exist on the information, consultation and participation of workers' representatives in cases of individual dismissal; exceptionally, consultation is imposed in all dismissals (Germany) or with the union to which the dismissed worker belongs (Spain). In collective dismissals, it has already been indicated that Community rules exist on consultation and negotiation.

8. The Form of Dismissal

It is also necessary to analyse the form or formalities of the dismissal, because the requirement of grounds and justification thereof implies the observance of formal and procedural requirements, regulated in most countries in the Law or in collective agreements. The various legal systems have been progressively introducing the requirement of written formalisation of notification of dismissal, which must be brought to the knowledge of the worker in a satisfactory manner. This has been followed by the addition of other formal requirements, to guarantee the knowledge by workers of the reasons for their dismissal or establishing prior controls which avoid unjustified dismissals, by means of an internal appeal system. The common element in the national legal systems is the requirement for written communication of the dismissal, accompanied in most cases by setting out the reasons for the employer's decision, with the variant of legislations that allow certain preliminary procedures – particularly The Netherlands, which requires prior approval of the Directorate of Employment, and Austria, which requires prior approval from the Labour Court for certain groups of employees (such as works council members or pregnant women). Also of interest is the rule in some systems obliging the employer to set out the criterion for selection of the workers affected in collective dismissals.

9. The Judicial Review of Dismissal

As a main consequence of the requirement of justification for dismissal, the possibility has been established of an external control over the employer's decision by the court. Apart from some exceptional cases, the system most commonly utilised for this subsequent control is that of judicial process through the courts, through an action initiated by the worker,[112] although the composition of these judicial bodies is different, depending upon the legal tradition of each system. The differences between the national systems consist in the presence or not of conciliatory mechanisms or of arbitration prior to recourse to the courts and, mainly, the degree of effectiveness of these pre-hearing mechanisms as a replacement for the courts. The widespread rule is that of institutionalisation of conciliatory procedures with the intervention of impartial third persons, who attempt to reach a prior agreement, on some occasions as an obligatory mechanism, in other cases in optional terms.

Access to the courts dealing with the justification for dismissal is subject in most countries to a brief prescribed period of grace,[113] which is different from the periods prescribed for breach by the worker. These requirements relate to the interval between the event that gave grounds for the dismissal and the decision to dismiss.

Another important topic is the rules concerning responsibility for proving the grounds for dismissal. Generally, the employer has the task of proving the grounds and genuineness of the dismissal, although in different forms in the national legislations.[114] This allows us to make reference to the

112 Or by the union, where this is allowed, as in Spain and Sweden.

113 For example, three weeks in Germany or 20 days in Spain.

114 Some of which expressly contain an inversion of the burden of proof to place it on the employer, although they refer to different contents (the existence of notice, concurrence of cause), and others envisage a certain weakening of the burden of proof on the worker.

employer's difficulty in obtaining judicial backing for their decisions and of a degree of uncertainty in the outcome of judicial proceedings.[115]

10. The Consequence of Unjustified Dismissal

A subject of special importance is the consequences of unjustified dismissal. In all the national systems, the intervention of the courts extends to control over the legality of the employer's decision to dismiss, differentiating between two basic models regarding the extent or effectiveness of this control over legality, taking the basic or substantial control as the point of differentiation. The first model applies in countries where some scope for freedom to dismiss still exists – countries in which the jurisdiction of the tribunals is limited to confirming that the required formalities have been carried out, with the dismissal being declared unlawful if the employer does not fulfil the requirements of form and/or notice. The second model occurs in practically all of the national legislations, where judicial control includes not only control over the requirements of form, but also involves investigating the concurrence between justifying or legitimising grounds for the dismissal.

As regards the consequences of unlawful dismissal, a traditional classification of the legal sanctions envisaged distinguishes between two alternative possibilities: the first, the imposition of compensatory damages, confirming the discharging effect produced at the time by the dismissal; the second, the ruling to reinstate the worker in his previous job, with continuity of the contract, as though no interruption had taken place. The different systems of the Member States include various combinations of possibilities, in a few cases envisaging only one of the alternatives presented. It is also quite common to establish various systems of sanctions depending on the groups or categories of workers, the size of companies, the decisive grounds for the legality of the dismissal, with special attention to discrimination or acts contrary to fundamental rights and public freedoms.

With these nuances, the existing models can be described as follows:

(a) Economic Compensation

This model is used by States which acknowledge the employer's right to discharge the employment contract unilaterally, even in the absence of justifying grounds, with the mere sanction of payment of a sum by way of compensation. Included in this group are the systems in which a right to discharge by the

115 It is sometimes suggested that employers' thought processes are not always logical, contrasting with the rigidity of the legal framework of the judicial bodies, which usually cannot opt for intermediate solutions between the lawfulness or the unlawfulness of the dismissal and its consequences.

employer is recognised "ad nutum",[116] although the Law already contains provision for a sanction of compensation when the employer dismisses without respecting the term of notice (which is generally lengthy), and without the dismissal being justified legally by the conduct or capacity of the worker. In Denmark, the doctrine and practice have moved away from these legal provisions, and in Belgium – apart from providing for the reinstatement for trade union delegates on company or safety committees – compensation varies depending on whether it concerns manual or white-collar workers and depending on the length of service or retribution; this may amount to the equivalent of six months' wages.

Also included in this group are the national systems which, denying the right to resolution "ad nutum" by the employer, do, however, envisage the imposition of economic compensation as the exclusive sanction for unlawful dismissal.[117] These cases envisage compensation with variables in the same way as in Belgium.

(b) Reinstatement to the Job or Economic Compensation

In the rest of the Member States, in one form or another, systems exist for the reinstatement of the worker into his former job, with compensation as an alternative, although with considerable differences as regards the extent to which the stability in employment is recognised, depending on who is given the option.

The option is given to the employer in the case of Spain (and, for small companies, in Italy), where dismissal without sufficient justification gives rise to a ruling on the part of the court for both the reinstatement of the worker and the payment of a legally assessed compensation as damages,[118] with the employer having the right to choose freely between reinstatement or payment of compensation. In Finland, the consequence of a failure to achieve a remedy of reinstatement is also economic compensation.[119]

In other cases, reinstatement is envisaged with a right of objection by the parties. This is the assumption of the legislation in France, Germany and the United Kingdom, which initially envisage a ruling of reinstatement of the worker into his former job – although, in the event of opposition to reinstatement by any of the parties, the judicial body may proceed to discharge the employment contract, ordering the employer to make payment of compensation for damages.

In some cases it is the judicial bodies which make the decision. This is the system in Ireland, The Netherlands, and, in accordance with the collective

116 Austria, Belgium, Denmark and Iceland.

117 This group includes Denmark, Greece and Luxembourg, as it has evolved so far.

118 This will be between 2 and 6 months' wages, with increments for length of service, in Italy; 1 month's wages per year of length of service with a maximum of 42 months, in Spain.

119 Between three and 24 months' wages, depending on the worker's length of service, age and likelihood of finding other employment.

agreements reached, in Denmark, with the alternatives of reinstatement or discharge with compensation both existing, although the choice is made by the Court which reviews the dismissal. In countries such as Denmark or Norway, judicial practice shows that the reinstatement or re-establishment of the relationship between the parties is rarely imposed, if it is proven that this has deteriorated or that its re-establishment is evidently unreasonable. Compensation is calculated, in these systems, according to the age and length of service of the worker or in accordance with equity. The Dutch legislation envisages nullification with mandatory reinstatement if the dismissal does not have the prior consent of the Directorate of Employment, but the courts have laid down the principles that they apply for the replacement of reinstatement with economic compensation, in accordance with criteria of fairness.

Finally, there are systems under which it is the worker who has the option. This is a variant on the systems where this option is envisaged, or where only reinstatement to the job is envisaged, subject to the important exception if the worker prefers personally to opt for discharge with compensation. This is the model for the legislation in Austria (for some groups of employees), Italy,[120] Portugal, Spain,[121] and Sweden.[122]

Together with these formulae on the "principle" ruling, it is quite common for national legislation to provide for other types of compensation or additional compensation. The most common formula is an order that the employer pay additional economic compensation equivalent to the stopped wages; *i.e.* those not received by the worker for the duration of the judicial process. Besides this order to make payment of so-called "procedure wages", in certain countries compensation is contemplated for termination of contract, irrespective of whether this is justified or contra legem. This is purely compensation for length of service in the company, compensating for the loss of the job *per se*.[123] Other jurisdictions, instead of procedure wages, envisage the receipt of unemployment benefit on account. Some systems establish supplementary compensation for cases of workers dismissed unlawfully who do not meet the conditions for receiving unemployment benefit; other systems have compensation for future losses or emotional damages. Exceptionally, there can be additional sanctions of an administrative nature for the employer's non-compliance with the regulations on dismissal.[124]

120 For cases of medium- or large-size companies and in discriminatory dismissals.

121 In both Austria and Spain, for dismissals *inter alia* of representatives of the workers and dismissals contrary to fundamental rights.

122 With compensation also in the form of "general damages" for non-financial loss.

123 "Severance pay" in Austria.

124 In Norway, we are informed of a special rule for the maintenance of the relationship during the negotiation procedure on the dismissal, which will remain in force until the final resolution of the dispute by a Court; this is not the case in extraordinary or summary dismissals on more serious grounds.

Exploitation of Workers

1. The Right to Health and Safety at Work

The national legal systems reviewed do not adopt a uniform approach to the constitutional recognition of the right to health and safety at work. For example, the Constitutions of Austria and Iceland do not contain any particular regulations referring to such rights, whereas those of Italy and Sweden make specific provision as to health and safety.[125] The constitutional position as to obligations relating to health and safety in Spain arises as a supporting element of social and economic policy,[126] while in Germany it derives from Article 1,[127] Article 2,[128] and Article 20.[129]

At the level of the European Union, Council Directive 89/891/EEC acknowledged that the legislative provisions in the Member States were very different as regards health and safety in the workplace.[130] The Directive requires an improvement in the protection afforded to workers and that such provisions do not lead to different levels of protection of health and safety allowing unfair competition to the detriment of health. Thus, the Directive, whose object is the application of measures to promote the improvement of the health and safety of workers at work, includes general principles relating to the prevention of professional risks and the protection of health and safety, the elimination of risk and accident factors, the provision of information as to health and safety, consultation with regard to it, balanced participation in its implementation in conformity with national legislation and uses, and the training of workers and their representatives.

The application of these principles allows Member States to introduce national provisions which are more favourable to the health and safety of workers than those provided for in the Directive. It may be noted that the

125 See, by way of example, Articles 32, 35, 41 and 42 of the Italian Constitution.

126 Article 40.2.

127 Protection of human dignity.

128 The right to integrity.

129 Which sets out the principle of "the social state".

130 Directive 89/391/EEC, on the introduction of measures to encourage improvements in the safety and health of workers at work.

period for implementation of the Directive into domestic law expired on 31 December 1992.[131]

2. Prevention of Labour Risks and Protection from Accidents at Work and Occupational Illnesses

2.1. Legislation

As has been mentioned, in most of the legal systems surveyed there are general rules to safeguard health and safety at work. In a similar way, there are provisions in those jurisdictions on the protection of workers in the event of accidents at work and occupational illnesses.[132]

2.2. Plans for the prevention or evaluation of risks

With the exception of Sweden, most of the national legal systems surveyed assume the development of prevention plans by employers. Instances of this type can be seen in Austria, where there is the obligation to evaluate risks and document the results of this evaluation and the preventive measures that are to be adopted, and in Spain, where the Law on the Prevention of Labour Risks requires the evaluation of risks, their documentation and the implementation of prevention activities to guarantee a greater level of protection of the health and safety of workers.[133] This envisages the adoption of special measures in connection with categories of workers with special risks, such as those who are pregnant or minors.

131 The Directive has been implemented by specific subsequent legislative action in Austria (Law on Protection for Workers, 1994), in Spain (Law on Prevention of Labour Risks, 1995) and in Italy (Decree 19 of September 1994). This is not the case in Sweden, where the Law on the Working Environment dates from 1977, nor in the United Kingdom, where this matter is regulated through various statutory laws (principally the Factories Act 1961, the Health and Safety at Work Act 1974, and the Installations in Offices, Shops and Railway Premises Act 1963) as well as the common law of negligence. In a similar way, in Germany there are a great number of provisions which confer protection on those at work.

These legislative requirements, and others such as the Laws in Iceland on the Working Environment and on Health and Safety at Work of 1980, state that work should take place in a healthy and safe environment. They place obligations on employers to ensure the effectiveness of such rights, as well as giving an important role to the public bodies and to the representatives of the workers in connection with health and safety at work.

132 Examples include the German Law on Protection at Work, the Law on Labour Safety, and the Industrial Code; the Austrian General Social Security Law; the Spanish General Social Security Law 1994 and the Regulation on Accidents at Work 1956 (now partially repealed); and the Italian Decree of 30 June 1956.

133 See Article 16 of the Law.

2.3 Safety Committees

The systems of most of the Member States contemplate the creation of safety committees or safety representatives. Whether or not these apply in a particular case may depend on the number of workers employed by the employer, and/or the existence of prevention services, which may be created within the employer's undertaking, or be contracted out to organisations or people outside the employing enterprise. In both cases, these must contain experts.

By way of example, it can be seen that, in Germany, the extent of the obligation depends on the size of the employer, the experience of the safety committee and the degree of danger of the activities performed by the employer. In Austria, meanwhile, employers with more than ten workers should have safety representatives and a safety committee, consisting of the employer, safety representatives, experts and specialist doctors.

In Spain, in relation to small employers with up to six workers, the employer himself can make provision for the prevention service, whereas, in other cases, the employer should make provision for this with multi-disciplinary experts, on the basis of the risks which may occur.[134]

Safety committees are formed by the employer and the workers in Iceland, and in Italy the safety committee must be composed of experts, either from within the employer's organisation, or from outside the employer hierarchy.

2.4. Action to Prevent Dangerous Activities

To ensure that obligations as to health and safety at work are fully effective, all the national legal systems considered provide for the rights of workers, both personally and through their representatives, to stop work, without loss of earnings, when there are circumstances of imminent danger. In Germany, employees may abandon their work if the employer does not fulfil his obligations to make available the protective measures required by the Decree on dangerous materials. In Austria, the employee is given the right to request the discharge of the employment contract. Spanish law provides that the prevention services and, failing this, the workers' representatives may do this.[135] It may also be appropriate to carry out an inspection of work in these circumstances.[136] Icelandic law confers a similar right and also places an obligation

134 Services external to the employer may be used, as may bodies created by Mutual Societies for Accidents at Work and Professional Illnesses, organisations collaborating in the management of the social security system.

135 See Article 9 of the Statute of Workers.

136 See, in this regard, Article 44 of the LPRL.

upon the worker.[137] In the United Kingdom and Austria, the worker may appeal against an employer's decision to dismiss him for abandoning the workplace, or any other measure taken against him as a reprisal, where the worker has acted so as to avoid imminent danger.

2.5. Control by Public Authorities of the Prevention of Labour Risks

With the intention of ensuring that health and safety legislation is effective in protecting employees the Member States surveyed assign powers of supervision and control over employers' activities to specific public bodies. The members of these bodies are granted rights of access to the centres of work, and have the right to review the employer's health and safety documentation. They may suspend working in the event of imminent risks to workers and/or have the power to propose and/or impose sanctions on a defaulting employer. In Germany, these functions are entrusted to the Industrial Inspection and Technical Inspection Services of the Associations for the Prevention of and Safety from Accidents at Work. In Austria, the Work Inspectors Unit – an independent administrative authority created by the Law on Work Inspections of 1993 – has these powers. In Spain, three classes of functions are assigned to the Public Administrations.[138] These include promotion and advice;[139] supervision and control;[140] and sanctions for non-compliance with the regulations.[141] In addition, pursuant to the new Criminal Code of 1995, infringement of the regulations for the prevention of risks at work (whether by malice or imprudence), if the lives, health or physical integrity of workers are placed in serious danger, is a crime.[142] Icelandic law entrusts the supervision of health and safety at work to a specific body, referred to as the Administration for Health and Safety at Work.[143] The criminal courts are used to enforce these provisions and there are financial penalties for non-compliance with them. Meanwhile, in Italy, the Law of 23 December 1978 establishes administrative controls over safety in the working environment and the prevention of accidents at work and professional illnesses, as well as administrative sanctions and, in the most serious cases, penal sanctions. The United Kingdom statute of 1974 assigns to the Health and

137 See Article 86 of the Icelandic Law 46/1980.

138 State and Autonomous Communities, which have these responsibilities transferred to them.

139 National Institute for Health and Safety.

140 Work Inspection and Social Security.

141 Labour Authorities of the Ministry of Employment and Social Security and of the Autonomous Communities with jurisdiction over the execution of employment legislation.

142 See Articles 316 and 317.

143 See Article 73 of Law 46/1980.

Safety Executive (HSE) the task of checking on the implementation of the law. The HSE carries out inspections into the causes of some accidents at work, and possesses enforcement powers to be exercised in addition to its general advisory role in this area. In certain specified circumstances, Local Authorities also have an enforcement role in this field.

2.6. *Responsibility of Employers for Non-compliance with Health and Safety Obligations*

Almost all of the national legal systems establish a right for workers to receive compensation for damage suffered as a consequence of non-compliance by the employer with provisions relating to health and safety at work. Although there are some variations, the offending employer will be responsible for any loss resulting from his default.

Thus, in Germany, the employer must pay compensation to the worker if the employee is injured due to infringement of the safety regulations. In Austria, this may only be applied in cases of damage caused intentionally, or by gross negligence, if the damage is caused by non-compliance with the safety regulations, and the person affected has the right to so-called "integrity compensation". However, in all cases in Austria where the labour relationship is concerned the employee will be entitled to the benefits of social insurance.

Spanish law obliges the employer to compensate the employee for damage caused by culpable non-compliance with the stated regulations. This obligation is enforceable before the employment courts, irrespective of the penal and/or civil responsibility, with foundations in the provision in Article 123 of the General Law on Social Security. This also establishes an additional payment above the social benefit for the accident at work when this has taken place with an infringement of the health and safety measures in the workplace – this can be as much as 50% of the sum for the benefit. In Iceland, the employer is responsible in accordance with the provisions of the principle of negligence in the Law on Compensation for Harmful Acts.[144]

Workers in the United Kingdom can make claims in the event of their suffering damage for non-compliance with statutory duties and negligence. To do this, they have to show that the infringement has taken place and that their loss has arisen as a result thereof. In Sweden, the 1970 Law of Torts makes the employer primarily responsible for compensation for damages and harm deriving from an accident.

2.7. *Public benefits paid as a result of accidents at work*

The social security systems of the Member States of the European Union and

144 Law 50/1993.

of the members of the European Economic Area provide for benefits for those injured as a result of accidents at work. In many cases,[145] the domestic law requires employers to subscribe to insurance arrangements to cover the risk of accidents at work.

Some examples may be given in relation to health assistance; the provision of benefit in the event of temporary disability; provision in relation to permanent disability; the provision of pensions for widows and orphans; and provisions in respect of pensions payable to other family members:

(i) Health Assistance

In Iceland (and Austria has similar provisions), the expenses for medical attention from the tenth day of the disability commencing are financed by insurance taken out by the employer, whereas in Spain and Sweden the benefit payable is that applicable to common or ordinary illness.

(ii) Benefit for Temporary Disability

In Austria, the base for the calculation of payment of benefit is the salary for the last year worked before the accident;[146] a daily wage is established for the family of hospitalised workers, with different percentages applicable in some circumstances. This compensation is not payable to the employee if the employer pays him his full wage during medical treatment. If the employer pays the employee half his wages, he receives half the accident sick list pay; there is also a right to receive transitional pay duringthe period of rehabilitation, at monthly levels equivalent to 60% of the base for calculation, which is increased according to the number of the employee's family members until it reaches 100%.

In Spain, the regulatory base of the benefit for temporary disability is calculated taking into account overtime worked over the previous 12 months. The benefit paid is at a level of 75% of the regulatory base from the date of the accident, and continues for a maximum duration of 30 months, no minimum period of absence being required.

In Iceland, payment is made from the eighth day of disability, provided this extends for more than 10 days, up to a maximum time of 52 weeks.[147] The employer receives the public payment if he continues paying the employee his wages. In Italy, the basis for calculation is the wages for the 12 months prior to the date of the accident, and the percentage of daily compensation

145 For instance, in Austria, Iceland and Spain.

146 At the time of the survey forming the basis of this Report, with a maximum of 36,000 ECUs annually.

147 The rate of daily compensation paid in Iceland in 1997 was 712 ISK (Icelandic kronor) for each worker, plus 153 ISK for each of his dependent minors.

varies, being 60% or 75% payment starting from the ninetieth day.

The benefit paid in Sweden is the same, and is subject to the same rules, as that for normal illness.

(iii) Permanent Disability

In Austria, payment for being on the sick list is made at the rate of 66% of the base for calculation for total disability. There is a proportional rate for partial disability, depending on the degree of incapacity, providing this is equal to, or more than, 20%. Austria also provides for an "orphan pension".

Absolute permanent disability (for all professions or trades) in Spain gives the right to a pension of 100% of the regulatory base. In the event of total permanent disability from the employee's habitual profession the pension varies, depending on age, from between 55% and 75%. Partial permanent disability (reduction of not less than 33% of working capacity) gives the right to lump-sum compensation.

Total disability in Iceland gives the right to receipt of an annual pension,[148] with no amount being paid if the disability is less than 10%.

In Italy, an income is established which is equivalent to the full wages which the worker received, if the degree of disability is more than 79%.

(iv) Pensions for Widows and Orphans

In Austria, as well as the possible pension from the pension insurance body, the widow (or widower) receives an annual amount calculated at 20% of the base, which rises to 40% if they have lost half their working capacity or they have reached 65 years of age (widower) or 60 (widow).

In Spain, the widow's pension received by the surviving spouse is at a level of 45% of the regulatory base; that for orphaned children aged less than 18 is at the rate of 20% until the age of 18, the cause of disability coming to an end, or the contracting of marriage.

An annual orphan's pension is paid in Iceland. In 1997 this was 132,210 ISK for each child. A monthly pension (in 1997 of 16,544 ISK) is paid for eight years to the widower when the accident at work leads to the death of the worker within a period of less than two years, if the deceased and widower were living together.

In Italy, the pension is paid to the spouse in such circumstances.

(v) Pensions to other Family Members

In some legal systems, economic benefits are contemplated for other family members. For example, in Austria and Spain, certain state benefits are paid

148 A figure of 163,380 ISK in 1997.

to others with economic dependence on, and with a specified certain degree of kinship to, the injured employee.

3. The Right to Equitable Working Conditions

3.1. Recognition of the Right in General

There are specific rights granted by Constitutions (for example, those of Germany, Italy and Spain), as well as other legal or regulatory provisions, which establish the right to equitable working conditions.[149] These regulations have a double purpose; on the one hand, to ensure decent working conditions for nationals and for foreigners working in their territory; and, on the other, to ensure that the health and safety of workers are not endangered by competition between employers.

The United Kingdom, which does not have a written constitution, has no equivalent constitutional provision.

Current examples of the areas covered include the following:

The Working Day

Except in the United Kingdom, where regulations do not exist to that effect, other than for limiting children's working days, most of the jurisdictions considered prescribe a maximum number of working hours for the employee. In these jurisdictions, when a maximum number of working hours is set, the employer does not have total freedom to determine the working day. The maximum in Germany is 8 hours a day from Monday to Saturday. This may be extended to ten, provided an average of eight hours per day is not exceeded over 24 weeks. The stipulation in Austria is 40 hours a week, with 8 normal, or up to 10 maximum, hours a day. In Spain, the limit is 40 hours a week

149 Examples of constitutional provisions include:

Austria:	The Law on Working Hours 1969 and the Law on Daily and Weekend Rest and Holidays 1983;
Germany:	Articles 1, 2 and 3 of the Constitution; the Law on the Working Day; and the Federal Law on Holidays;
Iceland:	The Law on the Working Environment and on Health and Safety at Work 46/1980; Law 88/1971; Law 20/1987; the Law on working Conditions and Social Rates 55/1980; and the Law on the Wage Guarantee Fund 53/1993;
Italy:	Article 36 of the Constitution; the Civil Code (Articles 2109, 2099 and 2751); the Decree of 15 March 1923; the Law of 10 April 1981; and the Law of 14 July 1959 (the so-called Vigorelli Law);
Spain:	Article 40 of the Constitution and the Statute of Workers.

and 9 per day, save for provisions to the contrary in collective agreements or in individual agreements reached between the employer and the workers. Iceland sets the maximum at 40 hours a week and eight hours a day, save for agreement between the parties, and with specific regulations for sailors. Italy lays down a maximum of 48 hours a week, although by collective agreement a figure of 40 hours a week is usually set. In Sweden, the maximum is 40 hours a week.

It should be noted that all of the Member States of the European Union have been obliged to review their arrangements in this area, in the light of Coouncil Directive 93/104/EC.[150]

Overtime

In many legal systems, limits are established for overtime, both by Law and by agreement. Those powers that exceed the normal maximum daily or weekly working hours are considered as overtime.

In Austria, the permissibility of overtime is conditional upon the existence of an increased workload or the need to complete tasks within a certain time.

In Spain, there is a maximum number of annual hours for full-time workers, but hours worked to prevent or repair faults, and other extraordinary and urgent damage, are not included within this limit.

In Iceland, overtime is considered to be the hours in excess of a working day of eight working hours between Monday and Friday.

Except in special situations, 48 hours a week, fifty a month, and an annual maximum of two hundred hours, may not be exceeded in Sweden.

In one Member State, Austria, overtime must be paid for at an increased rate of 50%, while in another, Spain, overtime must not be paid for at below the ordinary hourly rate. In practice, however, in all of the Member States considered in this Report, work during overtime is usually paid at a rate higher than the norm – although it may be noted that, in Germany, overtime only gives the right to additional payment if this is specified in the applicable collective agreement.

Holidays

Most of the domestic legal systems surveyed establish a minimum period for holidays, which the respective Laws usually set at 30 days a year, as in Italy and Spain. In Germany, the figure is 24 working days, and in Sweden 25 days, with the exclusion of weekends. In Austria, this increases to 35 days when the employee has more than 25 years' service. In some countries, the

150 Council Directive 93/104/EC concerning certain aspects of the organisation of working time.

period for holidays, in the absence of provisions in a collective agreement, will be set by agreement between the worker and the employer.[151] In other jurisdictions, the amount of holiday is set by the employer.[152] In Austria, Germany, Spain and Sweden, there are summary processes (at least, in the latter two countries mentioned) to lay down the holiday period where there is disagreement between the worker and the employer.

Wages: Wage Levels and Guarantees

State regulation of minimum wages does not exist either in Iceland or in the United Kingdom.[153] There is no such provision in Germany, where wages levels are regulated by what is established in collective agreements an approach also to be found in the Icelandic case. Nor is there any such provision in Austria, where the legal limit is the point of usury or agreements contrary to good custom. In Italy, the judges set wage levels, respecting provisions contained in Article 36 of the Constitution. In Spain, the Government sets the minimum inter-professional wage annually by means of Royal Decrees.[154]

All of the national laws surveyed have provision for the protection of workers' salaries and compensation for dismissal on the discharge of employment contracts in the event of the employer's insolvency. This is effected by the State, or through autonomous bodies created *ad hoc*.[155] In all of the cases analysed, financial limits are set to the protection given to employees. Usually, this is either temporal (number of days of salary owed) or quantitative (a sum is set, up to the level of which the State or autonomous body is responsible). In some Member States, a mixture of the two methods is used, as in Spain and the United Kingdom. In some jurisdictions the obligation on the insuring body arises on the declaration of the employer of its situation of insolvency or suspension of payments by it. In other Member States, the liability to make payment comes into existence on a declaration of insolvency of the employer by judicial process before the courts.

151 This is the case for Germany and Spain.

152 This is so in Italy and Sweden, with, in the latter case, an obligation to take the holidays during the Summer period.

153 In the case of the United Kingdom, the new Labour government elected in 1997 is in the course of introducing legislation to provide for a minimum wage, through the National Minimum Wage Act 1998.

154 For 1996 this was 5,509 ECUs, and for 1997 it was 5,654 ECUs, annual salary for workers aged over 18.

155 Which, in many cases, are supported by contributions from workers and/or employers, along with public contributions.

4. Judicial Protection of these Rights

In all of the Member States reviewed, workers have a right to go to the courts or tribunals to make claims in respect of the rights dealt with in this Part. Actions in relation to these kinds of claims will normally come before the courts having jurisdiction in employment issues, although there are some special cases.

In Austria and Spain, breaches of the regulations on health and safety at work give rise to administrative sanctions, which are justiciable before the courts of judicial review. If the worker has suffered injury, he may bring his claim before the courts with employment jurisdiction, irrespective of the outcome of the administrative sanction.

In the United Kingdom, industrial tribunals deal with the non-payment of wages, dismissal, and sanctions against workers for questions relating to health and safety at work. They also have power in relation to the application of the Community Working Time Directive, in so far as that instrument affects public employees. Claims for damages arising from injury at work are dealt with by the normal civil courts (the High Court and the County Courts).

Discrimination

1. Equality and Non-discrimination in General

1.1. The right of equality

The national legal systems surveyed contain a diversity of provisions on the rights of equality and non-discrimination. Many recognise the principle of equality of all people before the law. This has two aspects. First, a right to be treated equally by legal or other regulations – referred to as equality "in law", and, secondly, a right to the same application of the law by all public bodies – referred to as equality "in the application of the law". These rights stem from the concept of the need for equal treatment for those who are in the same situation. People should not be treated differently, or be required to satisfy different conditions to be entitled to some benefit, unless there is an objective and reasonable justification for the variation. In some legal systems, there is just explicit prohibition of specified types of discrimination.

The right to equality includes that of equitable treatment in legislative provisions. It also includes an equality of application of the regulations by judicial and governmental organs, especially when other fundamental rights are in issue. This aspect of equality in the application of laws lies easily in those legal systems where the binding force of precedent is recognised. It is an essential feature of such systems that a court confronted by similar circumstances will decide the issue before it in the same way as another court. In those systems where the doctrine of binding legal precedent does not apply, the concept of equality may appear to clash with the principle of the independence of each individual judicial body to decide the case before it anew. In reality, this difference appears to be more theoretical than practice. It appears to be a common requirement that, in the event of departure from precedents or from accepted legal doctrine, the departure must be justified, with an explicit or implicit reasoning showing that the solution adopted is not an exception or arbitrary unique case. In effect, in such systems the courts will require an objective justification for a departure from the approach previously adopted.

General statements on equality are frequently to be found, while specific references to equality between the sexes are to be found in the Constitutions of a majority of Member States. Particular note may be taken of the situation in Norway, where the principle of equality is not expressly provided for in general terms by the constitutional regulations but is considered as the inspiration behind the legal system in general and in many specific rules within that legal system.[156]

From these constitutional rules we will first consider the basis for determining those subject to this right. Some constitutions mention "all human beings" or "men", with generic reference to all people, a meaning imposed by the international provisions we are considering. Others limit the proclamation to "citizens" or to nationals, with explicit reference to "Spaniards", "Greeks", etc., although this is of limited effect because the subjective extension of a right and other fundamental rights depends on other constitutional rules which extend to "all people" or to "all". In some Constitutions, stipulations as to equality are brought together in a pronouncement of a universal nature on the subject of equality in general. Others restrict the obligations in connection with particular rights to nationals.

Secondly, the formula "equitable before the law" is generally repeated, but the expressions "before" and "law" are recognised with a broad meaning covering all the factors mentioned above and all classes of regulations, dispositions, resolutions and acts by all public powers. The Constitution or other primary source of law may be in general terms expressing the right of equality and no more. This may expressly provide for secondary legislation allowing limitation, restriction, or derogation, of or form the obligation in defined circumstances, or it may prohibit such limitation of the rights. Secondary legislation cannot limit a right granted in the primary source of the law unless this is expressly or impliedly authorised at the higher level. Although provisions requiring equality of treatment usually arise in a primary source of law, frequently this source provides for the adoption of regulations to deal with specific situation. The secondary source of law is subject to the requirements of the primary source, but can be used as a method of ensuring that the rules as to equality are applicable in particular circumstances.

156 For the individual national provisions see the following:

Austria:	Articles 7 and 9
Belgium:	Article 10
Denmark:	Articles 70, 83 and 87.
Finland:	Article 5
France:	Article 1 (Decl. 1979; Preamble C 1946, Articles 1, 2 and 77c, 1958)
Germany:	Articles 3 and 33.1
Greece:	Article 4.1 and 4.2
Iceland:	Article 65
Ireland:	Articles 9.3, 16.1.3, and 40.1
Italy:	Articles 3 and 37
Luxembourg:	Article 11.2
The Netherlands:	Article 1
Portugal:	Article 13.1
Spain:	Articles 1, 9.2, 14 and 139.1
Sweden:	Articles 2.1, 3 (Chap. I) and 16 (Chap. II).

It has been seen in Part I of this Report that the situation in Ireland is a special case, but, this notwithstanding, Ireland does have specific laws which prohibit inequality based on sex or civil status.

1.2. Prohibition of Discrimination

The legal systems surveyed prohibit discrimination or inequitable and unfavourable treatment, linked to concrete social, political or personal causes (referred to as "factors of discrimination") in addition to providing for the right to equality of treatment. When these factors of discrimination apply legal systems often strengthen the rule of equality by declaring unlawful all inequality which lacks objective and reasonable justification, requiring a greater degree of justification than that usually required. In Norway, although there is no constitutional rule prohibiting discrimination, a latent principle does exist, giving rise to a concept of non-discrimination. This says that discrimination is differential treatment arising form a given condition. It includes acts and omissions whose practical effect is that a factor of discrimination results in the person subject to it suffering unreasonable disadvantage in comparison with those who do not.

A right to equality is expressed in a positive manner requiring absolute equality of treatment. A right not to be discriminated against is expressed in a negative manner, forbidding inequality of treatment without reasonable, reasoned and objective grounds.

Almost all of the legal systems surveyed – with the exception of Luxembourg and Norway, where there is a tacit or implicit recognition – envisage an explicit prohibition of discrimination in general. All of them – except for Iceland – contain particular prohibitions in labour legislation. This extends to the abolition of privileges explicable on a historical basis.[157]

157 The Constitutional provisions referring to the prohibition of discrimination are as follows:

Austria:	Article 7 of the Constitution and 66.2 (State Convention 1919)
Belgium:	Articles 11 and 131
Denmark:	Article 70
Finland:	Article 5.2
France:	Preamble C. 1946, Article 2 C. 1958
Germany:	Articles 3.3, 6.5 and 33.3
Greece:	Article 5.2
Ireland:	Article 44.2.3
Italy:	Articles 3.1 and 30.2
The Netherlands:	Article 1
Portugal:	Articles 13.2, 36.4 and 41.2
Spain:	Articles 14 and 39.2
Sweden:	Articles 15 and 16 (Chap. II).

1.3. Factors of Discrimination

The factors of discrimination prohibited by the legal systems in general are very numerous, with Constitutions mentioning varied concepts or assumptions. Examining these constitutional regulations in detail, we can identify extensive agreement in relation to the following criteria: race (a term that is repeated, sometimes expressly including "colour of the skin" and "ethnic origin" in Sweden, or "colour" in Belgium); sex (with its repeated particularity in Ireland); religion (beliefs or religious practice); and political opinion.

There is less unanimity with regard to other factors where discrimination can occur. Some of these factors are: disability (in the United Kingdom, in accordance with the Disability Discrimination Act 1995, while Finland mentions "health"); origin (Germany and Portugal); language (Finland, Germany, Greece, Italy, Portugal and Sweden); nationality (Belgium, Germany and Greece); origin or birth (Austria, Denmark, Germany, Portugal and Spain); personal condition (Finland, Italy and Spain); social condition (Italy, Portugal and Spain); ideological reasons (Belgium, Finland, Portugal); affiliation (Portugal and Spain); and opinion (in general, Finland and Spain). There are also additional concepts used exclusively in Portugal (instruction, economic situation) and in Finland (age). In the United Kingdom, discrimination is prohibited on grounds of colour, race, nationality and ethnic or national backgrounds.

Residual clauses are to be found in the anti-discrimination provisions of many Member States. These forbid discrimination in general terms, referring to matters such as "any other condition or personal or social circumstance" or "any other consideration".

The factors of discrimination prohibited by the legal systems in connection with work and employment in particular include the following: origin (Finland, Germany and Spain); sex (in practically all of the systems, except for Norway, but in the sense of there being no prohibitive regulation referring specifically to this sphere, by referring to all areas); civil status (Ireland, Spain and the United Kingdom); race (in practically all of the systems); social condition (Spain); religious or political ideas (in many systems); membership or non-membership of unions (in many of the systems); relationship (in Spain); disability (United Kingdom); language (Italy and Spain); nationality and sexual orientation (The Netherlands); or "nationality of a state of the European Economic Area" (Norway).

The prohibition against discrimination by reason of sexual orientation is understood to be contained in other legal systems. It is clearly expressed in Sweden – where discrimination by reason of homosexuality is forbidden. In other Member States, it arises from a more generic formula, by the mention of sex or its explicit specification in other regulations – notably, such as those relating to unions – whose principles are understood to be referable to the working sphere.

One particular form of inequitable treatment which is prohibited is in relation to the exercise of fundamental rights in general, including especially that of having formulated actions or claims in defence of one's rights (United Kingdom – in cases of sexual, racial and disability discrimination; Austria; and Spain – inferred from ILO Convention No. 158 and Article 24 of the Spanish Constitution), by the understanding that no measure is allowed by the employer as a reprisal, sanction or damage for the fact that, previously, the worker has resorted to official or collective action to denounce, claim or make demands arising from non-compliance with the anti-discrimination rules by the employer.

In those Member States where there are general prohibitions on discrimination they apply to employment.

2. Equality and Non-discrimination in Employment

2.1. Conditions for and during employment

With the exception of Iceland, where specific rules are lacking, all the legal systems studied have regulations governing the rights of equality and non-discrimination in many facets of employment relationships, for instance as to access to employment and/or remuneration and/or professional conditions during employment.

In many legal systems, rules of equality and non-discrimination are established with general or residual clauses referring to "all phases of employment" (from the advertising of jobs offered until dismissal), "all working conditions" or "the other conditions" (also mentioning specific matters, such as the working day, pay or promotion). Some systems also make void or ineffective some classes of regulations or labour sources (regulatory precepts, clauses in collective agreements, individual agreements, and unilateral decisions by employers) if their effect is discriminatory or results in discriminatory treatment.

National rules in this respect are usually integrated into general employment regulations and in specific laws relating to equality.

2.2. Equality by Reason of Sex

In all of the national legal systems considered, equality between men and women in connection with work is especially recognised and guaranteed. In many of the Member States the principle of an equal wage for work of equal value is recognised. This usually applies to differences arising for reasons of sex, although some – exceptionally – extend it to some other factor of discrimination with a general character.

In this aspect of the law, the influence of Community legislation and the jurisprudence of the European Court of Justice is especially strong. Notably, this is to be seen in the development of the rule of using neutral, non-sexist criteria in the determining of working conditions existing in many legal systems.[158]

Some measures exist, or have existed (which are referred to as "positive discrimination", or "positive/affirmative action"), to promote real equality of opportunities for women in access to employment or during employment, where social reality shows that they have been disadvantaged. In these circumstances, rules are required to promote their placement in particular sectors of the labour market, or favourable conditions to encourage changes in other such sectors.

The principle of equality has been one of the essential concepts underlying political and social developments in Europe. Thus, the principle of the equality of the sexes has had an important part in the development of Community Law. Article 119 of the EC Treaty establishes the principle of equality of remuneration between workers without distinction for reasons of sex. In part this had an economic reason to avoid the unfair competition between competitors some of whom had a lower paid workforce. If originally the wide scope of Article 119 was not appreciated, it has evolved in its width and depth as a result of Ministerial Directives and decisions of the European Court of Justice.[159] The provisions of Protocol 14 to the Treaty on European Union, which deals with matters of social policy through the annexed Agreement on Social Policy (in which the Council will decide by majority), also deal with equality of opportunity on the labour market and equality of treatment between men and women.

The jurisprudence of the Court of Justice of the European Community has been of immense importance in defining the scope and meaning of the principle of sexual equality contained in the Treaty.

The legal rules and conceptual constructions relating to equality of the sexes in the national legal systems have been greatly influenced by Community Law and its development. Thus, the concept and limits of the principle of equality of men and women at work – both before the law (this must provide as equal what is equal) and in the administrative or judicial application of the same (equal cases must be resolved in the same way) – have developed much under the influence of the Community.

In many legal systems there is a coincidence of the following principles:

158 Although it may be noted that this does not extend to Iceland.

159 These include Directives 75/117/EEC, of 10 February 1975, 76/207/EEC, of 9 February 1976 (equality of treatment in access to employment, professional training and working conditions), 79/7/EEC, of 19 December 1978 (Social Security), 86/378/EEC, of 24 July 1986 (professional Social Security systems) and 86/613/EEC, of 11 December 1986 (autonomous activities and protection of maternity), together with that of 9 October 1992 (protection of the health and safety of pregnant or breast-feeding women).

(a) There are criteria which differentiate between people which are detrimental (in ways which may be explicit or implicit) to the principle of equality;

(b) All differences in treatment must serve a legitimate purpose or interest a purpose or object which is protected by the legal system;

and

(c) If there are permissible criteria of differentiation they must be appropriate to that purpose. Permissible differences must be proportionate to their purpose.

On the specific matter of equality of remuneration, there is also an appreciable agreement with the European doctrine on the concept of remuneration – all amounts in money or in kind directly or indirectly paid by the employer to the worker by reason of the working relationship – and on the meaning of equality of remuneration, including the identity of the unit of measurement used to establish the remuneration for unit of work and equality of the rate fixed for a job remunerated by unit of time for the same job.

Likewise, the distinction between "direct" and "indirect" discrimination is accepted in the national systems, although indirect discrimination is not seen as a uniform concept. For instance, in France it is considered to be one of hidden discrimination, and in the United Kingdom it is seen as applying where there is a disproportionate effect of an apparently objective action. These approaches can be contrasted with that in the United States of America, where indirect discrimination occurs when action has a "disparate impact" on the person subject to the discrimination.[160]

160 In the context of the present survey, the most extensive approach is to be found in the United Kingdom. There, several types of discrimination are considered unlawful.

Direct discrimination occurs when a person discriminates against another for certain reasons, treating him less favourably than others.

Indirect discrimination takes place when a person applies to another person a requirement or condition which they apply or would apply equally to people who are not of the same group as that person, when the requirement or condition (a) is such that the proportion of people in that group that may meet this is considerably smaller than the proportion of people that are not in that group and can meet it; (b) cannot be justified, without taking into account the race, sex, disability, nationality or ethnic origins of the person of whom it is required; (c) is to the detriment of the other person, as they are unable to meet it, and is not justifiable.

Victimisation (persecution or reprisals) is also forbidden. Victimisation takes place when one person discriminates against another by treating them in a less favourable manner than they would treat other people and do so because the person persecuted (a) has filed a claim against the discriminator or any other person for violation of the laws; (b) has offered testimony or information in connection with the claim presented by any person seeking protection in law; (c) has taken any initiative under the law concerning the discriminator or another person; and (d) alleges that the discriminator or another person has carried out an action that violates the laws.

Many systems recognise that the assessment of equality does not require compete coincidence of the situations being compared. This is of great importance when examining the pay of women and men who have occupied the same position at different times. Likewise, similarities occur in the application of the concept when comparing remuneration when the nature of the work which is undertaken differs. There is a general requirement for equality of payment for those undertaking work which is of equal value. In the same way, there is coincidence in the principle that evaluation of work should be undertaken in an objective manner which is not tainted by sex bias.

In developing this principle, set out in Article 2.1 of ILO Convention No. 100, measures must be adopted to promote the objective evaluation of work.[161]

Finally, it should be noted that criteria akin to measures of "affirmative action" or "positive discrimination" have begun to be seen more extensively – especially in the reservation of percentages or "quotas" of jobs or positions for women.[162]

2.3. Other measures for the integration of the disadvantaged

For similar reasons to those seen when considering the real and social inequality of persons because of their sex, many legal systems have measures to protect others who are members of disadvantaged groups. These include provisions to benefit the disabled, those from ethnic minorities, people with low incomes, and the unemployed. The purpose of this type of regulation is to alleviate particular disadvantages perceived to be suffered by the groups concerned. Types of measures

161 Article 3.1. It may also be noted that three rules have been taken from the jurisprudence of the European Court of Justice and applied literally by the Spanish Constitutional Court in its Decision No. 58/1994:

1. Where there are occupations predominantly occupied by workers of both sexes, who are unequally paid, if there is no transparency in the determination of the remuneration criteria, the employer is obliged to state clearly the reason for the differentials to exclude any indication that sex may have been the decisive factor;
2. To do so it is not sufficient to clearly state that the tasks are unequal in nature. This is because reasonableness and equality do not postulate an exact similarity in what is done but equality in the value of the work;
3. In the evaluation of the work the criteria of evaluation must not be, in themselves, discriminatory, but neutral, ensuring the equality of conditions of workers of both sexes. This is so unless there are exceptional circumstances and for reasons arising from the nature of the work. Different criteria are required. Features inherent in one of the sexes may not be considered to the detriment of the other, leading to the over-valuing of work – a good example being greater physical strength, which may naturally have a different impact on the sexes.

162 This controversial approach can be found in Austria, Germany (STJCE of 17 October 1995), Iceland, Italy and Spain – but not, it may be noted, in the United Kingdom.

adopted include improving facilities for workers or companies for access to employment, specific forms or methods of contracting, special bases for their labour relations, types of temporary contracting reserved for the disadvantaged, and facilitating their contracting. It must be appreciated that such measures will have a differing practical effect in legal systems which recognise a right to a minimum income for all people without resources.[163]

2.4. *Subjective sphere of protection according to nationality*

Recently, phenomena occurring in various European countries show the significance of the factor of nationality in social, political and legal problems – especially due to the legislative changes or social behaviour which affect non-nationals or foreigners. This has developed so that in certain States cases are being experienced of xenophobia, especially in relation to people of other races.

In the area covered by this Report it is important to consider whether a right of equality and non-discrimination only exists for nationals, or whether this also extends to citizens of other countries. If so, does it extend to those of other Member States of the European Union, or to all foreigners in general.

All Member States establish equality and non-discrimination both for nationals and for other foreigners from countries of the European Union – this is the obligation of Community legislation. As has also been mentioned, Norway, in its turn, has established the rule of equality and non-discrimination for all citizens of the European Economic Area. In The Netherlands, nationality is prohibited as a factor in employment discrimination.

Many Member States extend these rights of equality and non-discrimination in employment to other foreigners, for various reasons:

(i) due to historical links, such as those of the Latin American countries with respect to Spain, or the nationals of the former colonies of European countries; and
(ii) due to international regulations, such as the Agreements between the European Union and other States (for instance, Morocco).

Finally, for the rest of those who are non-nationals, member States usually establish the requirement of residence and/or work permits for their full harmonisation, or there are aspects of the employment regulations which are not applied to them.

163 Recently in Spain a reform has been agreed by the social partners, introducing a type of indefinite contract for the development of employment for those laid off, the young, the disabled, or those on temporary contracts. There is, in particular, a special rule as to the amount of compensation in the event of unfair dismissal of such persons. Action such as this raises interesting questions regarding the justification and proportion of the differential economic compensation for unjustified dismissal.

2.5. *Judicial procedure, measures and the burden of proof*

Emergency judicial procedures do not exist for the protection of the rights of equality examined in most of the countries, except in Italy for matters of equality between men and women,[164] and in Spain, for the claims founded on the violation of the rights of equality and non-discrimination.[165] As is indicated in some cases, judicial procedures to decide issues as to inequality of treatment are the general ones for labour disputes, without special procedures to correct inequality of treatment. It is noteworthy that, in some cases, a worker may appeal to Committees specialising in claims for equality of conditions with the function of making recommendations to resolve disputes. If this does not resolve the matter, the claimant may bring legal action to enforce his right (Iceland).

Generally, in cases where an individual claims to have been treated contrary to a requirement of equality the claimant is required to allege and prove the inequitable treatment which he has suffered. If he does so, the employer has the burden of demonstrating to the judicial body that the act or measure taken is not for discriminatory reasons or criteria, and he has to show a valid justification for it. Some legal systems envisage this rule specifically with regard to equality for reasons of sex.[166] In certain cases, it is envisaged that the claimant need not provide full proof of inequality, it being sufficient for him to present the facts constituting discrimination in a credible form (Germany). A judgment of the Supreme Court of Iceland of March 1997 has adopted a similar approach, and this is the rule in other States (for example, Spain). In Belgium, workers are required to prove discrimination, except for cases of improper dismissal – when it is for the employer to show lawful and non-discriminatory reasons for his action. In Ireland, the discrimination must be proved by the person who alleges it.

164 Article 15 of the Law of 9 December 1977.

165 Articles 175 onwards of the Law on Labour Procedure 1995, also applicable to other fundamental rights.

166 As is the case for Austria, Germany and Norway.

Rights of Association (Trade Union Freedom) and Collective Bargaining

1. Freedom to Join a Union

1.1. Recognition of the Right

All of the national legal systems recognise the right of employers and workers to associate freely, by setting up associations or unions. Although the picture is very varied, it is possible to distinguish the following categories:

(a) Systems in which only a general right of association is recognised, protecting employers and workers.

This is the case with Austria, Belgium, Denmark, Finland, The Netherlands, Norway,[167] Sweden, and the United Kingdom, with provision for the right of association or of free association – terms which demonstrate that we are dealing with a freedom or liberty which is recognised in favour of the individual, as the scope of his power or rights of action *vis-à-vis* the State, all public bodies and other citizens. However, the extent to which these benefits or rights come into conflict, when the rights of some clash with those of others, will have to be given due consideration.

(b) Systems in which the right of employers to form associations (in accordance with the general right of association or with the specifics of the associations of employers themselves) and the right of workers to form unions are both recognised.

This is the case in Germany, Iceland, Ireland (which, in fact, recognises the right to form "associations and unions"), Portugal and Spain. However, from this there does not derive any real inequality of powers, rights, functions or possibilities of action between some social persons and others, since each is generally treated as equal in their respective spheres, with similar requirements and treatment, except in the exclusive aspects of each in accordance with their legal, economic and social position and of their members in working relations. There are extreme cases in which, however, we can see signs of favouring the unions or compensating them for their prior situation of being prohibited or considered inferior.

167 Where there is no explicit recognition, but it is considered a basic general principle.

(c) Systems in which the right to unionise as such extends to both social agents. This is the situation which occurs in Italy.

This Report is primarily concerned, however, with the right to unionisation enjoyed and exercised by workers, rather than by employers.[168]

1.2. Those who Enjoy the Freedom to Join a Union

The right to trade union association is recognised, in the aforementioned terms, in relation to employers and workers. However, particularly with regard to workers, the recognition extends the scope of people to whom it applies in a different way in the various national legal systems, since it is attributed to the following persons:

(a) To all citizens without exception. This is the case of Austria (where self employed workers and pensioners are also included as holders of the right), Belgium, Denmark, Germany (where the right of association is also recognised for military and police personnel), Norway (as a logical consequence of the right of all citizens to associate) and Sweden.

(b) To all citizens in general, including public employees or officials, but excluding military and police personnel, who do not enjoy the right to unionise (United Kingdom), or where specific regulations with a non trade union character are applied to them (the case of Italy, with respect to members of the armed forces), or they have the right recognised, but limited to the negotiation of working conditions (Ireland, for civil and university officials). The prohibition on the right to join a union is extended, in some national legal systems, to other public employees (the case of Spain, with respect to judges and public prosecutors, while they remain active).

(c) To all salary earners in general, as is the case in Iceland.

1.3. Content of the Freedom to Join a Union

The wealth and variety of the legal systems are also enormous when we summarise or specify the concrete rights and powers or the content of the freedom to join a union. Some recognise all the rights stated below, and others only some of them.[169]

168 In relation to protection of the complementary right of the employer, see, for example, the decision of the European Court of Human Rights in *Gustafsson* v. *Sweden* (1996) 22 EHRR 409.

169 A more complete and extensive list can be found in the ILO Conventions to which reference has been made in Part I of this Report. See also the instruments set out in the Annex to this volume.

In the national legal systems, without doubt what particularly stands out is the extensive regulation in the Constitution of Portugal, in its Articles 55 and 56, which must be reflected by its regulatory maxim on the subject. Article 55 is entitled "on the freedom to join a union", and refers to the rights of "the workers" in this sphere, with an individual sense or category, therefore, recognising them:

"in the exercise of freedom to join a union:

(a) freedom of constitution of trade union association at all levels;
(b) freedom of membership, no worker being allowed to be forced to pay dues to a union of which they are not a member;
(c) freedom of organisation and internal regulation of trade union associations;
(d) the exercise of the right to trade union activity in the company; and
(e) the right to take part in the structures that decide the respective statutes".

This same Article 55 then goes on to mention *inter alia* the rights to establish relations with international organisations, to the internal principles of participation and democratic administration, and to that of independence to form other powers or groups. By contrast, Article 56 recognises as rights of "trade union associations" – with a collective sense or dimension – those to:

"(a) participate in the elaboration of employment legislation – apart from the role of negotiating collective agreements, which they are also granted;
(b) participate in the administration of Social Security institutions and other organisations whose function is to meet the interests of the working classes;
(c) participate in the execution of socio-economic plans; and
(d) be represented in the organisms of social agreement…".

This demonstrates the need to distinguish between "individual rights" and "collective rights".

Individual Rights

There is first the individual freedom to join a union, which may be said to include the following rights:

(a) The right to found unions: recognised in many national legal systems, such as Austria, Belgium, Finland, Germany, Spain, Sweden, or the United Kingdom.
(b) Freedom of positive affiliation or of affiliation to the union of free choice: recognised in some national legal systems, such as Austria, Belgium, Finland, Germany or Spain.
(c) Freedom of negative affiliation, or of non-affiliation to any union: also recognised in some legal systems, such as Austria, Belgium, Finland, Germany or Spain.
(d) The right to choose representatives within the union: also recognised in some legal systems, such as Austria, Belgium, Germany and Spain.
(e) The right to activity as a member of the union in the company and outside it: recognised in Austria, Belgium, Finland, Germany and Spain.

In Denmark, all of these rights are recognised – as they are in Ireland, where there is also mention of a right to remain separate from the association ("dissociation").

Collective Rights

A second aspect of trade union freedom is at the collective level, which includes the rights of unions or trade union organisations as collective persons. The following rights are included:

(a) The right to establish their own rules and programme of action: recognised *de facto* or in law in most national legal systems.
(b) The right to federate nationally or internationally: also recognised in most legal systems.
(c) The right to exercise the trade union activity of their own union, which is understood to include:

    (1) The right to negotiate collective agreements, recognised in most legal systems, with special emphasis on negotiation by public employees in some countries;
    (2) The right to strike: recognised in some legal systems, such as Germany, Iceland, Spain or Sweden – although the recognition is extensive and the legal basis very complex;[170]
    (3) The right to plan disputes or individual and collective claims: recognised in some legal systems, such as Austria, Germany or Spain;

170 As is indicated *infra*.

(4) The right to propose candidates as elected representatives in companies and professional associations: recognised in some legal systems, such as Austria, Germany and Spain, as well as in Belgium, with reference both to the general representatives bodies and the committees entrusted with matters of health and safety at work;

(5) The right to other activities, such as those relating to information about the company: which is expressly recognised in Finland, but is considered implicit in the right to trade union action in many others.

(d) The right to propose the appointment of some members of the administrative bodies of the company, as happens individually with some national legal systems (Sweden).

(e) The right to propose members for the national Employment Court (Sweden) or other Labour Courts (Finland), or to present them for appointment as consultants or experts of the courts (Germany).

1.4. Restrictive or Limiting Clauses on the Freedom to Join a Union

One of the classic examples of legal interference with trade unions, limiting the activities of companies and unions, are trade union protection clauses, signed by both parties on negotiating an accord or collective agreement. However, in some legal systems they are allowed in general terms (Norway), in accordance with a tradition and a conception that does not consider them unlawful – especially because of their origin, agreed between companies and unions.

"Closed shop" clauses – by which the employer is placed under an obligation not to allow into his company anybody other than the members of the union with which he has made an agreement, and no other – are expressly forbidden by many national legal systems,[171] although these are valid, if contained in collective agreements, in Finland, Norway or Sweden.

The "agency shop" clause – which allows the employer or the unions to raise contributions from all of the workers employed, whether they are members or not, for the benefit of the union with which the company has negotiated and made the agreement – is expressly permitted in certain national legal systems, notably those of Iceland or Spain.

1.5. Discrimination on the grounds of Trade Union Activity

In addition to restriction on the joint activities of unions and employers, the legal systems also envisage restrictions on the unilateral conduct or decisions of employers. Thus, many national legal systems prohibit discrimination in

171 Including Austria, Germany, Iceland, Ireland, Portugal, Spain and the United Kingdom.

employment and in working conditions on the basis of membership of a union or participation in trade union activities,[172] while there are, in some countries, special "fast-track" judicial procedures for dealing with conduct denounced as anti-trade union (as in the case of Italy and Spain).[173]

1.6. "Most Representative Unions"

Only in some legal systems is there special treatment given to the most representative unions – by which is meant those that have the largest trade union membership or affiliation, giving them more functions or rights than the others in respect of trade union action (the case of Italy or Spain), or rights of institutional participation (the case of Belgium or Spain). In Finland and Sweden, proposing members for Labour Courts is recognised for most representative trade union organisations.

This issue has generated polemics to no small degree, especially on account of the complaints by those unions which are not the "most representative", considering themselves to be discriminated against as a consequence of the lesser powers, functions, rights or possibilities of action that are granted them. This gives rise to questions affecting both the freedom to join a union and the prohibition of discrimination – generally resolved by requiring an objective and reasonable justification for differential treatment as between unions, with the need for a justifying cause being especially strong and appropriate in proportion to the differential introduced in connection with the function or faculty in question. The object of the measures favouring the "most representative" unions may be to avoid excessive trade union fragmentation, which would be counter to an effective role for the unions in exercising their function as protectors of workers' interests. In view of this, both absolute equality and simple proportionality are defensible – especially in the receipt of public assistance, which occurs in the form of direct grants, or paying the wages or expenses of persons designated by the union and released from their normal working duties (Finland or Spain). To this end, some legal systems distinguish a "hard core" or essential content of the right, which all unions gain equally, from an additional or "contingent" content, where there are differences depending upon the representation of the union. Included in the former are powers such as those of collective bargaining in general terms, the instigation of disputes or strikes, and trade union activity in companies in general. Included in the second are institutional participation, or action in elected representation, when these may not be constitutionally enforceable.

172 Austria, Belgium, Denmark, Finland, Germany, Iceland, Ireland, Italy, Norway, Portugal, Spain, Sweden and the United Kingdom.

173 See the detailed study on dismissal and the general prohibition against dismissals motivated by trade union affiliation or activity, to which reference is made in Part II of this Report.

1.7. Elected Representatives in the Company – Trade Union Freedom of these Representatives – Bodies for Representation of Workers in Companies with European Scope

Many legal systems envisage that there exist in companies both trade union representatives from the unions themselves, and others chosen by the workers, without those elected necessarily having to belong to unions – although in most cases these are, in practice, trade union representatives or those enjoying the freedom to join a union.[174]

Only in a few legal systems, at the time of writing, is there legislation on Works Councils or representatives of workers in companies with European scope, in Regulations putting into effect Directive 94/45/EC – even though this Directive allowed the application of the principle of subsidiarity in vertical or horizontal form.[175] This is the case for Austria, Belgium, Denmark,[176] Finland,[177] Germany and Sweden. In Spain, a Bill on "Rights of information and consultation of the workers in companies and groups of companies with a Community dimension", which envisages a European Works Council or an alternative procedure for information and consultation, was recently approved and published in final form.[178] In Norway, too, there have been regulations in force since 18 October 1996 on this subject, as a consequence of the obligations of that country as a signatory to the Agreement on the European Economic Area.[179]

2. Collective Bargaining

2.1. Company Agreements and those with larger scope than the Company

The negotiation of collective agreements may be carried out by a variety of social actors. In this respect, the following may be distinguished:

174 Only in one case (the United Kingdom) do such representatives not exist at the time of writing, although reference should be made to recent legislation introduced in the wake of the judgment of the European Court of Justice in Cases C-382/92 and C-383/92, *Commission of the European Communities* v. *United Kingdom of Great Britain and Northern Ireland.*

175 However, at the time of writing, progress towards implementation of the Works Council Directive can be seen in all of the signatory Member States.

176 Where the respective Laws were issued on this only in the last year (1996).

177 In the case of Finland, this is only the case for companies falling within the sphere of the European Economic Area.

178 The B.O.C.G. of 22 July 1996, enacted as Law 10/1997 of 24 April 1997.

179 (*Editor's note*). For more detailed information concerning developments in the various Member States as regards the introduction of national legislation implementing Directive 94/45/EC, see R.Blanpain (ed), *Labour Law and Industrial Relations in the European Union*, (1998) 32 Bulletin of Comparative Labour Relations [special edition, updating the material contained in R.Blanpain & T.Hanami (eds), *European Works Councils* (Peeters, Leuven 1995)].

(a) Company agreements: the employer and, as the other social partner, the representatives of the workers or unions.

In spite of the effectiveness of these agreements – as recognised in much of the information provided for the preparation of this Report – it is noteworthy that, in some other national reports, emphasis is placed on the limitation of the capacity of individual employers, by law or in practice, to attack collective bargaining.[180]

(b) Agreement with larger scope than the company: associations of employers and unions.

2.2. *Efficacy and Content of Collective Agreements*

This varies greatly as between national systems.[181] Thus, in some national legal systems, collective agreements have general efficacy when they are applied to all companies and workers included in their scope or dimensions. This general binding force is attributed to those negotiated by employers and unions with sufficient establishment or presence in the company, sector or sphere in question. This is widespread, with some legal systems specifying this sufficiency of representation in percentage or quantitative terms.[182] In cases such as Portugal or Spain, a subsequent agreement of assent is required from others who are not signatories, or an administrative or governmental decision extending the effect to non-members – which are ways of broadening their scope of application. Together with these, there are agreements whose effect is limited to signatories or those represented by the signatory parties – which is the only assumption mentioned in countries such as Norway. The legal systems with a less developed trade union tradition, with a background of less trade union power, or low numbers of affiliates, offer general negotiation rights to unions with a lower level of affiliation or representativeness.

The matters which are the subject of collective bargaining are highly varied, and, therefore, most national legal systems allow collective agreements to regulate all aspects of relations between company and workers – *e.g.* access to employment, working conditions, wages, professional structure, promotion, dismissals, discipline, and Social Security issues. In some legal systems, there is a distinction between two types of provisions or clauses in the agreements – some are described as "normative" clauses, especially concerning the methods of trade union action for the signatories, binding the negotiators, while along

180 Said to be the case for Austria or the United Kingdom.

181 For full treatment of this matter, see F.Schmidt & A.Neal, *Collective Agreements and Collective Bargaining* (Tübingen 1984).

182 Thus, for example, in Finland, the requirement is that the unions represent half, at least, of the workers in the sector.

with these there are "contractual" clauses, regulating the working relations of the persons included within the scope of the agreement.[183]

Most of the national legal systems recognise the collective agreement as having a value or force that is lower than the law, to which it is subject. This is without detriment to the validity of the provisions of the collective agreement which are more favourable or advantageous to the workers than those provided for by the law. In particular, the collective agreement is subject to constitutional regulations and principles, with some legal systems introducing rigorous rules into the agreements, such as forbidding mandatory retirement or discriminatory wage conditions, especially for reasons of sex. For the purposes of subjecting the Agreement to the law, there is a distinction between legal regulations of an imperative nature, which cannot be varied by agreement, and legal regulations, which can, instead, be modified by agreement.

3. Legal Basis of Strikes

Most European legal systems recognise the right to trade union action, including the right to strike, although few Constitutions refer specifically to the latter. However, there are both national legal systems which contain a detailed regulation of the matter, with complex and casuistic rules, and others in which the regulation of strike action is not developed in minute detail. This causes a difficulty in presenting a clear picture as to what are the requirements for calling a strike (which is fundamental, however, in some national legal systems, such as Finland, Germany, Iceland or Spain), or the legal basis of the exercise of strike action (although it is appropriate to point out that, in Germany, it is required that the measures of the strike comply with the law and with the principle of proportionality). In many legal systems, neither the Constitution nor the laws regulate the subject, as collective agreements are the main regulating source. Thus, the collective agreement may contain a "peace obligation" or undertaking which impedes the lawful exercise of strike action during the period of its validity – with exceptions in Denmark enabling release from this peace obligation, such as in the event of risks to life or health and the suspension of pay.

Many national legal systems state explicitly that the exercise of the right to strike leads to the suspension of the employment contract (Germany, Iceland) without the right of the worker to receive unemployment benefit from Social Security (Austria, Spain) and with employers being explicitly prohibited from replacing their striking workers with others contracted for that purpose (Spain).

183 For discussion of this division, which owes much to the writings of the German scholar Hugo Sinzheimer, see F.Schmidt & A.Neal, *Collective Agreements and Collective Bargaining* (Tübingen 1984).

Many legal systems also expressly prohibit strikes which are deemed illegal, whether due to serious irregularities in the convening process or by reason of the purpose for which the strike has been called. This is the case with political strikes in Germany (*i.e.* those founded on reasons which may not be included in collective agreements) or in Spain (*i.e.* those which do not affect the professional interests of those who promote or sustain them). Likewise, particular mention should be made of strikes called to alter arrangements agreed in collective agreements during the period of their validity – which action will be illegal in Austria, Finland, Norway, Spain and Sweden. The illegality of the strike carries as its effect the obligation to make reparation for the damage causes (Finland, Germany, Iceland, Norway, Sweden and the United Kingdom).

In many national legal systems, strikes are prohibited which affect the essential services of the community, such as health, safety or emergency services,[184] or there is some limitation.[185] In Italy, a Law has existed since 12 June 1990 regulating strikes in essential public services. In other legal systems, such a prohibition does not exist (Germany, Sweden and the United Kingdom).

In many systems, the Government has no power to impose mandatory or prohibitive solutions to certain strikes: this is the case in Austria, Denmark, Germany, Norway, Sweden and the United Kingdom – although, in the Scandinavian countries, the Parliament may approve an *ad hoc* Law which declares the illegality of industrial action or which imposes a solution. In Iceland, the Government may prohibit certain strikes in serious situations. In Spain, also in given serious circumstances, the Government is authorised to institute an obligatory process of arbitration (mandatory solution).

Only in a few legal systems is the establishment of minimum services provided for in a company for the safety and maintenance of installations and machinery during a strike which has been properly agreed upon and instituted by the parties in conflict (Germany, Iceland, Ireland, Spain and Sweden).

4. Judicial Protection of these Rights

In many legal systems, the right of unions to bring judicial proceedings in defence of their members, both individually and collectively, in relation to labour, trade union or Social Security rights, is expressly recognised. This is the case for Austria, Belgium, Denmark, Finland, Germany, Norway, Spain, Sweden, or the United Kingdom – although some systems limit this to cases of disputes or conflicts concerning collective agreements. In other cases, as happens in most countries,

184 Through the prohibition of their exercise by the personnel who perform such services, as is the case in Denmark or Iceland.

185 As is the case in Ireland or Spain.

the unions do provide means of assistance to their members.

Some systems envisage special and urgent procedures for the judicial resolution of this litigation when it concerns the freedom to join a union, the right to collective bargaining, or strike action.

As regards other fundamental rights, these may, in appropriate cases, justify recourse to the constitutional jurisdiction – where this exists – and to the European Court of Human Rights.

Summary of Conclusions

The starting point for the Seville Conference which gave rise to the present Report was the presentation entitled "For a Europe of civic and social rights", prepared by the *Comité des Sages*. In Part III, the Report distinguishes between those fundamental rights which are already contained within various international treaties and those which, while widely accepted, have not yet been agreed between the governments of the Member States. The Report recommended that the fundamental rights already incorporated in the various Treaties should simply be incorporated into a future Treaty so as to amount, in effect, to a Constitution of the European Union.

We now know that this did not happen in the Treaty of Amsterdam. The Seville Conference, consisting as it did of practising Judges, took a more pragmatic approach. We felt that an overview of those rights which are already incorporated into various Treaties, but which are not all equally enforceable in the courts of the Member States, should be no more than a starting point. Accordingly, this presentation set out with a review of those Treaties and the extent to which they give rise to enforceable rights. We moved from there to consider some of the more important rights which are, in practice, enforced in the Member States.

Our view is that any list of fundamental rights in a future Treaty should start from first principles, unencumbered by historic lists of fundamental rights. Although various rights may be set out in Treaties agreed at various dates in the past, they may be interpreted differently now, and, indeed, some may be seen as out-dated. Any statement in a future Treaty should set out a list of those rights which are, in practice, accepted in all Member States – both those set out in existing texts and those which our investigations have shown to be generally accepted.

In carrying out this exercise, it is vital to distinguish between those rights which are directly enforceable against employers and those "rights" which are really aspirations which the State aims to achieve.

On this basis, the following directly enforceable rights were identified by the Seville Conference:

(1) Rights in respect of working conditions. This right could be formulated either as a right not to have oppressive working conditions or as a right to equitable working conditions. While these two rights both contain subjective elements, there is a significant difference between them. The

latter comes from the International Agreement on Economic, Social and Cultural Rights, but it raises issues about the value of particular work, which are hard to define. There is a basis for suggesting that, while a right not to have oppressive working conditions is a right which every worker should be able to enforce against his or her employer, the right to equitable working conditions is an aspiration.

(2) The right to protection from arbitrary and unjustified dismissal. Although the texts refer only to arbitrary dismissal, it is clear from our discussions that all Member States accept the principle that employees cannot be dismissed without justification, and this is regarded as one of the most important safeguards.

(3) The right to health and safety at work.

(4) The right of association.

(5) The right of collective bargaining.

(6) The right not to be discriminated against on the grounds of sex, race, colour, nationality, politics or religion. This definition is significantly narrower than the definition of discrimination contained in the *Comité des Sages* Report, as being a right already established in international law. However, we believe that the definition set out above is likely to import a more practical effect.

The *Comité des Sages* definition includes also language, political, "or any other opinion", social origin, wealth, birth, "or any other situation". We consider that the breadth and vagueness of this statement renders it unenforceable, and that it quickly becomes apparent that this is not a true fundamental right, but an aspiration. Instead, we have tried to set out a prohibition on discrimination which could be directly enforced by workers against employers.

Some of the aspects of discrimination contained in our definition are not included in all Member States' existing legislation, but they are, nevertheless, largely accepted as an illegitimate basis for selecting employees or dealing with them in the workplace. There are other potential areas of discrimination which could be included – *e.g.* disability or sexual orientation – but these were not debated in detail at the Conference. It is, therefore, uncertain whether they would be accepted by all Member States. Some Constitutions, like the *Comité des Sages* proposals, contain a general reference forbidding discrimination "on any other grounds". This, however, is not acceptable. It is vague and misleading. Many grounds of discrimination – *e.g.* discrimination on the grounds of ability – are regarded as entirely acceptable. It is important that the prohibition of discrimination should set out clearly the different types of discrimination which are referred to.

The other "rights" contained in the *Comité des Sages* Report are really aspirations. In relation to the rights of workers they are:

(1) The right to work.

(2) The right to lifelong education and training.

(3) The right to protection of the family.

The most important of these is the "right to work". This is a right which cannot be enforced against the employer – except, perhaps, in a narrow situation where, for example, an employer retains a footballer or a photographer on contract in order to prevent him from working elsewhere. The "right to work" is really the proposition that all Member States should strive towards full employment. This is essentially a political matter, and not a matter of law. The right to education and training is, again, not a right which an individual can assert against an employer. The right to the protection of the family is more problematical. In practice, the right not to have oppressive working conditions is founded, in part, on the right of an employee to have time and money to protect his or her family. However, beyond such rights to limited hours and other social protection, the right to protection of the family is really no more than a general aspiration.

The right to equality before the law is a general right. It is dealt with in the Report as a matter of discrimination, but it differs from the right not to be discriminated against in that it is not enforceable, as such, against an employer. It is simply the right of all people to have equal access to the courts if they feel their rights are being breached. It is, therefore, not an employment right at all, but a general principle of civil liberties.

Finally, it is our belief that a "Statement of Fundamental Rights of Workers" is capable of agreement between all the Member States of the European Union without major changes to any of laws of those Member States. Such a Statement would differ from a "Statement of Fundamental Social Rights", in that it would consist of rights which any worker could enforce against his or her employer.

Part II

Selected International Instruments

United Nations
Declaration of Philadelphia (1944)[1]

DECLARATION CONCERNING THE AIMS AND PURPOSE OF THE INTERNATIONAL LABOUR ORGANISATION

The General Conference of the International Labour Organisation meeting in its Twenty-sixth Session in Philadelphia, hereby adopts this tenth day of May in the year nineteen hundred and forty-four the present Declaration of the aims and purposes of the International Labour Organisation and of the principles which should inspire the policy of its Members.

I

The Conference reaffirms the fundamental principles on which the Organisation is based and, in particular, that –

(a) labour is not a commodity;
(b) freedom of expression and of association are essential to sustained progress;
(c) poverty anywhere constitutes a danger to prosperity everywhere;
(d) the war against want requires to be carried on with unrelenting vigour within each nation, and by continuous and concerted international effort in which the representatives of workers and employers, enjoying equal status with those of governments, join with them in free discussion and democratic decision with a view to the promotion of the common welfare.

II

Believing that experience has fully demonstrated the truth of the statement in the Constitution of the International Labour Organisation that lasting peace can be established only if it is based on social justice, the Conference affirms that –

1. Annex to the Constitution of the International Labour Organisation, adopted in Philadelphia on 10 May 1944.

(a) all human beings, irrespective of race, creed or sex, have the right to pursue both their material well-being and their spiritual development in conditions of freedom and dignity, of economic security and equal opportunity;
(b) the attainment of the conditions in which this shall be possible must constitute the central aim of national and international policy;
(c) all national and international policies and measures, in particular those of an economic and financial character, should be judged in this light and accepted only in so far as they may be held to promote and not to hinder the achievement of this fundamental objective;
(d) it is a responsibility of the International Labour Organisation to examine and consider all international economic and financial policies and measures in the light of this fundamental objective;
(e) in discharging the tasks entrusted to it the International Labour Organisation, having considered all relevant economic and financial factors, may include in its decisions and recommendations any provisions which it considers appropriate.

III

The Conference recognises the solemn obligation of the International Labour Organisation to further among the nations of the world programmes which will achieve:

(a) full employment and the raising of standards of living;
(b) the employment of workers in the occupations in which they can have the satisfaction of giving the fullest measure of their skill and attainments and make their greatest contribution to the common well-being;
(c) the provision, as a means to the attainment of this end and under adequate guarantees for all concerned, of facilities for training and the transfer of labour, including migration for employment and settlement;
(d) policies in regard to wages and earnings, hours and other conditions of work calculated to ensure a just share of the fruits of progress to all, and a minimum living wage to all employed and in need of such protection;
(e) the effective recognition of the right of collective bargaining, the co-operation of management and labour in the continuous improvement of productive efficiency, and the collaboration of workers and employers in the preparation and application of social and economic measures;
(f) the extension of social security measures to provide a basic income to all in need of such protection and comprehensive medical care;
(g) adequate protection for the life and health of workers in all occupations;

(h) provision for child welfare and maternity protection;
(i) the provision of adequate nutrition, housing and facilities for recreation and culture;
(j) the assurance of equality of educational and vocational opportunity.

IV

Confident that the fuller and broader utilisation of the world's productive resources necessary for the achievement of the objectives set forth in this Declaration can be secured by effective international and national action, including measures to expand production and consumption, to avoid severe economic fluctuations to promote the economic and social advancement of the less developed regions of the world, to assure greater stability in world prices of primary products, and to promote a high and steady volume of international trade, the Conference pledges the full co-operation of the International Labour Organisation with such international bodies as may be entrusted with a share of the responsibility for this great task and for the promotion of the health, education and well-being of all peoples.

V

The conference affirms that the principles set forth in this Declaration are fully applicable to all peoples everywhere and that, while the manner of their application must be determined with due regard to the stage of social and economic development reached by each people, their progressive application to peoples who are still dependent, as well as to those who have already achieved self-government, is a matter of concern to the whole civilised world.

United Nations
Universal Declaration of Human Rights (1948)[1]

Preamble

Whereas recognition of the inherent dignity and of the equal and inalienable rights of all members of the human family is the foundation of freedom, justice and peace in the world,

Whereas disregard and contempt for human rights have resulted in barbarous acts which have outraged the conscience of mankind, and the advent of a world in which human beings shall enjoy freedom of speech and belief and freedom from fear and want has been proclaimed as the highest aspiration of the common people,

Whereas it is essential, if man is not to be compelled to have recourse, as a last resort, to rebellion against tyranny and oppression, that human rights should be protected by the rule of law,

Whereas it is essential to promote the development of friendly relations between nations,

Whereas the peoples of the United Nations have in the Charter reaffirmed their faith in fundamental human rights, in the dignity and worth of the human person and in the equal rights of men and women and have determined to promote social progress and better standards of life in larger freedom,

Whereas Member States have pledged themselves to achieve, in co-operation with the United Nations, the promotion of universal respect for and observance of human rights and fundamental freedoms,

Whereas a common understanding of these rights and freedoms is of the greatest importance for the full realisation of this pledge,

Now, therefore,

1. Adopted in New York on 10 December 1948.

THE GENERAL ASSEMBLY PROCLAIMS THIS UNIVERSAL DECLARATION OF HUMAN RIGHTS as a common standard of achievement for all peoples and all nations, to the end that every individual and every organ of society, keeping this Declaration constantly in mind, shall strive by teaching and education to promote respect for these rights and freedoms and by progressive measures, national and international, to secure their universal and effective recognition and observance, both among the peoples of Member States themselves and among the peoples of territories under their jurisdiction.

Article 1

All human beings are born free and equal in dignity and rights. They are endowed with reason and conscience and should act towards one another in a spirit of brotherhood.

Article 2

Everyone is entitled to all the rights and freedoms set forth in this Declaration, without distinction of any kind, such as race, colour, sex, language, religion, political or other opinion, national or social origin, property, birth or other status. Furthermore, no distinction shall be made on the basis of the political, jurisdictional or international status of the country or territory to which a person belongs, whether it be independent, trust, non-self-governing or under any other limitation of sovereignty.

Article 3

Everyone has the right to life, liberty and security of person.

Article 4

No one shall be held in slavery or servitude; slavery and the slave trade shall be prohibited in all their forms.

Article 5

No one shall be subjected to torture or to cruel, inhuman or degrading treatment or punishment.

Article 6

Everyone has the right to recognition everywhere as a person before the law.

Article 7

All are equal before the law and are entitled without any discrimination to equal protection of the law. All are entitled to equal protection against any discrimination in violation of this Declaration and against any incitement to such discrimination.

Article 8

Everyone has the right to an effective remedy by the competent national tribunals for acts violating the fundamental rights granted him by the constitution or by law.

Article 9

No one shall be subjected to arbitrary arrest, detention or exile.

Article 10

Everyone is entitled in full equality to a fair and public hearing by an independent and impartial tribunal, in the determination of his rights and obligations and of any criminal charge against him.

Article 11

(1) Everyone charged with a penal offence has the right to be presumed innocent until proved guilty according to law in a public trial at which he has had all the guarantees necessary for his defence.

(2) No one shall be held guilty of any penal offence on account of any act or omission which did not constitute a penal offence, under national or international law, at the time when it was committed. Nor shall a heavier penalty be imposed than the one that was applicable at the time the penal offence was committed.

Article 12

No one shall be subjected to arbitrary interference with his privacy, family, home or correspondence, nor to attacks upon his honour and reputation. Everyone has the right to the protection of the law against such interference or attacks.

Article 13

(1) Everyone has the right to freedom of movement and residence within the borders of each state.

(2) Everyone has the right to leave any country, including his own, and to return to his country.

Article 14

(1) Everyone has the right to seek and to enjoy in other countries asylum from persecution.

(2) This right may not be invoked in the case of prosecutions genuinely arising from non-political crimes or from acts contrary to the purposes and principles of the United Nations.

Article 15

(1) Everyone has the right to a nationality.

(2) No one shall be arbitrarily deprived of his nationality nor denied the right to change his nationality.

Article 16

(1) Men and women of full age, without any limitation due to race, nationality or religion, have the right to marry and to found a family. They are entitled to equal rights as to marriage, during marriage and at its dissolution.

(2) Marriage shall be entered into only with the free and full consent of the intending spouses.

(3) The family is the natural and fundamental group unit of society and is entitled to protection by society and the State.

Article 17

(1) Everyone has the right to own property alone as well as in association with others.

(2) No one shall be arbitrarily deprived of his property.

Article 18

Everyone has the right to freedom of thought, conscience and religion; this right includes freedom to change his religion or belief, and freedom, either alone or in community with others and in public or private, to manifest his religion or belief in teaching, practice, worship and observance.

Article 19

Everyone has the right to freedom of opinion and expression; this right includes freedom to hold opinions without interference and to seek, receive and impart information and ideas through any media and regardless of frontiers.

Article 20

(1) Everyone has the right to freedom of peaceful assembly and association.

(2) No one may be compelled to belong to an association.

Article 21

(1) Everyone has the right to take part in the government of his country, directly or through freely chosen representatives.

(2) Everyone has the right of equal access to public service in his country.

(3) The will of the people shall be the basis of the authority of government; this will shall be expressed in periodic and genuine elections which shall be by universal and equal suffrage and shall be held by secret vote or by equivalent free voting procedures.

Article 22

Everyone, as a member of society, has the right to social security and is entitled to realisation, through national effort and international co-operation and in accordance with the organisation and resources of each State, of the economic, social and cultural rights indispensable for his dignity and the free development of his personality.

Article 23

(1) Everyone has the right to work, to free choice of employment, to just and favourable conditions of work and to protection against unemployment.

(2) Everyone, without any discrimination, has the right to equal pay for equal work.

(3) Everyone who works has the right to just and favourable remuneration ensuring for himself and his family an existence worthy of human dignity, and supplemented, if necessary, by other means of social protection.

(4) Everyone has the right to form and to join trade unions for the protection of his interests.

Article 24

Everyone has the right to rest and leisure, including reasonable limitation of working hours and periodic holidays with pay.

Article 25

(1) Everyone has the right to a standard of living adequate for the health and well-being of himself and of his family, including food, clothing, housing and medical care and necessary social services, and the right to security in the event of unemployment, sickness, disability, widowhood, old age or other lack of livelihood in circumstances beyond his control.

(2) Motherhood and childhood are entitled to special care and assistance. All children, whether born in or out of wedlock, shall enjoy the same social protection.

Article 26

(1) Everyone has the right to education. Education shall be free, at least in the elementary and fundamental stages. Elementary education shall be compulsory. Technical and professional education shall be made generally available and higher education shall be equally accessible to all on the basis of merit.

(2) Education shall be directed to the full development of the human personality and to the strengthening of respect for human rights and

fundamental freedoms. It shall promote understanding, tolerance and friendship among all nations, racial or religious groups, and shall further the activities of the United Nations for the maintenance of peace.

(3) Parents have a prior right to choose the kind of education that shall be given to their children.

Article 27

(1) Everyone has the right freely to participate in the cultural life of the community, to enjoy the arts and to share in scientific advancement and its benefits.

(2) Everyone has the right to the protection of the moral and material interests resulting from any scientific, literary or artistic production of which he is the author.

Article 28

Everyone is entitled to a social and international order in which the rights and freedoms set forth in this Declaration can be fully realised.

Article 29

(1) Everyone has duties to the community in which alone the free and full development of his personality is possible.

(2) In the exercise of his rights and freedoms, everyone shall be subject only to such limitations as are determined by law solely for the purpose of securing due recognition and respect for the rights and freedoms of others and of meeting the just requirements of morality, public order and the general welfare in a democratic society.

(3) These rights and freedoms may in no case be exercised contrary to the purposes and principles of the United Nations.

Article 30

Nothing in this Declaration may be interpreted as implying for any State, group or person any right to engage in any activity or to perform any act aimed at the destruction of any of the rights and freedoms set forth herein.

ILO Convention No. 29 concerning Forced or Compulsory Labour (1930)[1]

PREAMBLE

The General Conference of the International Labour Organisation.

Having been convened at Geneva by the Governing Body of the International Labour Office, and having met in its Fourteenth Session on 10 June 1930, and

Having decided upon the adoption of certain proposals with regard to forced or compulsory labour, which is included in the first item on the agenda of the Session, and

Having determined that these proposals shall take the form of an international Convention.

Adopts the twenty-eighth day of June of the year one thousand nine hundred and thirty, the following Convention, which may be cited as the Forced Labour Convention, 1930, for ratification by the Members of the International Labour Organisation in accordance with the provisions of the Constitution of the International Labour Organisation:

ARTICLE 1

1. Each Member of the International Labour Organisation which ratifies this Convention undertakes to suppress the use of forced or compulsory labour in all its forms within the shortest possible period.

2. With a view to this complete suppression, recourse to forced or compulsory labour may be had, during the transitional period, for public purposes only and as an exceptional measure, subject to the conditions and guarantees hereinafter provided.

3. At the expiration of a period of five years after the coming into force of this Convention, and when the Governing Body of the International Labour Office prepares the report provided for in Article 31 below, the said Governing Body shall consider the possibility of the suppression of forced or compulsory labour in all its forms without a further transitional period and the desirability of placing this question on the agenda of the Conference.

1. Adopted in Geneva on 28 June 1930. Date of coming into force: 1 May 1932.

Article 2

For the purposes of this Convention the term "forced or compulsory labour" shall mean all work or service which is exacted from any person under the menace of any penalty and for which the said person has not offered himself voluntarily.

Nevertheless, for the purposes of this Convention, the term "forced or compulsory labour" shall not include –

(a) any work or service exacted in virtue of compulsory military service laws for work of a purely military character;
(b) any work or service which forms part of the normal civic obligations of the citizens of a fully self-governing country;
(c) any work or service exacted from any person as a consequence of a conviction in a court of law, provided that the said work or service is carried out under the supervision and control of a public authority and that the said person is not hired to or placed at the disposal of private individuals, companies or associations;
(d) any work or service exacted in cases of emergency, that is to say, in the event of war or of a calamity or threatened calamity, such as fire, flood, famine, earthquake, violent epidemic or epizootic diseases, invasion by animal, insect or vegetable pests, and in general any circumstance that would endanger the existence or the well-being of the whole or part of the population;
(e) minor communal services of a kind which, being performed by the members of the community in the direct interest of the said community, can therefore be considered as normal civic obligations incumbent upon the members of the community, provided that the members of the community or their direct representatives shall have the right to be consulted in regard to the need for such services.

Article 3

For the purposes of this Convention the term "competent authority" shall mean either an authority of the metropolitan country or the highest central authority in the territory concerned.

Article 4

1. The competent authority shall not impose or permit the imposition of forced or compulsory labour for the benefit of private individuals, companies or associations.

2. Where such forced or compulsory labour for the benefit of private individuals, companies or associations exists at the date on which a Member's ratification of this Convention is registered by the Director General of the International Labour Office, the Member shall completely suppress such forced or compulsory labour from the date on which this Convention comes into force for that Member.

Article 5

1. No concession granted to private individuals, companies or associations shall involve any form of forced or compulsory labour for the production or the collection of products which such private individuals, companies or associations utilise or in which they trade.

2. Where concessions exist containing provisions involving such forced compulsory labour, such provisions shall be rescinded as soon as possible, in order to comply with Article 1 of this Convention.

Article 6

Officials of the administration, even when they have the duty of encouraging the populations under their charge to engage in some form of labour, shall not put constraint upon the said populations or upon any individual members thereof to work for private individuals, companies or associations.

Article 7

1. Chiefs who do not exercise administrative functions shall not have recourse to forced or compulsory labour.

2. Chiefs who exercise administrative functions may, with the express permission of the competent authority, have recourse to forced or compulsory labour, subject to the provisions of Article 10 of this Convention.

3. Chiefs who are duly recognised and who do not receive adequate remuneration in other forms may have the enjoyment of personal services, subject to due regulation and provided that all necessary measures are taken to prevent abuses.

Article 8

1. The responsibility for every decision to have recourse to forced or compulsory labour shall rest with the highest civil authority in the territory concerned.

2. Nevertheless, that authority may delegate powers to the highest local authorities to exact forced or compulsory labour which does not involve the removal of the workers from their place of habitual residence. That authority may also delegate, for such periods and subject to such conditions as may be laid down in the regulations provided for in Article 23 of this Convention, powers to the highest local authorities to exact forced or compulsory labour which involves the removal of the workers from their place of habitual residence for the purpose of facilitating the movement of officials of the administration, when on duty, and for the transport of Government stores.

Article 9

Except as otherwise provided for in Article 10 of this Convention, any authority competent to exact forced or compulsory labour shall, before deciding to have recourse to such labour, satisfy itself –

(a) that the work to be done or the service to be rendered is of important direct interest for the community called upon to do work or render the service;
(b) that the work or service is of present or imminent necessity;
(c) that it has been impossible to obtain voluntary labour for carrying out the work or rendering the service by the offer of rates of wages and conditions of labour not less favourable than those prevailing in the area concerned for similar work or service; and
(d) that the work or service will not lay too heavy a burden upon the present population, having regard to the labour available and its capacity to undertake the work.

Article 10

1. Forced or compulsory labour exacted as a tax and forced or compulsory labour to which recourse is had for the execution of public works by chiefs who exercise administrative functions shall be progressively abolished.

2. Meanwhile, where forced or compulsory labour is exacted as a tax, and where recourse is had to forced or compulsory labour for the execution of public works by chiefs who exercise administrative functions, the authority concerned shall first satisfy itself –

   (a) that the work to be done or the service to be rendered is of important direct interest for the community called upon to do the work or render the service;
   (b) that the work or the service is of present or imminent necessity;
   (c) that the work or service will not lay too heavy a burden upon the present population, having regard to the labour available and its capacity to undertake the work;
   (d) that the work or service will not entail the removal of the workers from their place of habitual residence;
   (e) that the execution of the work or the rendering of the service will be directed in accordance with the exigencies of religion, social life and agriculture.

Article 11

1. Only adult able-bodied males who are of an apparent age of not less than 18 and not more than 45 years may be called upon for forced or compulsory labour. Except in respect of the kinds of labour provided for in Article 10 of this Convention, the following limitations and conditions shall apply:

   (a) whenever possible prior determination by a medical officer appointed by the administration that the persons concerned are not suffering from any infectious or contagious disease and that they are physically fit for the work required and for the conditions under which it is to be carried out;
   (b) exemption of school teachers and pupils and officials of the administration in general;
   (c) the maintenance in each community of the number of adult able bodied men indispensable for family and social life;
   (d) respect for conjugal and family ties.

2. For the purposes of subparagraph (c) of the preceding paragraph, the regulations provided for in Article 23 of this Convention shall fix the proportion of the resident adult able-bodied males who may be taken at any one time for forced or compulsory labour, provided always that this proportion shall in no case exceed 25 per cent. In fixing this proportion the competent authority shall take account of the density of the population,

of its social and physical development, of the seasons, and of the work which must be done by the persons concerned on their own behalf in their locality, and, generally, shall have regard to the economic and social necessities of the normal life of the community concerned.

Article 12

1. The maximum period for which any person may be taken for forced compulsory labour of all kinds in any one period of twelve months shall not exceed sixty days, including the time spent in going to and from the place of work.

2. Every person from whom forced or compulsory labour is exacted shall be furnished with a certificate indicating the periods of such labour which he has completed.

Article 13

1. The normal working hours of any person from whom forced or compulsory labour is exacted shall be the same as those prevailing in the case of voluntary labour, and the hours worked in excess of the normal working hours shall be remunerated at the rates prevailing in the case of overtime for voluntary labour.

2. A weekly day of rest shall be granted to all persons from whom forced or compulsory labour of any kind is exacted and this day shall coincide as far as possible with the day fixed by tradition or custom in the territories or regions concerned.

Article 14

1. With the exception of the forced or compulsory labour provided for in Article 10 of this Convention, forced or compulsory labour of all kinds shall be remunerated in cash at rates not less than those prevailing for similar kinds of work either in the district in which the labour is employed or in the district from which the labour is recruited, whichever may be the higher.

2. In the case of labour to which recourse is had by chiefs in the exercise of their administrative functions, payment of wages in accordance with the provisions of the preceding paragraph shall be introduced as soon as possible.

3. The wages shall be paid to each worker individually and not to his tribal chief or to any other authority.

4. For the purpose of payment of wages the days spent in travelling to and from the place of work shall be counted as working days.

5. Nothing in this Article shall prevent ordinary rations being given as a part of wages, such rations to be at least equivalent in value to the money payment they are taken to represent, but deductions from wages shall not be made either for the payment of taxes or for special food, clothing or accommodation supplied to a worker for the purpose of maintaining him in a fit condition to carry on his work under the special conditions of any employment, or for the supply of tools.

Article 15

1. Any laws or regulations relating to workmen's compensation for accidents or sickness arising out of the employment of the worker and any laws or regulations providing compensation for the dependants of deceased or incapacitated workers which are or shall be in force in the territory concerned shall be equally applicable to persons from whom forced or compulsory labour is exacted and to voluntary workers.

2. In any case it shall be an obligation on any authority employing any worker on forced or compulsory labour to ensure the subsistence of any such worker who, by accident or sickness arising out of his employment, is rendered wholly or partially incapable of providing for himself, and to take measures to ensure the maintenance of any persons actually dependent upon such a worker in the event of his incapacity or decease arising out of his employment.

Article 16

1. Except in cases of special necessity, persons from whom forced or compulsory labour is exacted shall not be transferred to districts where the food and climate differ so considerably from those to which they have been accustomed as to endanger their health.

2. In no case shall the transfer of such workers be permitted unless all measures relating to hygiene and accommodation which are necessary to adapt such workers to the conditions and to safeguard their health can be strictly applied.

3. When such transfer cannot be avoided, measures of gradual habituation to the new conditions of diet and of climate shall be adopted on competent medical advice.

4. In cases where such workers are required to perform regular work to which they are not accustomed, measures shall be taken to ensure their habituation to it, especially as regards progressive training, the hours of work and the provision of rest intervals, and any increase or amelioration of diet which may be necessary.

Article 17

Before permitting recourse to forced or compulsory labour for works of construction or maintenance which entail the workers remaining at the workplaces for considerable periods, the competent authority shall satisfy itself –

1. that all necessary measures are taken to safeguard the health of the workers and to guarantee the necessary medical care, and, in particular,

   (a) that the workers are medically examined before commencing the work and at fixed intervals during the period of service,
   (b) that there is an adequate medical staff, provided with the dispensaries, infirmaries, hospitals and equipment necessary to meet all requirements, and
   (c) that the sanitary conditions of the workplaces, the supply of drinking water, food, fuel, and cooking utensils, and, where necessary, of housing and clothing, are satisfactory;

2. that definite arrangements are made to ensure the subsistence of the families of the workers, in particular by facilitating the remittance, by a safe method, of part of the wages to the family, at the request or with the consent of the workers;

3. that the journeys of the workers to and from the work-places are made at the expense and under the responsibility of the administration, which shall facilitate such journeys by making the fullest use of all available means of transport;

4. that, in case of illness or accident causing incapacity to work of a certain duration, the worker is repatriated at the expense of the administration;

5. that any worker who may wish to remain as a voluntary worker at the end of his period of forced or compulsory labour is permitted to do so without, for a period of two years, losing his right to repatriation free of expense to himself.

Article 18

1. Forced or compulsory labour for the transport of persons or goods, such as the labour of porters or boatmen, shall be abolished within the shortest possible period. Meanwhile the competent authority shall promulgate regulations determining, inter alia,

   (a) that such labour shall only be employed for the purpose of facilitating the movement of officials of the administration, when on duty, or for the transport of Government stores, or, in cases of very urgent necessity, the transport of persons other than officials,
   (b) that the workers so employed shall be medically certified to be physically fit, where medical examination is possible, and that where such medical examination is not practicable the person employing such workers shall be held responsible for ensuring that they are physically fit and not suffering from any infectious or contagious disease,
   (c) the maximum load which these workers may carry,
   (d) the maximum distance from their homes to which they may be taken,
   (e) including the days spent in returning to their homes, and
   (f) the persons entitled to demand this form of forced or compulsory labour and the extent to which they are entitled to demand it.

2. In fixing the maxima referred to under (c), (d) and (e) in the foregoing paragraph, the competent authority shall have regard to all relevant factors, including the physical development of the population from which the workers are recruited, the nature of the country through which they must travel and the climatic conditions.

3. The competent authority shall further provide that the normal daily journey of such workers shall not exceed a distance corresponding to an average working day of eight hours, it being understood that account shall be taken not only of the weight to be carried and the distance to be covered, but also of the nature of the road, the season and all other relevant factors, and that, where hours of journey in excess of the normal daily journey are exacted, they shall be remunerated at rates higher than the normal rates.

Article 19

1. The competent authority shall only authorise recourse to compulsory cultivation as a method of precaution against famine or a deficiency of food supplies and always under the condition that the food or produce shall remain the property of the individuals or the community producing it.

2. Nothing in this Article shall be construed as abrogating the obligation on members of a community, where production is organised on a communal basis by virtue of law or custom and where the produce or any profit accruing from the sale thereof remain the property of the community, to perform the work demanded by the community by virtue of law or custom.

Article 20

Collective punishment laws under which a community may be punished for crimes committed by any of its members shall not contain provisions for forced or compulsory labour by the community as one of the methods of punishment.

Article 21

Forced or compulsory labour shall not be used for work underground in mines.

Article 22

The annual reports that Members which ratify this Convention agree to make to the International Labour Office, pursuant to the provisions of article 22 of the Constitution of the International Labour Organisation, on the measures they have taken to give effect to the provisions of this Convention, shall contain as full information as possible, in respect of each territory concerned, regarding the extent to which recourse has been had to forced or compulsory labour in that territory, the purposes for which it has been employed, the sickness and death rates, hours of work, methods of payment of wages and rates of wages, and any other relevant information.

Article 23

1. To give effect to the provisions of this Convention the competent authority shall issue complete and precise regulations governing the use of forced or compulsory labour.

2. These regulations shall contain, inter alia, rules permitting any person from whom forced or compulsory labour is exacted to forward all complaints relative to the conditions of labour to the authorities and ensuring that such complaints will be examined and taken into consideration.

Article 24

Adequate measures shall in all cases be taken to ensure that the regulations governing the employment of forced or compulsory labour are strictly applied, either by extending the duties of any existing labour inspectorate which has been established for the inspection of voluntary labour to cover the inspection of forced or compulsory labour or in some other appropriate manner. Measures shall also be taken to ensure that the regulations are brought to the knowledge of persons from whom such labour is exacted.

Article 25

The illegal exaction of forced or compulsory labour shall be punishable as a penal offence, and it shall be an obligation on any Member ratifying this Convention to ensure that the penalties imposed by law are really adequate and are strictly enforced.

Article 26

1. Each Member of the International Labour Organisation which ratifies this Convention undertakes to apply it to the territories placed under its sovereignty, jurisdiction, protection, suzerainty, tutelage or authority, so far as it has the right to accept obligations affecting matters of internal jurisdiction; provided that, if such Member may desire to take advantage of the provisions of article 35 of the Constitution of the International Labour Organisation, it shall append to its ratification a declaration stating –

   (1) the territories to which it intends to apply the provisions of this Convention without modification;
   (2) the territories to which it intends to apply the provisions of this Convention with modifications, together with details of the said modifications;
   (3) the territories in respect of which it reserves its decision.

2. The aforesaid declaration shall be deemed to be an integral part of the ratification and shall have the force of ratification. It shall be open to any Member, by a subsequent declaration, to cancel in whole or in part the reservations made, in pursuance of the provisions of subparagraphs (2) and (3) of this Article, in the original declaration.

FINAL

Article 27

The formal ratifications of this Convention under the conditions set forth in the Constitution of the International Labour Organisation shall be communicated to the Director-General of the International Labour Office for Registration.

Article 28

1. This Convention shall be binding only upon those Members whose ratifications have been registered with the International Labour Office.

2. It shall come into force twelve months after the date on which the ratifications of two members of the International Labour Organisation have been registered with the Director-General.

3. Thereafter, this Convention shall come into force for any Member twelve months after the date on which its ratification has been registered.

Article 29

As soon as the ratifications of two Members of the International Labour Organisation have been registered with the International Labour Office, the Director-General of the International Labour Office shall so notify all the Members of the International Labour Organisation. He shall likewise notify them of the registration of ratifications which may be communicated subsequently by other Members of the Organisation.

Article 30

1. A Member which has ratified this Convention may denounce it after the expiration of ten years from the date on which the Convention first comes into force, by an Act communicated to the Director-General of the International Labour Office for registration. Such denunciation shall not take effect until one year after the date on which it is registered with the International Labour Office.

2. Each member which has ratified this Convention and which does not, within the year following the expiration of the period of ten years mentioned in the preceding paragraph, exercise the right of denunciation provided for in this Article, will be bound for another period of five years and, thereafter,

may denounce this Convention at the expiration of each period of five years under the terms provided for in this Article.

Article 31

At the expiration of each period of five years after the coming into force of this Convention, the Governing Body of the International Labour Office shall present to the General Conference a report on the working of this Convention and shall consider the desirability of placing on the agenda of the Conference the question of its revision in whole or in part.

Article 32

1. Should the Conference adopt a new Convention revising this Convention in whole or in part, the ratification by a Member of the new revising Convention shall ipso jure involve denunciation of this Convention without any requirement of delay, notwithstanding the provisions of Article 30 above, if and when the new revising Convention shall have come into force.

2. As from the date of the coming into force of the new revising Convention, the present Convention shall cease to be open to ratification by the Members.

3. Nevertheless, this Convention shall remain in force in its actual form and content for those Members which have ratified it but have not ratified the revising convention.

Article 33

The French and English texts of this Convention shall both be authentic.

ILO Convention No. 87 concerning Freedom of Association and Protection of the Right to Organise (1948)[1]

Preamble

The General Conference of the International Labour Organisation.

Having been convened at San Francisco by the Governing Body of the International Labour Office, and having met in its Thirty-first Session on 17 June 1948;

Having decided to adopt, in the form of a Convention, certain proposals concerning freedom of association and protection of the right to organise, which is the seventh item on the agenda of the session; Considering that the Preamble to the Constitution of the International Labour Organisation declares recognition of the principle of freedom of association to be a means of improving conditions of labour and of establishing peace.

Considering that the Declaration of Philadelphia reaffirms that freedom of expression and of association are essential to sustained progress

Considering that the International Labour Conference, at its Thirtieth Session, unanimously adopted the principles which should form the basis for international regulation

Considering that the General Assembly of the United Nations, at its Second Session, endorsed these principles and requested the International Labour Organisation to continue every effort in order that it may be possible to adopt one or several international Conventions;

Adopts the ninth day of July of the year one thousand nine hundred and forty-eight, the following Convention, which may be cited as the Freedom of Association and Protection of the Right to Organise Convention, 1948:

Part I : Freedom of Association

Article 1

Each Member of the International Labour Organisation for which this Convention is in force undertakes to give effect to the following provisions.

1. Adopted in San Francisco on 9 July 1948. Date of coming into force: 4 July 1950.

Article 2

Workers and employers, without distinction whatsoever, shall have the right to establish and, subject only to the rules of the organisation concerned, to join organisations of their own choosing without previous authorisation.

Article 3

1. Workers' and employers' organisations shall have the right to draw up their constitutions and rules, to elect their representatives in full freedom, to organise their administration and activities and to formulate their programmes.

2. The public authorities shall refrain from any interference which would restrict this right or impede the lawful exercise thereof.

Article 4

Workers' and employers' organisations shall not be liable to be dissolved or suspended by administrative authority.

Article 5

Workers' and employers' organisations shall have the right to establish and join federations and confederations and any such organisation, federation or confederation shall have the right to affiliate with international organisations of workers and employers.

Article 6

The provisions of Articles 2, 3 and 4 hereof apply to federations and confederations of workers' and employers' organisations.

Article 7

The acquisition of legal personality by workers' and employers' organisations, federations and confederations shall not be made subject to conditions of such a character as to restrict the application of the provisions of Articles 2, 3 and 4 hereof.

Article 8

1. In exercising the rights provided for in this Convention workers and employers and their respective organisations, like other persons or organised collectivities, shall respect the law of the land.

2. The law of the land shall not be such as to impair, nor shall it be so applied as to impair, the guarantees provided for in this Convention.

Article 9

1. The extent to which the guarantees provided for in this Convention shall apply to the armed forces and the police shall be determined by national laws or regulations.

2. In accordance with the principle set forth in paragraph 8 of article 19 of the Constitution of the International Labour Organisation the ratification of this Convention by any Member shall not be deemed to affect any existing law, award, custom or agreement in virtue of which members of the armed forces or the police enjoy any right guaranteed by this Convention.

Article 10

In this Convention the term "organisation" means any organisation of workers or of employers for furthering and defending the interests of workers or of employers.

Part II : Protection of the Right to Organise

Article 11

Each Member of the International Labour Organisation for which this Convention is in force undertakes to take all necessary and appropriate measures to ensure that workers and employers may exercise freely the right to organise.

Part III : Miscellaneous Provisions

Article 12

1. In respect of the territories referred to in article 35 of the Constitution the International Labour Organisation as amended by the Constitution of the International Labour Organisation Instrument of Amendment 1946, other than the territories referred to in paragraphs 4 and 5 of the said article as so amended, each Member of the Organisation which ratifies this Convention shall communicate to the Director-General of the

International Labour Office as soon as possible after ratification a declaration stating:

(a) the territories in respect of which it undertakes that the provisions of the Convention shall be applied without modification;
(b) the territories in respect of which it undertakes that the provisions of the Convention shall be applied subject to modifications, together with details of the said modifications;
(c) the territories in respect of which the Convention is inapplicable and in such cases the grounds on which it is inapplicable;
(d) the territories in respect of which it reserves its decision.

2. The undertakings referred to in subparagraphs (a) and (b) of paragraph 1 of this Article shall be deemed to be an integral part of the ratification and shall have the force of ratification.

3. Any Member may at any time by a subsequent declaration cancel in whole or in part any reservations made in its original declaration in virtue of subparagraphs (b), (c) or (d) of paragraph 1 of this Article.

4. Any Member may, at any time at which the Convention is subject to denunciation in accordance with the provisions of Article 16, communicate to the Director-General a declaration modifying in any other respect the terms of any former declaration and stating the present position in respect of such territories as it may specify.

Article 13

1. Where the subject matter of this Convention is within the self-governing powers of any non-metropolitan territory, the Member responsible for the international relations of that territory may, in agreement with the Government of the territory, communicate to the Director-General of the International Labour Office a declaration accepting on behalf of the territory the obligations of this Convention.

2. A declaration accepting the obligations of this Convention may be communicated to the Director-General of the International Labour Office:

(a) by two or more Members of the Organisation in respect of any territory which is under their joint authority; or
(b) by any international authority responsible for the administration of any territory, in virtue of the Charter of the United Nations or otherwise, in respect of any such territory.

3. Declarations communicated to the Director-General of the International Labour Office in accordance with the preceding paragraphs of this Article shall indicate whether the provisions of the Convention will be applied in the territory concerned without modifications or subject to modification; when the declaration indicates that the provisions of the Convention will be applied subject to modifications it shall give details of the said modifications.

4. The Member, Members or international authority concerned may at any time by a subsequent declaration renounce in whole or in part the right to have recourse to any modification indicated in any former declaration.

5. The Member, Members or international authority concerned may, at any time at which this Convention is subject to denunciation in accordance with the provisions of Article 16, communicate to the Director-General a declaration modifying in any other respect the terms of any former declaration and stating the present position in respect of the application of the Convention.

FINAL

Part IV : Final Provisions

Article 14

The formal ratifications of this Convention shall be communicated to the Director-General of the International Labour Office for registration.

Article 15

1. This Convention shall be binding only upon those Members of the International Labour Organisation whose ratifications have been registered with the Director-General.

2. It shall come into force twelve months after the date on which the ratifications of two Members have been registered with the Director-General.

3. Thereafter, this Convention shall come into force for any Member twelve months after the date on which its ratifications has been registered.

Article 16

1. A Member which has ratified this Convention may denounce it after the expiration of ten years from the date on which the Convention first comes into force, by an Act communicated to the Director-General of the International Labour Office for registration. Such denunciation should not take effect until one year after the date on which it is registered.

2. Each Member which has ratified this Convention and which does not, within the year following the expiration of the period of ten years mentioned in the preceding paragraph, exercise the right of denunciation provided for in this Article, will be bound for another period of ten years and, thereafter, may denounce this Convention at the expiration of each period of ten years under the terms provided for in this Article.

Article 17

1. The Director-General of the International Labour Office shall notify all Members of the International Labour Organisation of the registration of all ratifications, declarations and denunciations communicated to him by the Members of the Organisation.

2. When notifying the Members of the Organisation of the registration of the second ratification communicated to him, the Director-General shall draw the attention of the Members of the Organisation to the date upon which the Convention will come into force.

Article 18

The Director-General of the International Labour Office shall communicate to the Secretary-General of the United Nations for registration in accordance with Article 102 of the Charter of the United Nations full particulars of all ratifications and acts of denunciation registered by him in accordance with the provisions of the preceding Articles.

Article 19

At the expiration of each period of ten years after the coming into force of this Convention, the Governing Body of the International Labour Office shall present to the General Conference a report on the working of this Convention and shall examine the desirability of placing on the agenda of the Conference the question of its revision in whole or in part.

ARTICLE 20

1. Should the Conference adopt a new Convention revising this Convention in whole or in part, then, unless the new Convention otherwise provides:

   (a) the ratification by a Member of the new revising Convention shall ipso jure involve the immediate denunciation of this Convention, notwithstanding the provisions of Article 16 above, if and when the new revising Convention shall have come into force;
   (b) as from the date when the new revising Convention comes into force this Convention shall cease to be open to ratification by the Members.

2. This Convention shall in any case remain in force in its actual form and content for those Members which have ratified it but have not ratified the revising Convention.

ARTICLE 21

The English and French versions of the text of this Convention are equally authoritative.

ILO Convention No. 98 concerning the Application of the Principles of the Right to Organise and to Bargain Collectively (1949)[1]

Preamble

The General Conference of the International Labour Organisation,

Having been convened at Geneva by the Governing Body of the International Labour Office, and having met in its Thirty-second Session on 8 June 1949, and

Having decided upon the adoption of certain proposals concerning the application of the principles of the right to organise and to bargain collectively, which is the fourth item on the agenda of the session, and

Having determined that these proposals shall take the form of an international Convention,

Adopts the first day of July of the year one thousand nine hundred and forty-nine, the following Convention,.which may be cited as the Right to Organise and Collective Bargaining Convention, 1949:

Article 1

1. Workers shall enjoy adequate protection against acts of anti-union discrimination in respect of their employment.

2. Such protection shall apply more particularly in respect of acts calculated to –

   (a) make the employment of a worker subject to the condition that shall not join a union or shall relinquish trade union membership;
   (b) cause the dismissal of or otherwise prejudice a worker by reason union membership or because of participation in union activities outside working hours or, with the consent of the employer, within working hours.

1. Adopted in Geneva on 1 July 1949. Date of coming into force: 18 July 1951.

ARTICLE 2

1. Workers' and employers' organisations shall enjoy adequate protection against any acts of interference by each other or each other's agents or members in their establishment, functioning or administration.

2. In particular, acts which are designed to promote the establishment of workers' organisations under the domination of employers or employers' organisations, or to support workers' organisations by financial or other means, with the object of placing such organisations under the control of employers or employers' organisations, shall be deemed to constitute acts of interference within the meaning of this Article.

ARTICLE 3

Machinery appropriate to national conditions shall be established, where necessary, for the purpose of ensuring respect for the right to organise as defined in the preceding Articles.

ARTICLE 4

Measures appropriate to national conditions shall be taken, where necessary, to encourage and promote the full development and utilisation of machinery for voluntary negotiation between employers or employers' organisations and workers' organisations, with a view to the regulation of terms and conditions of employment by means of collective agreements.

ARTICLE 5

1. The extent to which the guarantees provided for in this Convention shall apply to the armed forces and the police shall be determined by national laws or regulations.

2. In accordance with the principle set forth in paragraph 8 of article 19 of the Constitution of the International Labour Organisation the ratification of this Convention by any Member shall not be deemed to affect any existing law, award, custom or agreement in virtue of which members of the armed forces or the police enjoy any right guaranteed by this Convention.

Article 6

This Convention does not deal with the position of public servants engaged in the administration of the State, nor shall it be construed as prejudicing their rights or status in any way.

FINAL

Article 7

The formal ratifications of this Convention shall be communicated to the Director-General of the International Labour Office for registration.

Article 8

1. This Convention shall be binding only upon those Members of the International Labour Organisation whose ratifications have been registered with the Director-General.

2. It shall come into force twelve months after the date on which the ratifications of two Members have been registered with the Director-General.

3. Thereafter, this Convention shall come into force for any Member twelve months after the date on which its ratifications has been registered.

Article 9

1. Declarations communicated to the Director-General of the International Labour Office in accordance with paragraph 2 of article 35 of the Constitution of the International Labour Organisation shall indicate –

   (a) the territories in respect of which the Member concerned undertakes that the provisions of the Convention shall be applied without modification;
   (b) the territories in respect of which it undertakes that the provisions of the Convention shall be applied subject to modifications, together with details of the said modifications;
   (c) the territories in respect of which the Convention is inapplicable and in such cases the grounds on which it is inapplicable;
   (d) the territories in respect of which it reserves its decision pending further consideration of the position.

2. The undertakings referred to in subparagraphs (a) and (b) of paragraph 1 of this Article shall be deemed to be an integral part of the ratification and shall have the force of ratification.

3. Any Member may at any time by a subsequent declaration cancel in whole or in part any reservation made in its original declaration in virtue of subparagraph (b), (c) or (d) of paragraph 1 of this Article.

4. Any Member may, at any time at which the Convention is subject to denunciation in accordance with the provisions of Article 11, communicate to the Director-General a declaration modifying in any other respect the terms of any former declaration and stating the present position in respect of such territories as it may specify.

Article 10

1. Declarations communicated to the Director-General of the International Labour Office in accordance with paragraph 4 or 5 of article 35 of the Constitution of the International Labour Organisation shall indicate whether the provisions of the Convention will be applied in the territory concerned without modification or subject to modifications; when the declaration indicates that the provisions of the Convention will be applied subject to modifications, it shall give details of the said modifications.

2. The Member, Members or international authority concerned may at any time by a subsequent declaration renounce in whole or in part the right to have recourse to any modification indicated in any former declaration.

3. The Member, Members or international authority concerned may, at any time at which the Convention is subject to denunciation in accordance with the provisions of Article 11, communicate to the Director-General a declaration modifying in any other respect the terms of any former declaration and stating the present position in respect of the application of the Convention.

Article 11

1. A Member which has ratified this Convention may denounce it after the expiration of ten years from the date on which the Convention first comes into force, by an Act communicated to the Director-General of the International Labour Office for registration. Such denunciation should not take effect until one year after the date on which it is registered.

2. Each Member which has ratified this Convention and which does not, within the year following the expiration of the period of ten years mentioned in the preceding paragraph, exercise the right of denunciation provided for in this Article, will be bound for another period of ten years and, thereafter, may denounce this Convention at the expiration of each period of ten years under the terms provided for in this Article.

Article 12

1. The Director-General of the International Labour Office shall notify Members of the International Labour Organisation of the registration of all ratifications and denunciations communicated to him by the Members of the Organisation.

2. When notifying the Members of the Organisation of the registration of the second ratification communicated to him, the Director-General shall draw the attention of the Members of the Organisation to the date upon which the Convention will come into force.

Article 13

The Director-General of the International Labour Office shall communicate to the Secretary-General of the United Nations for registration in accordance with Article 102 of the Charter of the United Nations full particulars of all ratifications and acts of denunciation registered by him in accordance with the provisions of the preceding Articles.

Article 14

At such times as may consider necessary the Governing Body of the International Labour Office shall present to the General Conference a report on the working of this Convention and shall examine the desirability of placing on the agenda of the Conference the question of its revision in whole or in part.

Article 15

1. Should the Conference adopt a new Convention revising this Convention in whole or in part, then, unless the new Convention otherwise provides:

   (a) the ratification by a Member of the new revising Convention shall ipso jure involve the immediate denunciation of this Convention, notwithstanding the provisions of Article 11 above, if and when the new revising Convention shall have come into force;

(b) as from the date when the new revising Convention comes into force this Convention shall cease to be open to ratification by the Members.

2. This Convention shall in any case remain in force in its actual form and content for those Members which have ratified it but have not ratified the revising Convention.

Article 16

The English and French versions of the text of this Convention are equally authoritative.

ILO Convention No. 100 concerning Equal Remuneration for Men and Women Workers for Work of Equal Value (1951)[1]

Preamble

The General Conference of the International Labour Organisation,

Having been convened at Geneva by the Governing Body of the International Labour Office, and having met in its Thirty-fourth Session on 6 June 1951, and

Having decided upon the adoption of certain proposals with regard to the principle of equal remuneration for men and women workers for work of equal value, which is the seventh item on the agenda of the session, and

Having determined that these proposals shall take the form of an international Convention,

Adopts the twenty-ninth day of June of the year one thousand nine hundred and fifty-one, the following Convention, which may be cited as the Equal Remuneration Convention, 1951:

Article 1

For the purpose of this Convention –

(a) the term "remuneration" includes the ordinary, basic or minimum wage or salary and any additional emoluments whatsoever payable directly or indirectly, whether in cash or in kind, by the employer to the worker and arising out of the worker's employment;
(b) the term "equal remuneration for men and women workers for work of equal value" refers to rates of remuneration established without discrimination based on sex.

1. Adopted in Geneva on 29 June 1951. Date of coming into force: 23 May 1953.

Article 2

1. Each Member shall, by means appropriate to the methods in operation for determining rates of remuneration, promote and, in so far as is consistent with such methods, ensure the application to all workers of the principle of equal remuneration for men and women workers for work of equal value.

2. This principle may be applied by means of –

   (a) national laws or regulations;
   (b) legally established or recognised machinery for wage determination;
   (c) collective agreements between employers and workers; or
   (d) a combination of these various means.

Article 3

1. Where such action will assist in giving effect to the provisions of this Convention measures shall be taken to promote objective appraisal of jobs on the basis of the work to be performed.

2. The methods to be followed in this appraisal may be decided upon by the authorities responsible for the determination of rates of remuneration, or, where such rates are determined by collective agreements, by the partíes thereto.

3. Differential rates between workers which correspond, without regard to sex, to differences, as determined by such objective appraisal, in the work to be performed shall not be considered as being contrary to the principle of equal remuneration for men and women workers for work of equal value.

Article 4

Each Member shall co-operate as appropriate with the employers' and workers' organisations concerned for the purpose of giving effect to the provisions of this Convention.

FINAL

Article 5

The formal ratifications of this Convention shall be communicated to the Director-General of the International Labour Office for registration.

Article 6

1. This Convention shall be binding only upon those Members of the International Labour Organisation whose ratifications have been registered with the Director-General.

2. It shall come into force twelve months after the date on which the ratifications of two Members have been registered with the Director-General.

3. Thereafter, this Convention shall come into force for any Member twelve months after the date on which its ratifications has been registered.

Article 7

1. Declarations communicated to the Director-General of the International Labour Office in accordance with paragraph 2 of article 35 of the Constitution of the International Labour Organisation shall indicate –

   (a) the territories in respect of which the Member concerned undertakes that the provisions of the Convention shall be applied without modification;
   (b) the territories in respect of which it undertakes that the provisions of the Convention shall be applied subject to modifications, together with details of the said modifications;
   (c) the territories in respect of which the Convention is inapplicable and in such cases the grounds on which it is inapplicable;
   (d) the territories in respect of which it reserves its decision pending further consideration of the position.

2. The undertakings referred to in subparagraphs (a) and (b) of paragraph 1 of this Article shall be deemed to be an integral part of the ratification and shall have the force of ratification.

3. Any Member may at any time by a subsequent declaration cancel in whole or in part any reservation made in its original declaration in virtue of subparagraph (b), (c) or (d) of paragraph 1 of this Article.

4. Any Member may, at any time at which the Convention is subject to denunciation in accordance with the provisions of Article 9, communicate to the Director-General a declaration modifying in any other respect the terms of any former declaration and stating the present position in respect of such territories as it may specify.

Article 8

1. Declarations communicated to the Director-General of the International Labour Office in accordance with paragraph 4 or 5 of article 35 of the Constitution of the International Labour Organisation shall indicate whether the provisions of the Convention will be applied in the territory concerned without modification or subject to modifications; when the declaration indicates that the provisions of the Convention will be applied subject to modifications, it shall give details of the said modifications.

2. The Member, Members or international authority concerned may at any time by a subsequent declaration renounce in whole or in part the right to have recourse to any modification indicated in any former declaration.

3. The Member, Members or international authority concerned may, at any time at which the Convention is subject to denunciation in accordance with the provisions of Article 9, communicate to the Director-General a declaration modifying in any other respect the terms of any former declaration and stating the present position in respect of the application of the Convention.

Article 9

1. A Member which has ratified this Convention may denounce it after the expiration of ten years from the date on which the Convention first comes into force, by an Act communicated to the Director-General of the International Labour Office for registration. Such denunciation should not take effect until one year after the date on which it is registered.

2. Each Member which has ratified this Convention and which does not, within the year following the expiration of the period of ten years mentioned in the preceding paragraph, exercise the right of denunciation provided for in this Article, will be bound for another period of ten years and, thereafter, may denounce this Convention at the expiration of each period of ten years under the terms provided for in this Article.

Article 10

1. The Director-General of the International Labour Office shall notify all Members of the International Labour Organisation of the registration of all ratifications and denunciations communicated to him by the Members of the Organisation.

2. When notifying the Members of the Organisation of the registration of the second ratification communicated to him, the Director-General shall draw the attention of the Members of the Organisation to the date upon which the Convention will come into force.

Article 11

The Director-General of the International Labour Office shall communicate to the Secretary-General of the United Nations for registration in accordance with Article 102 of the Charter of the United Nations full particulars of all ratifications and acts of denunciation registered by him in accordance with the provisions of the preceding Articles.

Article 12

At such times as may consider necessary the Governing Body of the International Labour Office shall present to the General Conference a report on the working of this Convention and shall examine the desirability of placing on the agenda of the Conference the question of its revision in whole or in part.

Article 13

1. Should the Conference adopt a new Convention revising this Convention in whole or in part, then, unless the new Convention otherwise provides:

   (a) the ratification by a Member of the new revising Convention shall ipso jure involve the immediate denunciation of this Convention, notwithstanding the provisions of Article 9 above, if and when the new revising Convention shall have come into force;
   (b) as from the date when the new revising Convention comes into force this Convention shall cease to be open to ratification by the Members.

2. This Convention shall in any case remain in force in its actual form and content for those Members which have ratified it but have not ratified the revising Convention.

Article 14

The English and French versions of the text of this Convention are equally authoritative.

ILO Convention No. 105 concerning the Abolition of Forced Labour (1957)[1]

PREAMBLE

The General Conference of the International Labour Organisation,

Having been convened at Geneva by the Governing Body of the International Labour Office, and having met in its Fortieth Session on 5 June 1957, and

Having considered the question of forced labour, which is the fourth item on the agenda of the session, and Having noted the provisions of the Forced Labour Convention, 1930, and

Having noted that the Slavery Convention, 1926, provides that all necessary measures shall be taken to prevent compulsory or forced labour from developing into conditions analogous to slavery and that the Supplementary Convention on the Abolition of Slavery, the Slave Trade and Institutions and Practices Similar to Slavery, 1956, provides for the complete abolition of debt bondage and serfdom, and

Having noted that the Protection of Wages Convention, 1949, provides that wages shall be paid regularly and prohibits methods of payment which deprive the worker of a genuine possibility of terminating his employment, and

Having decided upon the adoption of further proposals with regard to the abolition of certain forms of forced or compulsory labour constituting a violation of the rights of man referred to in the Charter of the United Nations and enunciated by the Universal Declaration of Human Rights, and

Having determined that these proposals shall take the form of an international Convention,

Adopts the twenty-fifth day of June of the year one thousand nine hundred and fifty-seven, the following Convention, which may be cited as the Abolition of Forced Labour Convention, 1957:

ARTICLE 1

Each Member of the International Labour Organisation which ratifies this Convention undertakes to suppress and not to make use of any form of forced or compulsory labour –

1. Adopted in Geneva on 25 June 1957. Date of coming into force: 17 January 1959.

(a) as a means of political coercion or education or as a punishment for holding or expressing political views or views ideologically opposed to the established political, social or economic system;
(b) as a method of mobilising and using labour for purposes of economic development;
(c) as a means of labour discipline;
(d) as a punishment for having participated in strikes;
(e) as a means of racial, social, national or religious discrimination.

Article 2

Each Member of the International Labour Organisation which ratifies this Convention undertakes to take effective measures to secure the immediate and complete abolition of forced or compulsory labour as specified in Article 1 of this Convention.

FINAL

Article 3

The formal ratifications of this Convention shall be communicated to the Director-General of the International Labour Office for registration.

Article 4

1. This Convention shall be binding only upon those Members of the International Labour Organisation whose ratifications have been registered with the Director-General.

2. It shall come into force twelve months after the date on which the ratifications of two Members have been registered with the Director-General.

3. Thereafter, this Convention shall come into force for any Member twelve months after the date on which its ratifications has been registered.

Article 5

1. A Member which has ratified this Convention may denounce it after the expiration of ten years from the date on which the Convention first comes into force, by an Act communicated to the Director-General of the International Labour Office for registration. Such denunciation should not take effect until one year after the date on which it is registered.

2. Each Member which has ratified this Convention and which does not, within the year following the expiration of the period of ten years mentioned in the preceding paragraph, exercise the right of denunciation provided for in this Article, will be bound for another period of ten years and, thereafter, may denounce this Convention at the expiration of each period of ten years under the terms provided for in this Article.

Article 6

1. The Director-General of the International Labour Office shall notify all Members of the International Labour Organisation of the registration of all ratifications and denunciations communicated to him by the Members of the Organisation.

2. When notifying the Members of the Organisation of the registration of the second ratification communicated to him, the Director-General shall draw the attention of the Members of the Organisation to the date upon which the Convention will come into force.

Article 7

The Director-General of the International Labour Office shall communicate to the Secretary-General of the United Nations for registration in accordance with Article 102 of the Charter of the United Nations full particulars of all ratifications and acts of denunciation registered by him in accordance with the provisions of the preceding Articles.

Article 8

At such times as may consider necessary the Governing Body of the International Labour Office shall present to the General Conference a report on the working of this Convention and shall examine the desirability of placing on the agenda of the Conference the question of its revision in whole or in part.

Article 9

1. Should the Conference adopt a new Convention revising this Convention in whole or in part, then, unless the new Convention otherwise provides:

   (a) the ratification by a Member of the new revising Convention shall ipso jure involve the immediate denunciation of this Convention, notwithstanding the provisions of Article 5 above, if and when the new revising Convention shall have come into force;

(b) as from the date when the new revising Convention comes into force this Convention shall cease to be open to ratification by the Members.

2. This Convention shall in any case remain in force in its actual form and content for those Members which have ratified it but have not ratified the revising Convention.

Article 10

The English and French versions of the text of this Convention are equally authoritative.

ILO Convention No. 111 concerning Discrimination in Respect of Employment and Occupation (1958)[1]

Preamble

The General Conference of the International Labour Organisation,

Having been convened at Geneva by the Governing Body of the International Labour Office, and having met in its Forty-second Session on 4 June 1958, and

Having decided upon the adoption of certain proposals with regard to discrimination in the field of employment and occupation, which is the fourth item on the agenda of the session, and

Having determined that these proposals shall take the form of an international Convention, and

Considering that the Declaration of Philadelphia affirms that all human beings, irrespective of race, creed or sex, have the right to pursue both their material well-being and their spiritual development in conditions of freedom and dignity, of economic security and equal opportunity, and

Considering further that discrimination constitutes a violation of rights enunciated by the Universal Declaration of Human Rights,

Adopts the twenty-fifth day of June of the year one thousand nine hundred and fifty-eight, the following Convention, which may be cited as the Discrimination (Employment and Occupation) Convention, 1958:

Article 1

1. For the purpose of this Convention the term "discrimination" includes –

    (a) any distinction, exclusion or preference made on the basis of race, colour sex, religion, political opinion, national extraction or social origin, which has the effect of nullifying or impairing equality of opportunity or treatment in employment or occupation;
    (b) such other distinction, exclusion or preference which has the effect of nullifying or impairing equality of opportunity or treatment in

1. Adopted in Geneva on 25 June 1958. Date of coming into force: 15 June 1960.

employment or occupation as may be determined by the Member concerned after consultation with representative employers' and workers' organisations, where such exist, and with other appropriate bodies.

2. Any distinction, exclusion or preference in respect of a particular job based on the inherent requirements thereof shall not be deemed to be discrimination.

3. For the purpose of this Convention the terms "employment" and "occupation" include access to vocational training, access to employment and to particular occupations, and terms and conditions of employment.

Article 2

Each Member for which this Convention is in force undertakes to declare and pursue a national policy designed to promote, by methods appropriate to national conditions and practice, equality of opportunity and treatment in respect of employment and occupation, with a view to eliminating any discrimination in respect thereof.

Article 3

Each Member for which this Convention is in force undertakes, by methods appropriate to national conditions and practice –

(a) to seek the co-operation of employers' and workers' organisations and other appropriate bodies in promoting the acceptance and observance of this policy;
(b) to enact such legislation and to promote such educational programmes as may be calculated to secure the acceptance and observance of the policy;
(c) to repeal any statutory provisions and modify any administrative instructions or practices which are inconsistent with the policy;
(d) to pursue the policy in respect of employment under the direct control of a national authority;
(e) to ensure observance of the policy in the activities of vocational guidance, vocational training and placement services under the direction of a national authority;
(f) to indicate in its annual reports on the application of the Convention the action taken in pursuance of the policy and the results secured by such action.

Article 4

Any measures affecting an individual who is justifiably suspected of, or engaged in, activities prejudicial to the security of the State shall not be deemed to be discrimination, provided that the individual concerned shall have the right to appeal to a competent body established in accordance with national practice.

Article 5

1. Special measures of protection or assistance provided for in other Conventions or Recommendations adopted by the International Labour Conference shall not be deemed to be discrimination.

2. Any Member may, after consultation with representative employers' and workers' organisations, where such exist, determine that other special measures designed to meet the particular requirements of persons who, for reasons such as sex, age, disablement, family responsibilities or social or cultural status, are generally recognised to require special protection or assistance, shall not be deemed to be discrimination.

Article 6

Each Member which ratifies this Convention undertakes to apply it to non-metropolitan territories in accordance with the provisions of the Constitution of the International Labour Organisation.

Final

Article 7

The formal ratifications of this Convention shall be communicated to the Director-General of the International Labour Office for registration.

Article 8

1. This Convention shall be binding only upon those Members of the International Labour Organisation whose ratifications have been registered with the Director-General.

2. It shall come into force twelve months after the date on which the ratifications of two Members have been registered with the Director-General.

3. Thereafter, this Convention shall come into force for any Member twelve months after the date on which its ratifications has been registered.

Article 9

1. A Member which has ratified this Convention may denounce it after the expiration of ten years from the date on which the Convention first comes into force, by an Act communicated to the Director-General of the International Labour Office for registration. Such denunciation should not take effect until one year after the date on which it is registered.

2. Each Member which has ratified this Convention and which does not, within the year following the expiration of the period of ten years mentioned in the preceding paragraph, exercise the right of denunciation provided for in this Article, will be bound for another period of ten years and, thereafter, may denounce this Convention at the expiration of each period of ten years under the terms provided for in this Article.

Article 10

1. The Director-General of the International Labour Office shall notify all Members of the International Labour Organisation of the registration of all ratifications and denunciations communicated to him by the Members of the Organisation.

2. When notifying the Members of the Organisation of the registration of the second ratification communicated to him, the Director-General shall draw the attention of the Members of the Organisation to the date upon which the Convention will come into force.

Article 11

The Director-General of the International Labour Office shall communicate to the Secretary-General of the United Nations for registration in accordance with Article 102 of the Charter of the United Nations full particulars of all ratifications and acts of denunciation registered by him in accordance with the provisions of the preceding Articles.

Article 12

At such times as may consider necessary the Governing Body of the International Labour Office shall present to the General Conference a report on the working of this Convention and shall examine the desirability of placing on the agenda of the Conference the question of its revision in whole or in part.

ARTICLE 13

1. Should the Conference adopt a new Convention revising this Convention in whole or in part, then, unless the new Convention otherwise provides:

   (a) the ratification by a Member of the new revising Convention shall ipso jure involve the immediate denunciation of this Convention, notwithstanding the provisions of Article 9 above, if and when the new revising Convention shall have come into force;
   (b) as from the date when the new revising Convention comes into force this Convention shall cease to be open to ratification by the Members.

2. This Convention shall in any case remain in force in its actual form and content for those Members which have ratified it but have not ratified the revising Convention.

ARTICLE 14

The English and French versions of the text of this Convention are equally authoritative.

ILO Convention No. 138 concerning Minimum Age (1973)[1]

Preamble

The General Conference of the International Labour Organisation,

Having been convened at Geneva by the Governing Body of the International Labour Office, and having met in its Fifty-eighth Session on 6 June 1973, and

Having decided upon the adoption of certain proposals with regard to minimum age for admission to employment, which is the fourth item on the agenda of the session, and

Noting the terms of the Minimum Age (Industry) Convention, 1919, the Minimum Age (Sea) Convention, 1920, the Minimum Age (Agriculture) Convention, 1921, the Minimum Age (Trimmers and Stokers) Convention, 1921, the Minimum Age (Non-Industrial Employment) Convention, 1932, the Minimum Age (Sea) Convention (Revised), 1936, the Minimum Age (Industry) Convention (Revised), 1937, the Minimum Age (Non Industrial Employment) Convention (Revised), 1937, the Minimum Age (Fishermen) Convention, 1959, and the Minimum Age (Underground Work) Convention, 1965, and

Considering that the time has come to establish a general instrument on the subject, which would gradually replace the existing ones applicable to limited economic sectors, with a view to achieving the total abolition of child labour, and

Having determined that these proposals shall take the form of an international Convention,

Adopts the twenty-sixth day of June of the year one thousand nine hundred and seventy-three, the following Convention, which may be cited as the Minimum Age Convention, 1973:

Article 1

Each Member for which this Convention is in force undertakes to pursue a national policy designed to ensure the effective abolition of child labour and to raise progressively the minimum age for admission to employment or work to a level consistent with the fullest physical and mental development of young persons.

1. Adopted in Geneva on 26 June 1973. Date of coming into force: 19 June 1976.

Article 2

1. Each Member which ratifies this Convention shall specify, in a declaration appended to its ratification, a minimum age for admission to employment or work within its territory and on means of transport registered in its territory; subject to Articles 4 to 8 of this Convention, no one under that age shall be admitted to employment or work in any occupation.

2. Each Member which has ratified this Convention may subsequently notify the Director-General of the International Labour Office, by further declarations, that it specifies a minimum age higher than that previously specified.

3. The minimum age specified in pursuance of paragraph 1 of this Article shall not be less than the age of completion of compulsory schooling and, in any case, shall not be less than 15 years.

4. Notwithstanding the provisions of paragraph 3 of this Article, a Member whose economy and educational facilities are insufficiently developed may, after consultation with the organisations of employers and workers concerned, where such exist, initially specify a minimum age of 14 years.

5. Each Member which has specified a minimum age of 14 years in pursuance of the provisions of the preceding paragraph shall include in its reports on the application of this Convention submitted under Article 22 of the constitution of the International Labour Organisation a statement —

   (a) that its reason for doing so subsists; or
   (b) that it renounces its right to avail itself of the provisions in question as from a stated date.

Article 3

1. The minimum age for admission to any type of employment or work which by its nature or the circumstances in which it is carried out is likely to jeopardise the health, safety or morals of young persons shall not be less than 18 years.

2. The types of employment or work to which paragraph 1 of this Article applies shall be determined by national laws or regulations or by the competent authority, after consultation with the organisations of employers and workers concerned, where such exist.

3. Notwithstanding the provisions of paragraph 1 of this Article, national laws or regulations or the competent authority may, after consultation with the organisations of employers and workers concerned, where such exist, authorise employment or work as from the age of 16 years on condition that the health, safety and morals of the young persons concerned are fully protected and that the young persons have received adequate specific instruction or vocational training in the relevant branch of activity.

Article 4

1. In so far as necessary, the competent authority, after consultation with the organisations of employers and workers concerned, where such exist, may exclude from the application of this Convention limited categories of employment or work in respect of which special and substantial problems of application arise.

2. Each Member which ratifies this Convention shall list in its first report on the application of the Convention submitted under Article 22 of the Constitution of the International Labour Organisation any categories which may have been excluded in pursuance of paragraph 1 of this Article, giving the reasons for such exclusion, and shall state in subsequent reports the position of its law and practice in respect of the categories excluded and the extent to which effect has been given or is proposed to be given to the Convention in respect of such categories.

3. Employment or work covered by Article 3 of this Convention shall not be excluded from the application of the Convention in pursuance of this Article.

Article 5

1. A Member whose economy and administrative facilities are insufficiently developed may, after consultation with the organisations of employers and workers concerned, where such exist, initially limit the scope of application of this Convention.

2. Each Member which avails itself of the provisions of paragraph 1 of this Article shall specify, in a declaration appended to its ratification, the branches of economic activity or types of undertakings to which it will apply the provisions of the Convention.

3. The provisions of the Convention shall be applicable as a minimum to the following: mining and quarrying; manufacturing; construction; electricity, gas and water; sanitary services; transport, storage and communication; and plantations and other agricultural undertakings mainly producing for commercial purposes, but excluding family and small-scale holdings producing for local consumption and not regularly employing hired workers.

4. Any Member which has limited the scope of application of this Convention in pursuance of this Article —

   (a) shall indicate in its reports under Article 22 of the Constitution of the International Labour Organisation the general position as regards the employment or work of young persons and children in the branches of activity which are excluded from the scope of application of this Convention and any progress which may have been made towards wider application of the provisions of the Convention;
   (b) may at any time formally extend the scope of application by a declaration addressed to the Director-General of the International Labour Office.

Article 6

This Convention does not apply to work done by children and young persons in schools for general, vocational or technical education or in other training institutions, or to work done by persons at least 14 years of age in undertakings, where such work is carried out in accordance with conditions prescribed by the competent authority, after consultation with the organisations of employers and workers concerned, where such exist, and is an integral part of —

(a) a course of education or training for which a school or training institution is primarily responsible;
(b) a programme of training mainly or entirely in an undertaking, which programme has been approved by the competent authority; or
(c) a programme of guidance or orientation designed to facilitate the choice of an occupation or of a line of training.

Article 7

1. National laws or regulations may permit the employment or work of persons 13 to 15 years of age on light work which is —

   (a) not likely to be harmful to their health or development; and

(b) not such as to prejudice their attendance at school, their participation in vocational orientation or training programmes approved by the competent authority or their capacity to benefit from the instruction received.

2. National laws or regulations may also permit the employment or work of persons who are at least 15 years of age but have not yet completed their compulsory schooling on work which meets the requirements set forth in sub-paragraphs (a) and (b) of paragraph 1 of this Article.

3. The competent authority shall determine the activities in which employment or work may be permitted under paragraphs 1 and 2 of this Article and shall prescribe the number of hours during which and the conditions in which such employment or work may be undertaken.

4. Notwithstanding the provisions of paragraphs 1 and 2 of this Article, a Member which has availed itself of the provisions of paragraph 4 of Article 2 may, for as long as it continues to do so, substitute the ages 12 and 14 for the ages 13 and 15 in paragraph 1 and the age 14 for the age 15 in paragraph 2 of this Article.

Article 8

1. After consultation with the organisations of employers and workers concerned, where such exist, the competent authority may, by permits granted in individual cases, allow exceptions to the prohibition of employment or work provided for in Article 2 of this Convention, for such purposes as participation in artistic performances.

2. Permits so granted shall limit the number of hours during which and prescribe the conditions in which employment or work is allowed.

Article 9

1. All necessary measures, including the provision of appropriate penalties, shall be taken by the competent authority to ensure the effective enforcement of the provisions of this Convention.

2. National laws or regulations or the competent authority shall define the persons responsible for compliance with the provisions giving effect to the Convention.

3. National laws or regulations or the competent authority shall prescribe the registers or other documents which shall be kept and made available by the employer; such registers or documents shall contain the names and ages or dates of birth, duly certified wherever possible, of persons whom he employs or who work for him and who are less than 18 years of age.

Article 10

1. This Convention revises, on the terms set forth in this Article, the Minimum Age (Industry) Convention, 1919, the Minimum Age (Sea) Convention, 1920, the Minimum Age (Agriculture) Convention, 1921, the Minimum Age (Trimmers and Stokers) Convention, 1921, the Minimum Age (Non Industrial Employment) Convention, 1932, the Minimum Age (Sea) Convention (Revised), 1936, the Minimum Age (Industry) Convention (Revised), 1937, the Minimum Age (Non-Industrial Employment) Convention (Revised), 1937, the Minimum Age (Fishermen) Convention, 1959, and the Minimum Age (Underground Work) Convention, 1965.

2. The coming into force of this Convention shall not close the Minimum Age (Sea) Convention (Revised), 1936, the Minimum Age (Industry) Convention (Revised), 1937, the Minimum Age (Non-Industrial Employment) Convention (Revised), 1937, the Minimum Age (Fishermen) Convention, 1959, or the Minimum Age (Underground Work) Convention, 1965, to further ratification.

3. The Minimum Age (Industry) Convention, 1919, the Minimum Age (Sea) Convention, 1920, the Minimum Age (Agriculture) Convention, 1921, and the Minimum Age (Trimmers and Stokers) Convention, 1921, shall be closed to further ratification when all the parties thereto have consented to such closing by ratification of this Convention or by a declaration communicated to the Director-General of the International Labour Office.

4. When the obligations of this Convention are accepted —

   (a) by a Member which is a party to the Minimum Age (Industry) Convention (Revised), 1937, and a minimum age of not less than 15 years is specified in pursuance of Article 2 of this Convention, this shall ipso jure involve the immediate denunciation of that Convention,
   (b) in respect of non-industrial employment as defined in the Minimum Age (Non-Industrial Employment) Convention, 1932, by a Member which is a party to that Convention, this shall ipso jure involve the immediate denunciation of that Convention,

(c) in respect of non-industrial employment as defined in the Minimum Age (Non-Industrial Employment) Convention (Revised), 1937, by a Member which is a party to that Convention, and a minimum age of not less than 15 years is specified in pursuance of Article 2 of this Convention, this shall ipso jure involve the immediate denunciation of that Convention,

(d) in respect of maritime employment, by a Member which is a party to the Minimum Age (Sea) Convention (Revised), 1936, and a minimum age of not less than 15 years is specified in pursuance of Article 2 of this Convention or the Member specifies that Article 3 of this Convention applies to maritime employment, this shall ipso jure involve the immediate denunciation of that Convention,

(e) in respect of employment in maritime fishing, by a Member which is a party to the Minimum Age (Fishermen) Convention, 1959, and a minimum age of not less than 15 years is specified in pursuance of Article 2 of this Convention or the Member specifies that Article 3 of this Convention applies to employment in maritime fishing, this shall ipso jure involve the immediate denunciation of that Convention,

(f) by a Member which is a party to the Minimum Age (Underground Work) Convention, 1965, and a minimum age of not less than the age specified in pursuance of that Convention is specified in pursuance of Article 2 of this Convention or the Member specifies that such an age applies to employment underground in mines in virtue of Article 3 of this Convention, this shall ipso jure involve the immediate denunciation of that Convention, if and when this Convention shall have come into force.

5. Acceptance of the obligations of this Convention –

(a) shall involve the denunciation of the Minimum Age (Industry) Convention, 1919, in accordance with Article 12 thereof,

(b) in respect of agriculture shall involve the denunciation of the Minimum Age (Agriculture) Convention, 1921, in accordance with Article 9 thereof,

(c) in respect of maritime employment shall involve the denunciation of the Minimum Age (Sea) Convention, 1920, in accordance with Article 10 thereof, and of the Minimum Age (Trimmers and Stokers) Convention, 1921, in accordance with Article 12 thereof, if and when this Convention shall have come into force.

Article 11

The formal ratifications of this Convention shall be communicated to the Director-General of the International Labour Office for registration.

Article 12

1. This Convention shall be binding only upon those Members of the International Labour Organisation whose ratifications have been registered with the Director-General.

2. It shall come into force twelve months after the date on which the ratifications of two Members have been registered with the Director-General.

3. Thereafter, this Convention shall come into force for any Member twelve months after the date on which its ratifications has been registered.

Article 13

1. A Member which has ratified this Convention may denounce it after the expiration of ten years from the date on which the Convention first comes into force, by an Act communicated to the Director-General of the International Labour Office for registration. Such denunciation should not take effect until one year after the date on which it is registered.

2. Each Member which has ratified this Convention and which does not, within the year following the expiration of the period of ten years mentioned in the preceding paragraph, exercise the right of denunciation provided for in this Article, will be bound for another period of ten years and, thereafter, may denounce this Convention at the expiration of each period of ten years under the terms provided for in this Article.

Article 14

1. The Director-General of the International Labour Office shall notify all Members of the International Labour Organisation of the registration of all ratifications and denunciations communicated to him by the Members of the Organisation.

2. When notifying the Members of the Organisation of the registration of the second ratification communicated to him, the Director-General shall draw the attention of the Members of the Organisation to the date upon which the Convention will come into force.

ARTICLE 15

The Director-General of the International Labour Office shall communicate to the Secretary-General of the United Nations for registration in accordance with Article 102 of the Charter of the United Nations full particulars of all ratifications and acts of denunciation registered by him in accordance with the provisions of the preceding Articles.

ARTICLE 16

At such times as may consider necessary the Governing Body of the International Labour Office shall present to the General Conference a report on the working of this Convention and shall examine the desirability of placing on the agenda of the Conference the question of its revision in whole or in part.

ARTICLE 17

1. Should the Conference adopt a new Convention revising this Convention in whole or in part, then, unless the new Convention otherwise provides:

   (a) the ratification by a Member of the new revising Convention shall ipso jure involve the immediate denunciation of this Convention, notwithstanding the provisions of Article 13 above, if and when the new revising Convention shall have come into force;
   (b) as from the date when the new revising Convention comes into force this Convention shall cease to be open to ratification by the Members.

2. This Convention shall in any case remain in force in its actual form and content for those Members which have ratified it but have not ratified the revising Convention.

ARTICLE 18

The English and French versions of the text of this Convention are equally authoritative.

ILO Declaration on Fundamental Principles and Rights at Work and its Follow-up (1998)[1]

Whereas the ILO was founded in the conviction that social justice is essential to universal and lasting peace;

Whereas economic growth is essential but not sufficient to ensure equity, social progress and the eradication of poverty, confirming the need for the ILO to promote strong social policies, justice and democratic institutions;

Whereas the ILO should, now more than ever, draw upon all its standard-setting, technical co-operation and research resources in all its areas of competence, in particular employment, vocational training and working conditions, to ensure that, in the context of a global strategy for economic and social development, economic and social policies are mutually reinforcing components in order to create broad-based sustainable development;

Whereas the ILO should give special attention to the problems of persons with special social needs, particularly the unemployed and migrant workers, and mobilise and encourage international, regional and national efforts aimed at resolving their problems, and promote effective policies aimed at job creation;

Whereas, in seeking to maintain the link between social progress and economic growth, the guarantee of fundamental principles and rights at work is of particular significance in that it enables the persons concerned to claim freely and on the basis of equality of opportunity their fair share of the wealth which they have helped to generate, and to achieve fully their human potential;

Whereas the ILO is the constitutionally mandated international organisation and the competent body to set and deal with international labour standards, and enjoys universal support and acknowledgement in promoting fundamental rights at work as the expression of its constitutional principles;

Whereas it is urgent, in a situation of growing economic interdependence, to reaffirm the immutable nature of the fundamental principles and rights embodied in the Constitution of the Organisation and to promote their universal application;

1. Adopted in Geneva on 18 June 1998, at the 86 Session of the International Labour Conference.

THE INTERNATIONAL LABOUR CONFERENCE,

1. Recalls:

   (a) that in freely joining the ILO, all Members have endorsed the principles and rights set out in its Constitution and in the Declaration of Philadelphia, and have undertaken to work towards attaining the overall objectives of the Organisation to the best of their resources and fully in line with their specific circumstances;
   (b) that these principles and rights have been expressed and developed in the form of specific rights and obligations in Conventions recognised as fundamental both inside and outside the Organisation.

2. Declares that all Members, even if they have not ratified the Conventions in question, have an obligation arising from the very fact of membership in the Organisation, to respect, to promote and to realise, in good faith and in accordance with the Constitution, the principles concerning the fundamental rights which are the subject of those Conventions, namely:

   (a) freedom of association and the effective recognition of the right to collective bargaining;
   (b) the elimination of all forms of forced or compulsory labour;
   (c) the effective abolition of child labour; and
   (d) the elimination of discrimination in respect of employment and occupation.

3. Recognises the obligation on the Organisation to assist its Members, in response to their established and expressed needs, in order to attain these objectives by making full use of its constitutional, operational and budgetary resources, including by the mobilisation of external resources and support, as well as by encouraging other international organisations with which the ILO has established relations, pursuant to Article 12 of its Constitution, to support these efforts:

   (a) by offering technical co-operation and advisory services to promote the ratification and implementation of the fundamental Conventions;
   (b) by assisting those Members not yet in a position to ratify some or all of these Conventions in their efforts to respect, to promote and to realise the principles concerning fundamental rights which are the subject of those Conventions; and
   (c) by helping the Members in their efforts to create a climate for economic and social development.

4. Decides that, to give full effect to this Declaration, a promotional follow up, which is meaningful and effective, shall be implemented in accordance with the measures specified in the Annex hereto, which shall be considered as an integral part of this Declaration.

5. Stresses that labour standards should not be used for protectionist trade purposes, and that nothing in this Declaration and its follow-up shall be invoked or otherwise used for such purposes; in addition, the comparative advantage of any country should in no way be called into question by this Declaration and its follow-up.

Annex

Follow-up to the Declaration

I. Overall Purpose

1. The aim of the follow-up described below is to encourage the efforts made by the Members of the Organisation to promote the fundamental principles and rights enshrined in the Constitution of the ILO and the Declaration of Philadelphia and reaffirmed in this Declaration.

2. In line with this objective, which is of a strictly promotional nature, this follow-up will allow the identification of areas in which the assistance of the Organisation through its technical co-operation activities may prove useful to its Members to help them implement these fundamental principles and rights. It is not a substitute for the established supervisory mechanisms, nor shall it impede their functioning; consequently, specific situations within the purview of those mechanisms shall not be examined or re-examined within the framework of this follow-up.

3. The two aspects of this follow-up, described below, are based on existing procedures: the annual follow-up concerning non-ratified fundamental Conventions will entail merely some adaptation of the present modalities of application of Article 19, paragraph 5(e) of the Constitution; and the global report will serve to obtain the best results from the procedures carried out pursuant to the Constitution.

II. Annual follow-up concerning non-ratified fundamental Conventions

A. Purpose and scope

1. The purpose is to provide an opportunity to review each year, by means of simplified procedures to replace the four-year review introduced by the Governing Body in 1995, the efforts made in accordance with the Declaration by Members which have not yet ratified all the fundamental Conventions.

2. The follow-up will cover each year the four areas of fundamental principles and rights specified in the Declaration.

B. Modalities

1. The follow-up will be based on reports requested from Members under article 19, paragraph 5(e) of the Constitution. The report forms will be drawn up so as to obtain information from governments which have not ratified one or more of the fundamental Conventions, on any changes which may have taken place in their law and practice, taking due account of Article 23 of the Constitution and established practice.

2. These reports, as compiled by the Office, will be reviewed by the Governing Body.

3. With a view to presenting an introduction to the reports thus compiled, drawing attention to any aspects which might call for a more in-depth discussion, the Office may call upon a group of experts appointed for this purpose by the Governing Body.

4. Adjustments to the Governing Body's existing procedures should be examined to allow Members which are not represented on the Governing Body to provide, in the most appropriate way, clarifications which might prove necessary or useful during Governing Body discussions to supplement the information contained in their reports.

III. Global report

A. Purpose and scope

1. The purpose of this report is to provide a dynamic global picture relating to each category of fundamental principles and rights noted during the preceding four-year period, and to serve as a basis for assessing the

effectiveness of the assistance provided by the Organisation, and for determining priorities for the following period, in the form of action plans for technical co-operation designed in particular to mobilise the internal and external resources necessary to carry them out.

2. The report will cover, each year, one of the four categories of fundamental principles and rights in turn.

B. Modalities

1. The report will be drawn up under the responsibility of the Director General on the basis of official information, or information gathered and assessed in accordance with established procedures. In the case of States which have not ratified the fundamental Conventions, it will be based in particular on the findings of the aforementioned annual follow-up. In the case of Members which have ratified the Conventions concerned, the report will be based in particular on reports as dealt with pursuant to Article 22 of the Constitution.

2. This report will be submitted to the Conference for tripartite discussion as a report of the Director-General. The Conference may deal with this report separately from reports under Article 12 of its Standing Orders, and may discuss it during a sitting devoted entirely to this report, or in any other appropriate way. It will then be for the Governing Body, at an early session, to draw conclusions from this discussion concerning the priorities and plans of action for technical co-operation to be implemented for the following four-year period.

IV. It is understood that:

1. Proposals shall be made for amendments to the Standing Orders of the Governing Body and the Conference which are required to implement the preceding provisions.

2. The Conference shall, in due course, review the operation of this follow up in the light of the experience acquired to assess whether it has adequately fulfilled the overall purpose articulated in Part I.

Council of Europe Convention for Protection of Human Rights and Fundamental Freedoms (1950)[1]

The governments signatory hereto, being members of the Council of Europe,

Considering the Universal Declaration of Human Rights proclaimed by the General Assembly of the United Nations on 10th December 1948;

Considering that this Declaration aims at securing the universal and effective recognition and observance of the Rights therein declared;

Considering that the aim of the Council of Europe is the achievement of greater unity between its members and that one of the methods by which that aim is to be pursued is the maintenance and further realisation of human rights and fundamental freedoms;

Reaffirming their profound belief in those fundamental freedoms which are the foundation of justice and peace in the world and are best maintained on the one hand by an effective political democracy and on the other by a common understanding and observance of the human rights upon which they depend;

Being resolved, as the governments of European countries which are like-minded and have a common heritage of political traditions, ideals, freedom and the rule of law, to take the first steps for the collective enforcement of certain of the rights stated in the Universal Declaration,

Have agreed as follows:

Article 1

The High Contracting Parties shall secure to everyone within their jurisdiction the rights and freedoms defined in Section I of this Convention.

1. Adopted in Rome on 4 November 1950. Text completed by Protocol No. 2 (ETS N° 44) of 6 May 1963 and amended by Protocol No. 3 (ETS N° 45) of 6 May 1963, Protocol No. 5 (ETS N° 55) of 20 January 1966 and Protocol No. 8 (ETS N° 118) of 19 March 1985.

SECTION I

ARTICLE 2

1. Everyone's right to life shall be protected by law. No one shall be deprived of his life intentionally save in the execution of a sentence of a court following his conviction of a crime for which this penalty is provided by law.

2. Deprivation of life shall not be regarded as inflicted in contravention of this article when it results from the use of force which is no more than absolutely necessary:

   (a) in defence of any person from unlawful violence;
   (b) in order to effect a lawful arrest or to prevent the escape of a person lawfully detained;
   (c) in action lawfully taken for the purpose of quelling a riot or insurrection.

ARTICLE 3

No one shall be subjected to torture or to inhuman or degrading treatment or punishment.

ARTICLE 4

1. No one shall be held in slavery or servitude.

2. No one shall be required to perform forced or compulsory labour.

3. For the purpose of this article the term "forced or compulsory labour" shall not include:

   (a) any work required to be done in the ordinary course of detention imposed according to the provisions of Article 5 of this Convention or during conditional release from such detention;
   (b) any service of a military character or, in case of conscientious objectors in countries where they are recognised, service exacted instead of compulsory military service;
   (c) any service exacted in case of an emergency or calamity threatening the life or well-being of the community;
   (d) any work or service which forms part of normal civic obligations.

Article 5

1. Everyone has the right to liberty and security of person. No one shall be deprived of his liberty save in the following cases and in accordance with a procedure prescribed by law:

   (a) the lawful detention of a person after conviction by a competent court;
   (b) the lawful arrest or detention of a person for non-compliance with the lawful order of a court or in order to secure the fulfilment of any obligation prescribed by law;
   (c) the lawful arrest or detention of a person effected for the purpose of bringing him before the competent legal authority on reasonable suspicion of having committed an offence or when it is reasonably considered necessary to prevent his committing an offence or fleeing after having done so;
   (d) the detention of a minor by lawful order for the purpose of educational supervision or his lawful detention for the purpose of bringing him before the competent legal authority;
   (e) the lawful detention of persons for the prevention of the spreading of infectious diseases, of persons of unsound mind, alcoholics or drug addicts or vagrants;
   (f) the lawful arrest or detention of a person to prevent his effecting an unauthorised entry into the country or of a person against whom action is being taken with a view to deportation or extradition.

2. Everyone who is arrested shall be informed promptly, in a language which he understands, of the reasons for his arrest and of any charge against him.

3. Everyone arrested or detained in accordance with the provisions of paragraph 1 (c) of this article shall be brought promptly before a judge or other officer authorised by law to exercise judicial power and shall be entitled to trial within a reasonable time or to release pending trial. Release may be conditioned by guarantees to appear for trial.

4. Everyone who is deprived of his liberty by arrest or detention shall be entitled to take proceedings by which the lawfulness of his detention shall be decided speedily by a court and his release ordered if the detention is not lawful.

5. Everyone who has been the victim of arrest or detention in contravention of the provisions of this article shall have an enforceable right to compensation.

Article 6

1. In the determination of his civil rights and obligations or of any criminal charge against him, everyone is entitled to a fair and public hearing within a reasonable time by an independent and impartial tribunal established by law. Judgment shall be pronounced publicly but the press and public may be excluded from all or part of the trial in the interests of morals, public order or national security in a democratic society, where the interests of juveniles or the protection of the private life of the parties so require, or to the extent strictly necessary in the opinion of the court in special circumstances where publicity would prejudice the interests of justice.

2. Everyone charged with a criminal offence shall be presumed innocent until proved guilty according to law.

3. Everyone charged with a criminal offence has the following minimum rights:

    (a) to be informed promptly, in a language which he understands and in detail, of the nature and cause of the accusation against him;
    (b) to have adequate time and facilities for the preparation of his defence;
    (c) to defend himself in person or through legal assistance of his own choosing or, if he has not sufficient means to pay for legal assistance, to be given it free when the interests of justice so require;
    (d) to examine or have examined witnesses against him and to obtain the attendance and examination of witnesses on his behalf under the same conditions as witnesses against him;
    (e) to have the free assistance of an interpreter if he cannot understand or speak the language used in court.

Article 7

1. No one shall be held guilty of any criminal offence on account of any act or omission which did not constitute a criminal offence under national or international law at the time when it was committed. Nor shall a heavier penalty be imposed than the one that was applicable at the time the criminal offence was committed.

2. This article shall not prejudice the trial and punishment of any person for any act or omission which, at the time when it was committed, was criminal according to the general principles of law recognised by civilised nations.

Article 8

1. Everyone has the right to respect for his private and family life, his home and his correspondence.

2. There shall be no interference by a public authority with the exercise of this right except such as is in accordance with the law and is necessary in a democratic society in the interests of national security, public safety or the economic well-being of the country, for the prevention of disorder or crime, for the protection of health or morals, or for the protection of the rights and freedoms of others.

Article 9

1. Everyone has the right to freedom of thought, conscience and religion; this right includes freedom to change his religion or belief and freedom, either alone or in community with others and in public or private, to manifest his religion or belief, in worship, teaching, practice and observance.

2. Freedom to manifest one's religion or beliefs shall be subject only to such limitations as are prescribed by law and are necessary in a democratic society in the interests of public safety, for the protection of public order, health or morals, or for the protection of the rights and freedoms of others.

Article 10

1. Everyone has the right to freedom of expression. This right shall include freedom to hold opinions and to receive and impart information and ideas without interference by public authority and regardless of frontiers. This article shall not prevent States from requiring the licensing of broadcasting, television or cinema enterprises.

2. The exercise of these freedoms, since it carries with it duties and responsibilities, may be subject to such formalities, conditions, restrictions or penalties as are prescribed by law and are necessary in a democratic society, in the interests of national security, territorial integrity or public safety, for the prevention of disorder or crime, for the protection of health or morals, for the protection of the reputation or rights of others, for preventing the disclosure of information received in confidence, or for maintaining the authority and impartiality of the judiciary.

Article 11

1. Everyone has the right to freedom of peaceful assembly and to freedom of association with others, including the right to form and to join trade unions for the protection of his interests.

2. No restrictions shall be placed on the exercise of these rights other than such as are prescribed by law and are necessary in a democratic society in the interests of national security or public safety, for the prevention of disorder or crime, for the protection of health or morals or for the protection of the rights and freedoms of others. This article shall not prevent the imposition of lawful restrictions on the exercise of these rights by members of the armed forces, of the police or of the administration of the State.

Article 12

Men and women of marriageable age have the right to marry and to found a family, according to the national laws governing the exercise of this right.

Article 13

Everyone whose rights and freedoms as set forth in this Convention are violated shall have an effective remedy before a national authority notwithstanding that the violation has been committed by persons acting in an official capacity.

Article 14

The enjoyment of the rights and freedoms set forth in this Convention shall be secured without discrimination on any ground such as sex, race, colour, language, religion, political or other opinion, national or social origin, association with a national minority, property, birth or other status.

Article 15

1. In time of war or other public emergency threatening the life of the nation any High Contracting Party may take measures derogating from its obligations under this Convention to the extent strictly required by the exigencies of the situation, provided that such measures are not inconsistent with its other obligations under international law.

2. No derogation from Article 2, except in respect of deaths resulting from lawful acts of war, or from Articles 3, 4 (paragraph 1) and 7 shall be made under this provision.

3. Any High Contracting Party availing itself of this right of derogation shall keep the Secretary General of the Council of Europe fully informed of the measures which it has taken and the reasons therefor. It shall also inform the Secretary General of the Council of Europe when such measures have ceased to operate and the provisions of the Convention are again being fully executed.

Article 16

Nothing in Articles 10, 11 and 14 shall be regarded as preventing the High Contracting Parties from imposing restrictions on the political activity of aliens.

Article 17

Nothing in this Convention may be interpreted as implying for any State, group or person any right to engage in any activity or perform any act aimed at the destruction of any of the rights and freedoms set forth herein or at their limitation to a greater extent than is provided for in the Convention.

Article 18

The restrictions permitted under this Convention to the said rights and freedoms shall not be applied for any purpose other than those for which they have been prescribed.

SECTION II

Article 19

To ensure the observance of the engagements undertaken by the High Contracting Parties in the present Convention, there shall be set up:

(a) a European Commission of Human Rights, hereinafter referred to as "the Commission";
(b) a European Court of Human Rights, hereinafter referred to as "the Court".

SECTION III

Article 20.1

1. The Commission shall consist of a number of members equal to that of the High Contracting Parties. No two members of the Commission may be nationals of the same State.

2. The Commission shall sit in plenary session. It may, however, set up Chambers, each composed of at least seven members. The Chambers may examine petitions submitted under Article 25 of this Convention which can be dealt with on the basis of established case law or which raise no serious question affecting the interpretation or application of the Convention. Subject to this restriction and to the provisions of paragraph 5 of this article, the Chambers shall exercise all the powers conferred on the Commission by the Convention. The member of the Commission elected in respect of a High Contracting Party against which a petition has been lodged shall have the right to sit on a Chamber to which the petition has been referred.

3. The Commission may set up committees, each composed of at least three members, with the power, exercisable by a unanimous vote, to declare inadmissible or strike from its list of cases a petition submitted under Article 25, when such a decision can be taken without further examination.

4. A chamber or committee may at any time relinquish jurisdiction in favour of the plenary Commission which may also order the transfer to it of any petition referred to a Chamber or committee.

5. Only the plenary Commission can exercise the following powers:

   (a) the examination of applications submitted under Article 24;
   (b) the bringing of a case before the Court in accordance with Article 48 (a);
   (c) the drawing up of rules of procedure in accordance with Article 36.

Article 21.1

1. The members of the Commission shall be elected by the Committee of Ministers by an absolute majority of votes, from a list of names drawn up by the Bureau of the Consultative Assembly; each group of the Representatives of the High Contracting Parties in the Consultative Assembly shall put forward three candidates, of whom two at least shall be its nationals.

2. As far as applicable, the same procedure shall be followed to complete the Commission in the event of other States subsequently becoming Parties to this Convention, and in filling casual vacancies.

3. The candidates shall be of high moral character and must either possess the qualifications required for appointment to high judicial office or be persons of recognised competence in national or international law.

Article 22.2

1. The members of the Commission shall be elected for a period of six years. They may be re-elected. However, of the members elected at the first election, the terms of seven members shall expire at the end of three years.

2. The members whose terms are to expire at the end of the initial period of three years shall be chosen by lot by the Secretary General of the Council of Europe immediately after the first election has been completed.

3. In order to ensure that, as far as possible, one half of the membership of the Commission shall be renewed every three years, the Committee of Ministers may decide, before proceeding to any subsequent election, that the term or terms of office of one or more members to be elected shall be for a period other than six years but not more than nine and not less than three years.

4. In cases where more than one term of office is involved and the Committee of Ministers applies the preceding paragraph, the allocation of the terms of office shall be effected by the drawing of lots by the Secretary General, immediately after the election.

5. A member of the Commission elected to replace a member whose term of office has not expired shall hold office for the remainder of his predecessor's term.

6. The members of the Commission shall hold office until replaced. After having been replaced, they shall continue to deal with such cases as they already have under consideration.

Article 23.1

The members of the Commission shall sit on the Commission in their individual capacity. During their term of office they shall not hold any position which is incompatible with their independence and impartiality as members of the Commission or the demands of this office.

Article 24

Any High Contracting Party may refer to the Commission, through the Secretary General of the Council of Europe, any alleged breach of the provisions of the Convention by another High Contracting Party.

Article 25

1. The Commission may receive petitions addressed to the Secretary General of the Council of Europe from any person, non-governmental organisation or group of individuals claiming to be the victim of a violation by one of the High Contracting Parties of the rights set forth in this Convention, provided that the High Contracting Party against which the complaint has been lodged has declared that it recognises the competence of the Commission to receive such petitions. Those of the High Contracting Parties who have made such a declaration undertake not to hinder in any way the effective exercise of this right.

2. Such declarations may be made for a specific period.

3. The declarations shall be deposited with the Secretary General of the Council of Europe who shall transmit copies thereof to the High Contracting Parties and publish them.

4. The Commission shall only exercise the powers provided for in this article when at least six High Contracting Parties are bound by declarations made in accordance with the preceding paragraphs.

Article 26

The Commission may only deal with the matter after all domestic remedies have been exhausted, according to the generally recognised rules of international law, and within a period of six months from the date on which the final decision was taken.

Article 27

1. The Commission shall not deal with any petition submitted under Article 25 which:

   (a) is anonymous, or
   (b) is substantially the same as a matter which has already been examined by the Commission or has already been submitted to another

procedure of international investigation or settlement and if it contains no relevant new information.

2. The Commission shall consider inadmissible any petition submitted under Article 25 which it considers incompatible with the provisions of the present Convention, manifestly ill-founded, or an abuse of the right of petition.

3. The Commission shall reject any petition referred to it which it considers inadmissible under Article 26.

Article 28.1

1. In the event of the Commission accepting a petition referred to it:

   (a) it shall, with a view to ascertaining the facts, undertake together with the representatives of the parties an examination of the petition and, if need be, an investigation, for the effective conduct of which the States concerned shall furnish all necessary facilities, after an exchange of views with the Commission;
   (b) it shall at the same time place itself at the disposal of the parties concerned with a view to securing a friendly settlement of the matter on the basis of respect for human rights as defined in this Convention.

2. If the Commission succeeds in effecting a friendly settlement, it shall draw up a report which shall be sent to the States concerned, to the Committee of Ministers and to the Secretary General of the Council of Europe for publication. This report shall be confined to a brief statement of the facts and of the solution reached.

Article 29.3

After it has accepted a petition submitted under Article 25, the Commission may nevertheless decide by a majority of two-thirds of its members to reject the petition if, in the course of its examination, it finds that the existence of one of the grounds for non-acceptance provided for in Article 27 has been established.

In such a case, the decision shall be communicated to the Parties.

Article 30.1

1. The Commission may at any stage of the proceedings decide to strike a petition out of its list of cases where the circumstances lead to the conclusion that:

(a) the applicant does not intend to pursue his petition, or
(b) the matter has been resolved, or
(c) for any other reason established by the Commission, it is no longer justified to continue the examination of the petition. However, the Commission shall continue the examination of a petition if respect for human rights as defined in this Convention so requires.

2. If the Commission decides to strike a petition out of its list after having accepted it, it shall draw up a report which shall contain a statement of the facts and the decision striking out the petition together with the reasons therefor. The report shall be transmitted to the Parties, as well as to the Committee of Ministers for information. The Commission may publish it.

3. The Commission may decide to restore a petition to its list of cases if it considers that the circumstances justify such a course.

Article 31.1

1. If the examination of a petition has not been completed in accordance with Article 28 (paragraph 2), 29 or 30, the Commission shall draw up a report on the facts and state its opinion as to whether the facts found disclose a breach by the State concerned of its obligations under the Convention. The individual opinions of members of the Commission on this point may be stated in the report.

2. The report shall be transmitted to the Committee of Ministers. It shall also be transmitted to the States concerned, who shall not be at liberty to publish it.

3. In transmitting the report to the Committee of Ministers the Commission may make such proposals as it thinks fit.

Article 32

1. If the question is not referred to the Court in accordance with Article 48 of this Convention within a period of three months from the date of the transmission of the report to the Committee of Ministers, the Committee of Ministers shall decide by a majority of two-thirds of the members entitled to sit on the Committee whether there has been a violation of the Convention.

2. In the affirmative case the Committee of Ministers shall prescribe a period during which the High Contracting Party concerned must take the measures required by the decision of the Committee of Ministers.

3. If the High Contracting Party concerned has not taken satisfactory measures within the prescribed period, the Committee of Ministers shall decide by the majority provided for in paragraph 1 above what effect shall be given to its original decision and shall publish the report.

4. The High Contracting Parties undertake to regard as binding on them any decision which the Committee of Ministers may take in application of the preceding paragraphs.

Article 33

The Commission shall meet in camera.

Article 34.1

Subject to the provisions of Articles 20 (paragraph 3) and 29, the Commission shall take its decisions by a majority of the members present and voting.

Article 35

The Commission shall meet as the circumstances require. The meetings shall be convened by the Secretary General of the Council of Europe.

Article 36

The Commission shall draw up its own rules of procedure.

Article 37

The Secretariat of the Commission shall be provided by the Secretary General of the Council of Europe.

SECTION IV

Article 38

The European Court of Human Rights shall consist of a number of judges equal to that of the members of the Council of Europe. No two judges may be nationals of the same State.

Article 39

1. The members of the Court shall be elected by the Consultative Assembly by a majority of the votes cast from a list of persons nominated by the

members of the Council of Europe; each member shall nominate three candidates, of whom two at least shall be its nationals.

2. As far as applicable, the same procedure shall be followed to complete the Court in the event of the admission of new members of the Council of Europe, and in filling casual vacancies.

3. The candidates shall be of high moral character and must either possess the qualifications required for appointment to high judicial office or be jurisconsults of recognised competence.

Article 40.4

1. The members of the Court shall be elected for a period of nine years. They may be re-elected. However, of the members elected at the first election the terms of four members shall expire at the end of three years, and the terms of four more members shall expire at the end of six years.

2. The members whose terms are to expire at the end of the initial periods of three and six years shall be chosen by lot by the Secretary General immediately after the first election has been completed.

3. In order to ensure that, as far as possible, one-third of the membership of the Court shall be renewed every three years, the Consultative Assembly may decide, before proceeding to any subsequent election, that the term or terms of office of one or more members to be elected shall be for a period other than nine years but not more than twelve and not less than six years.

4. In cases where more than one term of office is involved and the Consultative Assembly applies the preceding paragraph, the allocation of the terms of office shall be effected by the drawing of lots by the Secretary General, immediately after the election.

5. A member of the Court elected to replace a member whose term of office has not expired shall hold office for the remainder of his predecessor's term.

6. The members of the Court shall hold office until replaced. After having been replaced, they shall continue to deal with such cases as they already have under consideration.

7. The members of the Court shall sit on the Court in their individual capacity. During their term of office they shall not hold any position which is incompatible with their independence and impartiality as members of the Court or the demands of this office.

Article 41.1

The Court shall elect its President and one or two Vice-Presidents for a period of three years. They may be re-elected.

Article 42

The members of the Court shall receive for each day of duty a compensation to be determined by the Committee of Ministers.

Article 43.1

For the consideration of each case brought before it the Court shall consist of a Chamber composed of nine judges. There shall sit as an ex officio member of the Chamber the judge who is a national of any State party concerned, or, if there is none, a person of its choice who shall sit in the capacity of judge; the names of the other judges shall be chosen by lot by the President before the opening of the case.

Article 44

Only the High Contracting Parties and the Commission shall have the right to bring a case before the Court.

Article 45

The jurisdiction of the Court shall extend to all cases concerning the interpretation and application of the present Convention which the High Contracting Parties or the Commission shall refer to it in accordance with Article 48.

Article 46

1. Any of the High Contracting Parties may at any time declare that it recognises as compulsory ipso facto and without special agreement the jurisdiction of the Court in all matters concerning the interpretation and application of the present Convention.

2. The declarations referred to above may be made unconditionally or on condition of reciprocity on the part of several or certain other High Contracting Parties or for a specified period.

3. These declarations shall be deposited with the Secretary General of the Council of Europe who shall transmit copies thereof to the High Contracting Parties.

Article 47

The Court may only deal with a case after the Commission has acknowledged the failure of efforts for a friendly settlement and within the period of three months provided for in Article 32.

Article 48

The following may bring a case before the Court, provided that the High Contracting Party concerned, if there is only one, or the High Contracting Parties concerned, if there is more than one, are subject to the compulsory jurisdiction of the Court or, failing that, with the consent of the High Contracting Party concerned, if there is only one, or of the High Contracting Parties concerned if there is more than one:

(a) the Commission;
(b) a High Contracting Party whose national is alleged to be a victim;
(c) a High Contracting Party which referred the case to the Commission;
(d) a High Contracting Party against which the complaint has been lodged.

Article 49

In the event of dispute as to whether the Court has jurisdiction, the matter shall be settled by the decision of the Court.

Article 50

If the Court finds that a decision or a measure taken by a legal authority or any other authority of a High Contracting Party is completely or partially in conflict with the obligations arising from the present Convention, and if the internal law of the said Party allows only partial reparation to be made for the consequences of this decision or measure, the decision of the Court shall, if necessary, afford just satisfaction to the injured party.

Article 51

1. Reasons shall be given for the judgment of the Court.

2. If the judgment does not represent in whole or in part the unanimous opinion of the judges, any judge shall be entitled to deliver a separate opinion.

Article 52

The judgment of the Court shall be final.

Article 53

The High Contracting Parties undertake to abide by the decision of the Court in any case to which they are Parties.

Article 54

The judgment of the Court shall be transmitted to the Committee of Ministers which shall supervise its execution.

Article 55

The Court shall draw up its own rules and shall determine its own procedure.

Article 56

1. The first election of the members of the Court shall take place after the declarations by the High Contracting Parties mentioned in Article 46 have reached a total of eight.

2. No case can be brought before the Court before this election.

SECTION V

Article 57

On receipt of a request from the Secretary General of the Council of Europe any High Contracting Party shall furnish an explanation of the manner in which its internal law ensures the effective implementation of any of the provisions of the Convention.

Article 58

The expenses of the Commission and the Court shall be borne by the Council of Europe.

Article 59

The members of the Commission and of the Court shall be entitled, during the discharge of their functions, to the privileges and immunities provided for in Article 40 of the Statute of the Council of Europe and in the agreements made there under.

Article 60

Nothing in this Convention shall be construed as limiting or derogating from any of the human rights and fundamental freedoms which may be ensured under the laws of any High Contracting Party or under any other agreement to which it is a Party.

Article 61

Nothing in this Convention shall prejudice the powers conferred on the Committee of Ministers by the Statute of the Council of Europe.

Article 62

The High Contracting Parties agree that, except by special agreement, they will not avail themselves of treaties, conventions or declarations in force between them for the purpose of submitting, by way of petition, a dispute arising out of the interpretation or application of this Convention to a means of settlement other than those provided for in this Convention.

Article 63

1. Any State may at the time of its ratification or at any time thereafter declare by notification addressed to the Secretary General of the Council of Europe that the present Convention shall extend to all or any of the territories for whose international relations it is responsible.

2. The Convention shall extend to the territory or territories named in the notification as from the thirtieth day after the receipt of this notification by the Secretary General of the Council of Europe.

3. The provisions of this Convention shall be applied in such territories with due regard, however, to local requirements.

4. Any State which has made a declaration in accordance with paragraph 1 of this article may at any time thereafter declare on behalf of one or more of the territories to which the declaration relates that it accepts the competence of the Commission to receive petitions from individuals, non governmental organisations or groups of individuals in accordance with Article 25 of the present Convention.

Article 64

1. Any State may, when signing this Convention or when depositing its instrument of ratification, make a reservation in respect of any particular provision of the Convention to the extent that any law then in force in its territory is not in conformity with the provision. Reservations of a general character shall not be permitted under this article.

2. Any reservation made under this article shall contain a brief statement of the law concerned.

Article 65

1. A High Contracting Party may denounce the present Convention only after the expiry of five years from the date on which it became a party to it and after six months' notice contained in a notification addressed to the Secretary General of the Council of Europe, who shall inform the other High Contracting Parties.

2. Such a denunciation shall not have the effect of releasing the High Contracting Party concerned from its obligations under this Convention in respect of any act which, being capable of constituting a violation of such obligations, may have been performed by it before the date at which the denunciation became effective.

3. Any High Contracting Party which shall cease to be a member of the Council of Europe shall cease to be a Party to this Convention under the same conditions.

4. The Convention may be denounced in accordance with the provisions of the preceding paragraphs in respect of any territory to which it has been declared to extend under the terms of Article 63.

Article 66

1. This Convention shall be open to the signature of the members of the Council of Europe. It shall be ratified. Ratifications shall be deposited with the Secretary General of the Council of Europe.

2. The present Convention shall come into force after the deposit of ten instruments of ratification.

3. As regards any signatory ratifying subsequently, the Convention shall come into force at the date of the deposit of its instrument of ratification.

4. The Secretary General of the Council of Europe shall notify all the members of the Council of Europe of the entry into force of the Convention, the names of the High Contracting Parties who have ratified it, and the deposit of all instruments of ratification which may be effected subsequently. Done at Rome this 4th day of November 1950, in English and French, both texts being equally authentic, in a single copy which shall remain deposited in the archives of the Council of Europe. The Secretary General shall transmit certified copies to each of the signatories.

Council of Europe Protocol No.2 to the Convention for the Protection of Human Rights and Fundamental Freedoms, conferring upon the European Court of Human Rights Competence to give Advisory Opinions (1963)[1]

PREAMBLE

The member States of the Council of Europe signatory hereto,

Having regard to the provisions of the Convention for the Protection of Human Rights and Fundamental Freedoms signed at Rome on 4th November 1950 (hereinafter referred to as "the Convention") and, in particular, Article 19 instituting, among other bodies, a European Court of Human Rights (hereinafter referred to as "the Court");

Considering that it is expedient to confer upon the Court competence to give advisory opinions subject to certain conditions,

Have agreed as follows:

ARTICLE 1

1. The Court may, at the request of the Committee of Ministers, give advisory opinions on legal questions concerning the interpretation of the Convention and the Protocols thereto.

2. Such opinions shall not deal with any question relating to the content or scope of the rights or freedoms defined in Section 1 of the Convention and in the Protocols thereto, or with any other question which the Commission, the Court or the Committee of Ministers might have to consider in consequence of any such proceedings as could be instituted in accordance with the Convention.

1. Adopted in Strasbourg on 6 May 1963.

3. Decisions of the Committee of Ministers to request an advisory opinion of the Court shall require a two-thirds majority vote of the representatives entitled to sit on the Committee.

Article 2

The Court shall decide whether a request for an advisory opinion submitted by the Committee of Ministers is within its consultative competence as defined in Article 1 of this Protocol.

Article 3

1. For the consideration of requests for an advisory opinion, the Court shall sit in plenary session.

2. Reasons shall be given for advisory opinions of the Court.

3. If the advisory opinion does not represent in whole or in part the unanimous opinion of the judges, any judge shall be entitled to deliver a separate opinion.

4. Advisory opinions of the Court shall be communicated to the Committee of Ministers.

Article 4

The powers of the Court under Article 55 of the Convention shall extend to the drawing up of such rules and the determination of such procedure as the Court may think necessary for the purposes of this Protocol.

Article 5

1. This Protocol shall be open to signature by member States of the Council of Europe, signatories to the Convention, who may become Parties to it by:

   (a) signature without reservation in respect of ratification or acceptance;
   (b) signature with reservation in respect of ratification or acceptance, followed by ratification or acceptance.

   Instruments of ratification or acceptance shall be deposited with the Secretary General of the Council of Europe.

2. This Protocol shall enter into force as soon as all States Parties to the Convention shall have become Parties to the Protocol, in accordance with the provisions of paragraph 1 of this Article.

3. From the date of the entry into force of this Protocol, Articles 1 to 4 shall be considered an integral part of the Convention.

4. The Secretary General of the Council of Europe shall notify the member States of the Council of:

    (a) any signature without reservation in respect of ratification or acceptance;
    (b) any signature with reservation in respect of ratification or acceptance;
    (c) the deposit of any instrument of ratification or acceptance;
    (d) the date of entry into force of this Protocol in accordance with paragraph 2 of this Article.

In witness whereof, the undersigned, being duly authorised thereto, have signed this Protocol.

Done at Strasbourg, this 6th day of May 1963, in English and in French, both texts being equally authoritative, in a single copy which shall remain deposited in the archives of the Council of Europe. The Secretary General shall transmit certified copies to each of the signatory States.

Council of Europe European Social Charter (Revised 1996 version)[1]

Preamble

The governments signatory hereto, being members of the Council of Europe,

Considering that the aim of the Council of Europe is the achievement of greater unity between its members for the purpose of safeguarding and realising the ideals and principles which are their common heritage and of facilitating their economic and social progress, in particular by the maintenance and further realisation of human rights and fundamental freedoms;

Considering that in the European Convention for the Protection of Human Rights and Fundamental Freedoms signed at Rome on 4 November 1950, and the Protocols thereto, the member States of the Council of Europe agreed to secure to their populations the civil and political rights and freedoms therein specified;

Considering that in the European Social Charter opened for signature in Turin on 18 October 1961 and the Protocols thereto, the member States of the Council of Europe agreed to secure to their populations the social rights specified therein in order to improve their standard of living and their social well-being;

Recalling that the Ministerial Conference on Human Rights held in Rome on 5 November 1990 stressed the need, on the one hand, to preserve the indivisible nature of all human rights, be they civil, political, economic, social or cultural and, on the other hand, to give the European Social Charter fresh impetus;

Resolved, as was decided during the Ministerial Conference held in Turin on 21 and 22 October 1991, to update and adapt the substantive contents of the Charter in order to take account in particular of the funda-mental social changes which have occurred since the text was adopted;

Recognising the advantage of embodying in a Revised Charter, designed progressively to take the place of the European Social Charter, the rights guaranteed by the Charter as amended, the rights guaranteed by the Additional Protocol of 1988 and to add new rights,

Have agreed as follows:

1. Adopted in Geneva on 18 June 1998, at the 86th Session of the International Labour Conference.

PART I

The Parties accept as the aim of their policy, to be pursued by all appropriate means both national and international in character, the attainment of conditions in which the following rights and principles may be effectively realised:

1. Everyone shall have the opportunity to earn his living in an occupation freely entered upon.

2. All workers have the right to just conditions of work.

3. All workers have the right to safe and healthy working conditions.

4. All workers have the right to a fair remuneration sufficient for a decent standard of living for themselves and their families.

5. All workers and employers have the right to freedom of association in national or international organisations for the protection of their economic and social interests.

6. All workers and employers have the right to bargain collectively.

7. Children and young persons have the right to a special protection against the physical and moral hazards to which they are exposed.

8. Employed women, in case of maternity, have the right to a special protection.

9. Everyone has the right to appropriate facilities for vocational guidance with a view to helping him choose an occupation suited to his personal aptitude and interests.

10. Everyone has the right to appropriate facilities for vocational training.

11. Everyone has the right to benefit from any measures enabling him to enjoy the highest possible standard of health attainable.

12. All workers and their dependents have the right to social security.

13. Anyone without adequate resources has the right to social and medical assistance.

14. Everyone has the right to benefit from social welfare services.

15. Disabled persons have the right to independence, social integration and participation in the life of the community.

16. The family as a fundamental unit of society has the right to appropriate social, legal and economic protection to ensure its full development.

17. Children and young persons have the right to appropriate social, legal and economic protection.

18. The nationals of any one of the Parties have the right to engage in any gainful occupation in the territory of any one of the others on a footing of equality with the nationals of the latter, subject to restrictions based on cogent economic or social reasons.

19. Migrant workers who are nationals of a Party and their families have the right to protection and assistance in the territory of any other Party.

20. All workers have the right to equal opportunities and equal treatment in matters of employment and occupation without discrimination on the grounds of sex.

21. Workers have the right to be informed and to be consulted within the undertaking.

22. Workers have the right to take part in the determination and improvement of the working conditions and working environment in the undertaking.

23. Every elderly person has the right to social protection.

24. All workers have the right to protection in cases of termination of employment.

25. All workers have the right to protection of their claims in the event of the insolvency of their employer.

26. All workers have the right to dignity at work.

27. All persons with family responsibilities and who are engaged or wish to engage in employment have a right to do so without being subject to discrimination and as far as possible without conflict between their employment and family responsibilities.

28. Workers' representatives in undertakings have the right to protection against acts prejudicial to them and should be afforded appropriate facilities to carry out their functions.

29. All workers have the right to be informed and consulted in collective redundancy procedures.

30. Everyone has the right to protection against poverty and social exclusion.

31. Everyone has the right to housing.

PART II

The Parties undertake, as provided for in Part III, to consider themselves bound by the obligations laid down in the following articles and paragraphs.

Article 1 - The right to work

With a view to ensuring the effective exercise of the right to work, the Parties undertake:

1. to accept as one of their primary aims and responsibilities the achievement and maintenance of as high and stable a level of employment as possible, with a view to the attainment of full employment;

2. to protect effectively the right of the worker to earn his living in an occupation freely entered upon;

3. to establish or maintain free employment services for all workers;

4. to provide or promote appropriate vocational guidance, training and rehabilitation.

Article 2 - The right to just conditions of work

With a view to ensuring the effective exercise of the right to just conditions of work, the Parties undertake:

1. to provide for reasonable daily and weekly working hours, the working week to be progressively reduced to the extent that the increase of productivity and other relevant factors permit;

2. to provide for public holidays with pay;

3. to provide for a minimum of four weeks' annual holiday with pay;

4. to eliminate risks in inherently dangerous or unhealthy occupations, and where it has not yet been possible to eliminate or reduce sufficiently these risks, to provide for either a reduction of working hours or additional paid holidays for workers engaged in such occupations;

5. to ensure a weekly rest period which shall, as far as possible, coincide with the day recognised by tradition or custom in the country or region concerned as a day of rest;

6. to ensure that workers are informed in written form, as soon as possible, and in any event not later than two months after the date of commencing their employment, of the essential aspects of the contract or employment relationship;

7. to ensure that workers performing night work benefit from measures which take account of the special nature of the work.

ARTICLE 3 - THE RIGHT TO SAFE AND HEALTHY WORKING CONDITIONS

With a view to ensuring the effective exercise of the right to safe and healthy working conditions, the Parties undertake, in consultation with employers' and workers' organisations:

1. to formulate, implement and periodically review a coherent national policy on occupational safety, occupational health and the working environment. The primary aim of this policy shall be to improve occupational safety and health and to prevent accidents and injury to health arising out of, linked with or occurring in the course of work, particularly by minimising the causes of hazards inherent in the working environment;

2. to issue safety and health regulations;

3. to provide for the enforcement of such regulations by measures of supervision;

4. to promote the progressive development of occupational health services for all workers with essentially preventive and advisory functions.

Article 4 - The right to a fair remuneration

With a view to ensuring the effective exercise of the right to a fair remuneration, the Parties undertake:

1. to recognise the right of workers to a remuneration such as will give them and their families a decent standard of living;

2. to recognise the right of workers to an increased rate of remuneration for overtime work, subject to exceptions in particular cases;

3. to recognise the right of men and women workers to equal pay for work of equal value;

4. to recognise the right of all workers to a reasonable period of notice for termination of employment;

5. to permit deductions from wages only under conditions and to the extent prescribed by national laws or regulations or fixed by collective agreements or arbitration awards.

The exercise of these rights shall be achieved by freely concluded collective agreements, by statutory wage-fixing machinery, or by other means appropriate to national conditions.

Article 5 - The right to organise

With a view to ensuring or promoting the freedom of workers and employers to form local, national or international organisations for the protection of their economic and social interests and to join those organisations, the Parties undertake that national law shall not be such as to impair, nor shall it be so applied as to impair, this freedom. The extent to which the guarantees provided for in this article shall apply to the police shall be determined by national laws or regulations. The principle governing the application to the members of the armed forces of these guarantees and the extent to which they shall apply to persons in this category shall equally be determined by national laws or regulations.

Article 6 - The right to bargain collectively

With a view to ensuring the effective exercise of the right to bargain collectively, the Parties undertake:

1. to promote joint consultation between workers and employers;

2. to promote, where necessary and appropriate, machinery for voluntary negotiations between employers or employers' organisations and workers' organisations, with a view to the regulation of terms and conditions of employment by means of collective agreements;

3. to promote the establishment and use of appropriate machinery for conciliation and voluntary arbitration for the settlement of labour disputes; and recognise:

4. the right of workers and employers to collective action in cases of conflicts of interest, including the right to strike, subject to obligations that might arise out of collective agreements previously entered into.

Article 7 - The right of children and young persons to protection

With a view to ensuring the effective exercise of the right of children and young persons to protection, the Parties undertake:

1. to provide that the minimum age of admission to employment shall be 15 years, subject to exceptions for children employed in prescribed light work without harm to their health, morals or education;

2. to provide that the minimum age of admission to employment shall be 18 years with respect to prescribed occupations regarded as dangerous or unhealthy;

3. to provide that persons who are still subject to compulsory education shall not be employed in such work as would deprive them of the full benefit of their education;

4. to provide that the working hours of persons under 18 years of age shall be limited in accordance with the needs of their development, and particularly with their need for vocational training;

5. to recognise the right of young workers and apprentices to a fair wage or other appropriate allowances;

6. to provide that the time spent by young persons in vocational training during the normal working hours with the consent of the employer shall be treated as forming part of the working day;

7. to provide that employed persons of under 18 years of age shall be entitled to a minimum of four weeks' annual holiday with pay;

8. to provide that persons under 18 years of age shall not be employed in night work with the exception of certain occupations provided for by national laws or regulations;

9. to provide that persons under 18 years of age employed in occupations prescribed by national laws or regulations shall be subject to regular medical control;

10. to ensure special protection against physical and moral dangers to which children and young persons are exposed, and particularly against those resulting directly or indirectly from their work.

Article 8 - The right of employed women to protection of maternity

With a view to ensuring the effective exercise of the right of employed women to the protection of maternity, the Parties undertake:

1. to provide either by paid leave, by adequate social security benefits or by benefits from public funds for employed women to take leave before and after childbirth up to a total of at least fourteen weeks;

2. to consider it as unlawful for an employer to give a woman notice of dismissal during the period from the time she notifies her employer that she is pregnant until the end of her maternity leave, or to give her notice of dismissal at such a time that the notice would expire during such a period;

3. to provide that mothers who are nursing their infants shall be entitled to sufficient time off for this purpose;

4. to regulate the employment in night work of pregnant women, women who have recently given birth and women nursing their infants;

5. to prohibit the employment of pregnant women, women who have recently given birth or who are nursing their infants in underground mining and all other work which is unsuitable by reason of its dangerous, unhealthy or arduous nature and to take appropriate measures to protect the employment rights of these women.

Article 9 - The right to vocational guidance

With a view to ensuring the effective exercise of the right to vocational guidance, the Parties undertake to provide or promote, as necessary, a service which will assist all persons, including the handicapped, to solve problems related to occupational choice and progress, with due regard to the individual's characteristics and their relation to occupational opportunity: this assistance should be available free of charge, both to young persons, including schoolchildren, and to adults.

Article 10 - The right to vocational training

With a view to ensuring the effective exercise of the right to vocational training, the Parties undertake:

1. to provide or promote, as necessary, the technical and vocational training of all persons, including the handicapped, in consultation with employers' and workers' organisations, and to grant facilities for access to higher technical and university education, based solely on individual aptitude;

2. to provide or promote a system of apprenticeship and other systematic arrangements for training young boys and girls in their various employments;

3. to provide or promote, as necessary:

   (a) adequate and readily available training facilities for adult workers;
   (b) special facilities for the retraining of adult workers needed as a result of technological development or new trends in employment;

4. to provide or promote, as necessary, special measures for the retraining and reintegration of the long-term unemployed;

5. to encourage the full utilisation of the facilities provided by appropriate measures such as:

   (a) reducing or abolishing any fees or charges;
   (b) granting financial assistance in appropriate cases;
   (c) including in the normal working hours time spent on supplementary training taken by the worker, at the request of his employer, during employment;

(d) ensuring, through adequate supervision, in consultation with the employers' and workers' organisations, the efficiency of apprenticeship and other training arrangements for young workers, and the adequate protection of young workers generally.

Article 11 - The right to protection of health

With a view to ensuring the effective exercise of the right to protection of health, the Parties undertake, either directly or in co-operation with public or private organisations, to take appropriate measures designed inter alia:

1. to remove as far as possible the causes of ill-health;

2. to provide advisory and educational facilities for the promotion of health and the encouragement of individual responsibility in matters of health;

3. to prevent as far as possible epidemic, endemic and other diseases, as well as accidents.

Article 12 - The right to social security

With a view to ensuring the effective exercise of the right to social security, the Parties undertake:

1. to establish or maintain a system of social security;

2. to maintain the social security system at a satisfactory level at least equal to that necessary for the ratification of the European Code of Social Security;

3. to endeavour to raise progressively the system of social security to a higher level;

4. to take steps, by the conclusion of appropriate bilateral and multilateral agreements or by other means, and subject to the conditions laid down in such agreements, in order to ensure:

   (a) equal treatment with their own nationals of the nationals of other Parties in respect of social security rights, including the retention of benefits arising out of social security legislation, whatever movements the persons protected may undertake between the territories of the Parties;

(b) the granting, maintenance and resumption of social security rights by such means as the accumulation of insurance or employment periods completed under the legislation of each of the Parties.

Article 13 - The right to social and medical assistance

With a view to ensuring the effective exercise of the right to social and medical assistance, the Parties undertake:

1. to ensure that any person who is without adequate resources and who is unable to secure such resources either by his own efforts or from other sources, in particular by benefits under a social security scheme, be granted adequate assistance, and, in case of sickness, the care necessitated by his condition;

2. to ensure that persons receiving such assistance shall not, for that reason, suffer from a diminution of their political or social rights;

3. to provide that everyone may receive by appropriate public or private services such advice and personal help as may be required to prevent, to remove, or to alleviate personal or family want;

4. to apply the provisions referred to in paragraphs 1, 2 and 3 of this article on an equal footing with their nationals to nationals of other Parties lawfully within their territories, in accordance with their obligations under the European Convention on Social and Medical Assistance, signed at Paris on 11 December 1953.

Article 14 - The right to benefit from social welfare services

With a view to ensuring the effective exercise of the right to benefit from social welfare services, the Parties undertake:

1. to promote or provide services which, by using methods of social work, would contribute to the welfare and development of both individuals and groups in the community, and to their adjustment to the social environment;

2. to encourage the participation of individuals and voluntary or other organisations in the establishment and maintenance of such services.

Article 15 - The right of persons with disabilities to independence, social integration and participation in the life of the community

With a view to ensuring to persons with disabilities, irrespective of age and the nature and origin of their disabilities, the effective exercise of the right to independence, social integration and participation in the life of the community, the Parties undertake, in particular:

1. to take the necessary measures to provide persons with disabilities with guidance, education and vocational training in the framework of general schemes wherever possible or, where this is not possible, through specialised bodies, public or private;

2. to promote their access to employment through all measures tending to encourage employers to hire and keep in employment persons with disabilities in the ordinary working environment and to adjust the working conditions to the needs of the disabled or, where this is not possible by reason of the disability, by arranging for or creating sheltered employment according to the level of disability. In certain cases, such measures may require recourse to specialised placement and support services;

3. to promote their full social integration and participation in the life of the community in particular through measures, including technical aids, aiming to overcome barriers to communication and mobility and enabling access to transport, housing, cultural activities and leisure.

Article 16 - The right of the family to social, legal and economic protection

With a view to ensuring the necessary conditions for the full development of the family, which is a fundamental unit of society, the Parties undertake to promote the economic, legal and social protection of family life by such means as social and family benefits, fiscal arrangements, provision of family housing, benefits for the newly married and other appropriate means.

Article 17 - The right of children and young persons to social, legal and economic protection

With a view to ensuring the effective exercise of the right of children and young persons to grow up in an environment which encourages the full development of their personality and of their physical and mental capacities, the Parties undertake, either directly or in co-operation with public and private organisations, to take all appropriate and necessary measures designed:

1. (a) to ensure that children and young persons, taking account of the rights and duties of their parents, have the care, the assistance, the education and the training they need, in particular by providing for the establishment or maintenance of institutions and services sufficient and adequate for this purpose;
   (b) to protect children and young persons against negligence, violence or exploitation;
   (c) to provide protection and special aid from the state for children and young persons temporarily or definitively deprived of their family's support;

2. to provide to children and young persons a free primary and secondary education as well as to encourage regular attendance at schools.

Article 18 - The right to engage in a gainful occupation in the territory of other Parties

With a view to ensuring the effective exercise of the right to engage in a gainful occupation in the territory of any other Party, the Parties undertake:

1. to apply existing regulations in a spirit of liberality;

2. to simplify existing formalities and to reduce or abolish chancery dues and other charges payable by foreign workers or their employers;

3. to liberalise, individually or collectively, regulations governing the employment of foreign workers; and recognise:

4. the right of their nationals to leave the country to engage in a gainful occupation in the territories of the other Parties.

Article 19 - The right of migrant workers and their families to protection and assistance

With a view to ensuring the effective exercise of the right of migrant workers and their families to protection and assistance in the territory of any other Party, the Parties undertake:

1. to maintain or to satisfy themselves that there are maintained adequate and free services to assist such workers, particularly in obtaining accurate

information, and to take all appropriate steps, so far as national laws and regulations permit, against misleading propaganda relating to emigration and immigration;

2. to adopt appropriate measures within their own jurisdiction to facilitate the departure, journey and reception of such workers and their families, and to provide, within their own jurisdiction, appropriate services for health, medical attention and good hygienic conditions during the journey;

3. to promote co-operation, as appropriate, between social services, public and private, in emigration and immigration countries;

4. to secure for such workers lawfully within their territories, insofar as such matters are regulated by law or regulations or are subject to the control of administrative authorities, treatment not less favourable than that of their own nationals in respect of the following matters:

   (a) remuneration and other employment and working conditions;
   (b) membership of trade unions and enjoyment of the benefits of collective bargaining;
   (c) accommodation;

5. to secure for such workers lawfully within their territories treatment not less favourable than that of their own nationals with regard to employment taxes, dues or contributions payable in respect of employed persons;

6. to facilitate as far as possible the reunion of the family of a foreign worker permitted to establish himself in the territory;

7. to secure for such workers lawfully within their territories treatment not less relating to matters referred to in this article;

8. interest or morality;

9. to permit, within legal limits, the transfer of such parts of the earnings and savings of such workers as they may desire;

10. employed migrants insofar as such measures apply;

11. to promote and facilitate the teaching of the national language of the receiving members of their families;

12. worker's mother tongue to the children of the migrant worker.

Article 20 - The right to equal opportunities and equal treatment in matters of employment and occupation without discrimination on the grounds of sex

With a view to ensuring the effective exercise of the right to equal opportunities and equal treatment in matters of employment and occupation without discrimination on the grounds of sex, the Parties undertake to recognise that right and to take appropriate measures to ensure or promote its application in the following fields:

(a) access to employment, protection against dismissal and occupational reintegration;
(b) vocational guidance, training, retraining and rehabilitation;
(c) terms of employment and working conditions, including remuneration;
(d) career development, including promotion.

Article 21 - The right to information and consultation

With a view to ensuring the effective exercise of the right of workers to be informed and consulted within the undertaking, the Parties undertake to adopt or encourage measures enabling workers or their representatives, in accordance with national legislation and practice:

(a) to be informed regularly or at the appropriate time and in a comprehensible way about the economic and financial situation of the undertaking employing them, on the understanding that the disclosure of certain information which could be prejudicial to the undertaking may be refused or subject to confidentiality; and
(b) to be consulted in good time on proposed decisions which could substantially affect the interests of workers, particularly on those decisions which could have an important impact on the employment situation in the undertaking.

Article 22 - The right to take part in the determination and improvement of the working conditions and working environment

With a view to ensuring the effective exercise of the right of workers to take part in the determination and improvement of the working conditions and working environment in the undertaking, the Parties undertake to adopt or encourage measures enabling workers or their representatives, in accordance with national legislation and practice, to contribute:

(a) to the determination and the improvement of the working conditions, work organisation and working environment;

(b) to the protection of health and safety within the undertaking;
(c) to the organisation of social and socio-cultural services and facilities within the undertaking;
(d) to the supervision of the observance of regulations on these matters.

Article 23 - The right of elderly persons to social protection

With a view to ensuring the effective exercise of the right of elderly persons to social protection, the Parties undertake to adopt or encourage, either directly or in co-operation with public or private organisations, appropriate measures designed in particular:

- to enable elderly persons to remain full members of society for as long as possible, by means of:
  (a) adequate resources enabling them to lead a decent life and play an active part in public, social and cultural life;
  (b) provision of information about services and facilities available for elderly persons and their opportunities to make use of them;

- to enable elderly persons to choose their life-style freely and to lead independent lives in their familiar surroundings for as long as they wish and are able, by means of:
  (a) provision of housing suited to their needs and their state of health or of adequate support for adapting their housing;
  (b) the health care and the services necessitated by their state;

- to guarantee elderly persons living in institutions appropriate support, while respecting their privacy, and participation in decisions concerning living conditions in the institution.

Article 24 - The right to protection in cases of termination of employment

With a view to ensuring the effective exercise of the right of workers to protection in cases of termination of employment, the Parties undertake to recognise:

(a) the right of all workers not to have their employment terminated without valid reasons for such termination connected with their capacity or conduct or based on the operational requirements of the undertaking, establishment or service;

(b) the right of workers whose employment is terminated without a valid reason to adequate compensation or other appropriate relief.

To this end the Parties undertake to ensure that a worker who considers that his employment has been terminated without a valid reason shall have the right to appeal to an impartial body.

Article 25 - The right of workers to the protection of their claims in the event of the insolvency of their employer

With a view to ensuring the effective exercise of the right of workers to the protection of their claims in the event of the insolvency of their employer, the Parties undertake to provide that workers' claims arising from contracts of employment or employment relationships be guaranteed by a guarantee institution or by any other effective form of protection.

Article 26 - The right to dignity at work

With a view to ensuring the effective exercise of the right of all workers to protection of their dignity at work, the Parties undertake, in consultation with employers' and workers' organisations:

1. to promote awareness, information and prevention of sexual harassment in the workplace or in relation to work and to take all appropriate measures to protect workers from such conduct;

2. to promote awareness, information and prevention of recurrent reprehensible or distinctly negative and offensive actions directed against individual workers in the workplace or in relation to work and to take all appropriate measures to protect workers from such conduct.

Article 27 - The right of workers with family responsibilities to equal opportunities and equal treatment

With a view to ensuring the exercise of the right to equality of opportunity and treatment for men and women workers with family responsibilities and between such workers and other workers, the Parties undertake:

1. to take appropriate measures:

   (a) to enable workers with family responsibilities to enter and remain in employment, as well as to re-enter employment after an absence due to those responsibilities, including measures in the field of vocational guidance and training;

(b) to take account of their needs in terms of conditions of employment and social security;
(c) to develop or promote services, public or private, in particular child daycare services and other childcare arrangements;

2. to provide a possibility for either parent to obtain, during a period after maternity leave, parental leave to take care of a child, the duration and conditions of which should be determined by national legislation, collective agreements or practice;

3. to ensure that family responsibilities shall not, as such, constitute a valid reason for termination of employment.

Article 28 - The right of workers' representatives to protection in the undertaking and facilities to be accorded to them

With a view to ensuring the effective exercise of the right of workers' representatives to carry out their functions, the Parties undertake to ensure that in the undertaking:

(a) they enjoy effective protection against acts prejudicial to them, including dismissal, based on their status or activities as workers' representatives within the undertaking;
(b) they are afforded such facilities as may be appropriate in order to enable them to carry out their functions promptly and efficiently, account being taken of the industrial relations system of the country and the needs, size and capabilities of the undertaking concerned.

Article 29 - The right to information and consultation in collective redundancy procedures

With a view to ensuring the effective exercise of the right of workers to be informed and consulted in situations of collective redundancies, the Parties undertake to ensure that employers shall inform and consult workers' representatives, in good time prior to such collective redundancies, on ways and means of avoiding collective redundancies or limiting their occurrence and mitigating their consequences, for example by recourse to accompanying social measures aimed, in particular, at aid for the redeployment or retraining of the workers concerned.

Article 30 - The right to protection against poverty and social exclusion

With a view to ensuring the effective exercise of the right to protection against poverty and social exclusion, the Parties undertake:

(a) to take measures within the framework of an overall and co-ordinated approach to promote the effective access of persons who live or risk living in a situation of social exclusion or poverty, as well as their families, to, in particular, employment, housing, training, education, culture and social and medical assistance;
(b) to review these measures with a view to their adaptation if necessary.

Article 31 - The right to housing

With a view to ensuring the effective exercise of the right to housing, the Parties undertake to take measures designed:

1. to promote access to housing of an adequate standard;

2. to prevent and reduce homelessness with a view to its gradual elimination;

3. to make the price of housing accessible to those without adequate resources.

PART III

Article A - Undertakings

1. Subject to the provisions of Article B below, each of the Parties undertakes:

    (a) to consider Part I of this Charter as a declaration of the aims which it will pursue by all appropriate means, as stated in the introductory paragraph of that part;
    (b) to consider itself bound by at least six of the following nine articles of Part II of this Charter: Articles 1, 5, 6, 7, 12, 13, 16, 19 and 20;
    (c) to consider itself bound by an additional number of articles or numbered paragraphs of Part II of the Charter which it may select, provided that the total number of articles or numbered paragraph by which it is bound is not less than sixteen articles or sixty-three numbered paragraphs.

2. The articles or paragraphs selected in accordance with sub-paragraphs b and c of paragraph 1 of this article shall be notified to the Secretary General of the Council of Europe at the time when the instrument of ratification acceptance or approval is deposited.

3. Any Party may, at a later date, declare by notification addressed to the Secretary General that it considers itself bound by any articles or any numbered paragraphs of Part II of the Charter which it has not already accepted under the terms of paragraph 1 of this article. Such undertakings subsequently given shall be deemed to be an integral part of the ratification, acceptance or approval and shall have the same effect as from the first day of the month following the expiration of a period of one month after the date of the notification.

4. Each Party shall maintain a system of labour inspection appropriate to national conditions.

Article B - Links with the European Social Charter and the 1988 Additional Protocol

No Contracting Party to the European Social Charter or Party to the Additional Protocol of 5 May 1988 may ratify, accept or approve this Charter without considering itself bound by at least the provisions corresponding to the provisions of the European Social Charter and, where appropriate, of the Additional Protocol, to which it was bound.

Acceptance of the obligations of any provision of this Charter shall, from the date of entry into force of those obligations for the Party concerned, result in the corresponding provision of the European Social Charter and, where appropriate, of its Additional Protocol of 1988 ceasing to apply to the Party concerned in the event of that Party being bound by the first of those instruments or by both instruments.

PART IV

Article C - Supervision of the implementation of the undertakings contained in this Charter

The implementation of the legal obligations contained in this Charter shall be submitted to the same supervision as the European Social Charter.

Article D - Collective complaints

1. The provisions of the Additional Protocol to the European Social Charter providing for a system of collective complaints shall apply to the undertakings given in this Charter for the States which have ratified the said Protocol.

2. Any State which is not bound by the Additional Protocol to the European Social Charter providing for a system of collective complaints may when depositing its instrument of ratification, acceptance or approval of this Charter or at any time thereafter, declare by notification addressed to the Secretary General of the Council of Europe, that it accepts the supervision of its obligations under this Charter following the procedure provided for in the said Protocol.

PART V

Article E - Non-discrimination

The enjoyment of the rights set forth in this Charter shall be secured without discrimination on any ground such as race, colour, sex, language, religion, political or other opinion, national extraction or social origin, health, association with a national minority, birth or other status.

Article F - Derogations in time of war or public emergency

1. In time of war or other public emergency threatening the life of the nation any Party may take measures derogating from its obligations under this Charter to the extent strictly required by the exigencies of the situation, provided that such measures are not inconsistent with its other obligations under international law.

2. Any Party which has availed itself of this right of derogation shall, within a reasonable lapse of time, keep the Secretary General of the Council of Europe fully informed of the measures taken and of the reasons therefor. It shall likewise inform the Secretary General when such measures have ceased to operate and the provisions of the Charter which it has accepted are again being fully executed.

Article G - Restrictions

1. The rights and principles set forth in Part I when effectively realised, and their effective exercise as provided for in Part II, shall not be subject to any restrictions or limitations not specified in those parts, except such as are prescribed by law and are necessary in a democratic society for the protection of the rights and freedoms of others or for the protection of public interest, national security, public health, or morals.

2. The restrictions permitted under this Charter to the rights and obligations set forth herein shall not be applied for any purpose other than that for which they have been prescribed.

Article H - Relations between the Charter and domestic law or international agreements

The provisions of this Charter shall not prejudice the provisions of domestic law or of any bilateral or multilateral treaties, conventions or agreements which are already in force, or may come into force, under which more favourable treatment would be accorded to the persons protected.

Article I - Implementation of the undertakings given

1. Without prejudice to the methods of implementation foreseen in these articles the relevant provisions of Articles 1 to 31 of Part II of this Charter shall be implemented by:

   (a) laws or regulations;
   (b) agreements between employers or employers' organisations and workers' organisations;
   (c) a combination of those two methods;
   (d) other appropriate means.

2. Compliance with the undertakings deriving from the provisions of paragraphs 1, 2, 3, 4, 5 and 7 of Article 2, paragraphs 4, 6 and 7 of Article 7, paragraphs 1, 2, 3 and 5 of Article 10 and Articles 21 and 22 of Part II of this Charter shall be regarded as effective if the provisions are applied, in accordance with paragraph 1 of this article, to the great majority of the workers concerned.

Article J - Amendments

1. Any amendment to Parts I and II of this Charter with the purpose of extending the rights guaranteed in this Charter as well as any amendment to Parts III to VI, proposed by a Party or by the Governmental Committee, shall be communicated to the Secretary General of the Council of Europe and forwarded by the Secretary General to the Parties to this Charter.

2. Any amendment proposed in accordance with the provisions of the preceding paragraph shall be examined by the Governmental Committee which shall submit the text adopted to the Committee of Ministers for

approval after consultation with the Parliamentary Assembly. After its approval by the Committee of Ministers this text shall be forwarded to the Parties for acceptance.

3. Any amendment to Part I and to Part II of this Charter shall enter into force, in respect of those Parties which have accepted it, on the first day of the month following the expiration of a period of one month after the date on which three Parties have informed the Secretary General that they have accepted it.
   In respect of any Party which subsequently accepts it, the amendment shall enter into force on the first day of the month following the expiration of a period of one month after the date on which that Party has informed the Secretary General of its acceptance.

4. Any amendment to Parts III to VI of this Charter shall enter into force on the first day of the month following the expiration of a period of one month after the date on which all Parties have informed the Secretary General that they have accepted it.

PART VI

ARTICLE K - SIGNATURE, RATIFICATION AND ENTRY INTO FORCE

1. This Charter shall be open for signature by the member States of the Council of Europe. It shall be subject to ratification, acceptance or approval. Instruments of ratification, acceptance or approval shall be deposited with the Secretary General of the Council of Europe.

2. This Charter shall enter into force on the first day of the month following the expiration of a period of one month after the date on which three member States of the Council of Europe have expressed their consent to be bound by this Charter in accordance with the preceding paragraph.

3. In respect of any member State which subsequently expresses its consent to be bound by this Charter, it shall enter into force on the first day of the month following the expiration of a period of one month after the date of the deposit of the instrument of ratification, acceptance or approval.

Article L - Territorial application

1. This Charter shall apply to the metropolitan territory of each Party. Each signatory may, at the time of signature or of the deposit of its instrument of ratification, acceptance or approval, specify, by declaration addressed to the Secretary General of the Council of Europe, the territory which shall be considered to be its metropolitan territory for this purpose.

2. Any signatory may, at the time of signature or of the deposit of its instrument of ratification, acceptance or approval, or at any time thereafter, declare by notification addressed to the Secretary General of the Council of Europe, that the Charter shall extend in whole or in part to a non metropolitan territory or territories specified in the said declaration for whose international relations it is responsible or for which it assumes international responsibility. It shall specify in the declaration the articles or paragraphs of Part II of the Charter which it accepts as binding in respect of the territories named in the declaration.

3. The Charter shall extend its application to the territory or territories named in the aforesaid declaration as from the first day of the month following the expiration of a period of one month after the date of receipt of the notification of such declaration by the Secretary General.

4. Any Party may declare at a later date by notification addressed to the Secretary General of the Council of Europe that, in respect of one or more of the territories to which the Charter has been applied in accordance with paragraph 2 of this article, it accepts as binding any articles or any numbered paragraphs which it has not already accepted in respect of that territory or territories. Such undertakings subsequently given shall be deemed to be an integral part of the original declaration in respect of the territory concerned, and shall have the same effect as from the first day of the month following the expiration of a period of one month after the date of receipt of such notification by the Secretary General.

Article M - Denunciation

1. Any Party may denounce this Charter only at the end of a period of five years from the date on which the Charter entered into force for it, or at the end of any subsequent period of two years, and in either case after giving six months' notice to the Secretary General of the Council of Europe who shall inform the other Parties accordingly.

2. Any Party may, in accordance with the provisions set out in the preceding paragraph, denounce any article or paragraph of Part II of the Charter accepted by it provided that the number of articles or paragraphs by which this Party is bound shall never be less than sixteen in the former case and sixty-three in the latter and that this number of articles or paragraphs shall continue to include the articles selected by the Party among those to which special reference is made in Article A, paragraph 1, sub-paragraph b.

3. Any Party may denounce the present Charter or any of the articles or paragraphs of Part II of the Charter under the conditions specified in paragraph 1 of this article in respect of any territory to which the said Charter is applicable, by virtue of a declaration made in accordance with paragraph 2 of Article L.

Article N - Appendix

The appendix to this Charter shall form an integral part of it.

Article O - Notifications

The Secretary General of the Council of Europe shall notify the member States of the Council and the Director General of the International Labour Office of:

(a) any signature;
(b) the deposit of any instrument of ratification, acceptance or approval;
(c) any date of entry into force of this Charter in accordance with Article K;
(d) any declaration made in application of Articles A, paragraphs 2 and 3, D, paragraphs 1 and 2, F, paragraph 2, L, paragraphs 1, 2, 3 and 4;
(e) any amendment in accordance with Article J;
(f) any denunciation in accordance with Article M;
(g) any other act, notification or communication relating to this Charter.

In witness whereof, the undersigned, being duly authorised thereto, have signed this revised Charter.

Done at Strasbourg, this 3rd day of May 1996, in English and French, both texts being equally authentic, in a single copy which shall be deposited in the archives of the Council of Europe. The Secretary General of the Council of Europe shall transmit certified copies to each member State of the Council of Europe and to the Director General of the International Labour Office.

APPENDIX

To The Revised European Social Charter

Scope of the Revised European Social Charter in terms of persons protected

1. Without prejudice to Article 12, paragraph 4, and Article 13, paragraph 4, the persons covered by Articles 1 to 17 and 20 to 31 include foreigners only in so far as they are nationals of other Parties lawfully resident or working regularly within the territory of the Party concerned, subject to the understanding that these articles are to be interpreted in the light of the provisions of Articles 18 and 19. This interpretation would not prejudice the extension of similar facilities to other persons by any of the Parties.

2. Each Party will grant to refugees as defined in the Convention relating to the Status of Refugees, signed in Geneva on 28 July 1951 and in the Protocol of 31 January 1967, and lawfully staying in its territory, treatment as favourable as possible, and in any case not less favourable than under the obligations accepted by the Party under the said convention and under any other existing international instruments applicable to those refugees.

3. Each Party will grant to stateless persons as defined in the Convention on the Status of Stateless Persons done in New York on 28 September 1954 and lawfully staying in its territory, treatment as favourable as possible and in any case not less favourable than under the obligations accepted by the Party under the said instrument and under any other existing international instruments applicable to those stateless persons.

Part I, paragraph 18, and Part II, Article 18, paragraph 1

It is understood that these provisions are not concerned with the question of entry into the territories of the Parties and do not prejudice the provisions of the European Convention on Establishment, signed in Paris on 13 December 1955.

PART II

Article 1, paragraph 2

This provision shall not be interpreted as prohibiting or authorising any union security clause or practice.

Article 2, paragraph 6

Parties may provide that this provision shall not apply:

(a) to workers having a contract or employment relationship with a total duration not exceeding one month and/or with a working week not exceeding eight hours;
(b) where the contract or employment relationship is of a casual and/or specific nature, provided, in these cases, that its non-application is justified by objective considerations.

Article 3, paragraph 4

It is understood that for the purposes of this provision the functions, organisation and conditions of operation of these services shall be determined by national laws or regulations, collective agreements or other means appropriate to national conditions.

Article 4, paragraph 4

This provision shall be so understood as not to prohibit immediate dismissal for any serious offence.

Article 4, paragraph 5

It is understood that a Party may give the undertaking required in this paragraph if the great majority of workers are not permitted to suffer deductions from wages either by law or through collective agreements or arbitration awards, the exceptions being those persons not so covered.

Article 6, paragraph 4

It is understood that each Party may, insofar as it is concerned, regulate the exercise of the right to strike by law, provided that any further restriction that this might place on the right can be justified under the terms of Article G.

Article 7, paragraph 2

This provision does not prevent Parties from providing in their legislation that young persons not having reached the minimum age laid down may perform work in so far as it is absolutely necessary for their vocational training where such work is carried out in accordance with conditions prescribed by the competent authority and measures are taken to protect the health and safety of these young persons.

Article 7, paragraph 8

It is understood that a Party may give the undertaking required in this paragraph if it fulfils the spirit of the undertaking by providing by law that the great majority of persons under eighteen years of age shall not be employed in night work.

Article 8, paragraph 2

This provision shall not be interpreted as laying down an absolute prohibition. Exceptions could be made, for instance, in the following cases:

(a) if an employed woman has been guilty of misconduct which justifies breaking off the employment relationship;
(b) if the undertaking concerned ceases to operate;
(c) if the period prescribed in the employment contract has expired.

Article 12, paragraph 4

The words "and subject to the conditions laid down in such agreements" in the introduction to this paragraph are taken to imply inter alia that with regard to benefits which are available independently of any insurance contribution, a Party may require the completion of a prescribed period of residence before granting such benefits to nationals of other Parties.

Article 13, paragraph 4

Governments not Parties to the European Convention on Social and Medical Assistance may ratify the Charter in respect of this paragraph provided that they grant to nationals of other Parties a treatment which is in conformity with the provisions of the said convention.

Article 16

It is understood that the protection afforded in this provision covers single-parent families.

Article 17

It is understood that this provision covers all persons below the age of 18 years, unless under the law applicable to the child majority is attained earlier, without prejudice to the other specific provisions provided by the Charter, particularly Article 7.

This does not imply an obligation to provide compulsory education up to the above-mentioned age.

Article 19, paragraph 6

For the purpose of applying this provision, the term "family of a foreign worker" is understood to mean at least the worker's spouse and unmarried children, as long as the latter are considered to be minors by the receiving State and are dependent on the migrant worker.

Article 20

1. It is understood that social security matters, as well as other provisions relating to unemployment benefit, old age benefit and survivor's benefit, may be excluded from the scope of this article.

2. Provisions concerning the protection of women, particularly as regards pregnancy, confinement and the post-natal period, shall not be deemed to be discrimination as referred to in this article.

3. This article shall not prevent the adoption of specific measures aimed at removing de facto inequalities.

4. Occupational activities which, by reason of their nature or the context in which they are carried out, can be entrusted only to persons of a particular sex may be excluded from the scope of this article or some of its provisions. This provision is not to be interpreted as requiring the Parties to embody in laws or regulations a list of occupations which, by reason of their nature or the context in which they are carried out, may be reserved to persons of a particular sex.

Articles 21 and 22

1. For the purpose of the application of these articles, the term "workers' representatives" means persons who are recognised as such under national legislation or practice.

2. The terms "national legislation and practice" embrace as the case may be, in addition to laws and regulations, collective agreements, other agreements between employers and workers' representatives, customs as well as relevant case law.

3. For the purpose of the application of these articles, the term "undertaking" is understood as referring to a set of tangible and intangible components, with or without legal personality, formed to produce goods or provide services for financial gain and with power to determine its own market policy.

4. It is understood that religious communities and their institutions may be excluded from the application of these articles, even if these institutions are "undertakings" within the meaning of paragraph 3. Establishments pursuing activities which are inspired by certain ideals or guided by certain moral concepts, ideals and concepts which are protected by national legislation, may be excluded from the application of these articles to such an extent as is necessary to protect the orientation of the undertaking.

5. It is understood that where in a state the rights set out in these articles are exercised in the various establishments of the undertaking, the Party concerned is to be considered as fulfilling the obligations deriving from these provisions.

6. The Parties may exclude from the field of application of these articles, those undertakings employing less than a certain number of workers, to be determined by national legislation or practice.

Article 22

1. This provision affects neither the powers and obligations of states as regards the adoption of health and safety regulations for workplaces, nor the powers and responsibilities of the bodies in charge of monitoring their application.

2. The terms "social and socio-cultural services and facilities" are understood as referring to the social and/or cultural facilities for workers provided by some undertakings such as welfare assistance, sports fields, rooms for nursing mothers, libraries, children's holiday camps, etc.

Article 23, paragraph 1

For the purpose of the application of this paragraph, the term "for as long as possible" refers to the elderly person's physical, psychological and intellectual capacities.

Article 24

1. It is understood that for the purposes of this article the terms "termination of employment" and "terminated" mean termination of employment at the initiative of the employer.

2. It is understood that this article covers all workers but that a Party may exclude from some or all of its protection the following categories of employed persons:

   (a) workers engaged under a contract of employment for a specified period of time or a specified task;
   (b) workers undergoing a period of probation or a qualifying period of employment, provided that this is determined in advance and is of a reasonable duration;
   (c) workers engaged on a casual basis for a short period.

3. For the purpose of this article the following, in particular, shall not constitute valid reasons for termination of employment:

   (a) trade union membership or participation in union activities outside working hours, or, with the consent of the employer, within working hours;
   (b) seeking office as, acting or having acted in the capacity of a workers' representative;
   (c) the filing of a complaint or the participation in proceedings against an employer involving alleged violation of laws or regulations or recourse to competent administrative authorities;
   (d) race, colour, sex, marital status, family responsibilities, pregnancy, religion, political opinion, national extraction or social origin;
   (e) maternity or parental leave;
   (f) temporary absence from work due to illness or injury.

4. It is understood that compensation or other appropriate relief in case of termination of employment without valid reasons shall be determined by national laws or regulations, collective agreements or other means appropriate to national conditions.

Article 25

1. It is understood that the competent national authority may, by way of exemption and after consulting organisations of employers and workers,

exclude certain categories of workers from the protection provided in this provision by reason of the special nature of their employment relationship.

2. It is understood that the definition of the term "insolvency" must be determined by national law and practice.

3. The workers' claims covered by this provision shall include at least:

   (a) the workers' claims for wages relating to a prescribed period, which shall not be less than three months under a privilege system and eight weeks under a guarantee system, prior to the insolvency or to the termination of employment;
   (b) the workers' claims for holiday pay due as a result of work performed during the year in which the insolvency or the termination of employment occurred;
   (c) the workers' claims for amounts due in respect of other types of paid absence relating to a prescribed period, which shall not be less than three months under a privilege system and eight weeks under a guarantee system, prior to the insolvency or the termination of the employment.

PART V

Article E

A differential treatment based on an objective and reasonable justification shall not be deemed discriminatory.

Article F

The terms "in time of war or other public emergency" shall be so understood as to cover also the threat of war.

Article I

It is understood that workers excluded in accordance with the appendix to Articles 21 and 22 are not taken into account in establishing the number of workers concerned.

Article J

The term "amendment" shall be extended so as to cover also the addition of new articles to the Charter.

For Product Safety Concerns and Information please contact our EU representative GPSR@taylorandfrancis.com Taylor & Francis Verlag GmbH, Kaufingerstraße 24, 80331 München, Germany

Batch number: 10725923

Printed by Printforce, the Netherlands